C0-AUB-429

295

28 R

JEHOVAH'S WITNESSES

THE NEW WORLD SOCIETY

Marley Cole

VANTAGE PRESS • NEW YORK

289.9
J388col
J388

128066

FIRST PRINTING—MAY, 1955
SECOND PRINTING—JUNE, 1955

*All rights reserved, including the right of
reproduction in whole or in part in any form*
Copyright, 1955, by Marley Cole
Published by Vantage Press, Inc.
120 West 31st Street, New York 1, N. Y.
Manufactured in the United States of America
Library of Congress Catalog Card Number: 54-12633

CONTENTS

*The New World Society Assembles— "Not forsaking the gathering of ourselves together, as some have the custom, but encouraging one another, and all the more as you behold the day drawing near."—*HEBREWS *10:25, New World Translation of the Christian Greek Scriptures*

CHAPTER ONE

THE NEW WORLD SOCIETY ASSEMBLES

AT three o'clock Sunday, July 26, 1953, a small cabin plane and a helicopter circled round and round over Yankee Stadium, in the Bronx, New York. Photographers from the metropolitan press, the newsreels, TV stations, and a national magazine focused their cameras earthward upon a scene never witnessed before. The mammoth amphitheater was not only jammed solid with humanity to the last bleacher seat, but thousands of people, in orderly droves, were thronging the outfield grass. Presently, they were settled down quietly, right on the grass, in vast flowerbeds of color, filling the

3

playing field to within a few yards of a gigantic half-moon stage anchored at second base. Ninety-one thousand people were down there in the Stadium.

The photographers tried to work into their view finders the scenes just outside the Stadium. On one side there were two city lots covered by circus-size tents. Up toward the elevated railroad line, a few blocks away, there were more lots covered with tents. So many people had gathered in the tent areas that, as in the Stadium, the seats within tents could not accommodate them all. There were 25,240 people out there, within and around the tents, a total of 116,802 people—sixteen solid acres of humanity.

Then one of the planes zoomed off toward New Jersey. Forty miles away, near Plainfield, it hovered over a still stranger spectacle. It appeared to be a city—the largest city in the county. But it was a trailer city, a tent city. It was laid out in the conventional pattern of streets and avenues. It had materialized, as if out of nowhere, only eight or nine days before, and it would vanish in two or three more days. But right then there were 49,027 people down there.

They were really part of the audience at Yankee Stadium, audibly connected by direct wire and loud-speaker system. At that moment the trailer-city population was listening to the program in progress on the stage at second base, in the Yankees' ball park.

This was the aerial photographer's pictorial report of the New World Society Assembly of Jehovah's Witnesses, 1953 style.

Ground cameras, grinding and flashing, were recording the scenes inside Yankee Stadium. Plump, apple-cheeked Percy Chapman, supervisor of the Canadian Branch of Jehovah's Witnesses, in his present role of assembly chairman, was conducting the Witnesses' spokesman, Nathan H. Knorr, to the podium.

"Mr. Knorr is a world traveler and internationally recognized Bible authority," Chapman was saying. "He will speak to us on his widely advertised Bible subject, 'After Armageddon—God's New World.'"

Thunderous hand clapping filled the Stadium. Mr. Knorr, who is president of the Watch Tower Bible and Tract Society, international directive agency of Jehovah's witnesses, waited while an attendant adjusted his microphone. He looked out toward as many of the 165,829 people as he could see from the stage. He commenced to speak, and his words were carried simultaneously to another invisible audience over the Witnesses' own 5,000-watt radio station WBBR. Other wires transmitted his message to tape-recording technicians, who recorded it for replaying on a mass scale to no telling how many more people associated with the 14,000 congregations of Jehovah's witnesses scattered among 150 countries, in the days and years to come.

"Armageddon," Knorr was saying, "is no mere stormy conflict between two political parties within a nation; it is no mere atomic war between blocs of nations for the domination of the earth—the much-feared World War III; it is not the climax of the fight between the hateful Communist camp and Christendom's most powerful religious system and its political, commercial and religious allies."

Wrapping all the world and its nations up together as Armageddon's target, Knorr's voice warmed dramatically. "Armageddon is what the sacred Scriptures of divine prophecy call it, 'the war of the great day of God the Almighty,' the war in which the Creator of heaven and earth will face all his foes and will fight as he did in the days of old. God the Almighty foresaw the necessity for that war in due time and he foretold its coming. That war is therefore unavoidable."

His audience sensed his approaching climax. "The facts of modern history prove we are in 'the day of God the Almighty' and his war is very near."

Again a resounding peal of hand clapping filled the air. No shouting, no hooting, no whistling, but a vibrant sensitive response to every word. And every word pointed to Armageddon as ringing down the curtain on this present living generation.

Yankee Stadium had been the scene of such a demon-

stration only once before—in 1950, when Jehovah's witnesses
held a similar world convention there.

More than 20,000 of these people came from foreign
countries—ninety-six countries in all. Jehovah's witnesses,
as a rule, live on the humbler side of life. But one fourth
of their total membership—510,228 as of July, 1953—had
managed to get to New York from places as far off as New
Zealand, Chile, and Ethiopia. The total cost for transportation, food, and lodging, must have been about ten million
dollars.

To stage the eight-day convention the Witnesses had to
organize and operate a metropolis bigger in area than modern Jerusalem, and with more people in it than in the
whole state of Nevada.

"So far as we are concerned, you people are running
your own convention," Stadium Assistant Superintendent
John Anderson told John Groh, the Witnesses' convention
manager. Maintenance Supervisor James Regan turned a
set of master keys over to them to do with as they pleased.
The Stadium's union labor force handed over the job of
keeping the grounds clean to the Witnesses' cleaning department of 962 workers. A city police unit of not less than
35 and, at times, up to 80 men, under Captain Albert Dunn,
of the Bronx, reported "no problems." They had little more
to do than look on, while a corps of 4,400 Witness attendants
manipulated the throngs in and out of the Stadium, and to
and from the cafeteria.

The United States Navy, the Civil Defense Administration, and the New York City Department of Health were
among those who sent observers to study the crowd-handling
methods and the mass-feeding techniques used by Jehovah's
witnesses.

"Their methods are marvelous," they reported. "But
don't expect them to work as well for anybody else."

"Why not?" their superiors demanded.

"Because Jehovah's witnesses work voluntarily. Who else
would do all that work for nothing?"

Volunteered, for example, was a trucking fleet of sixty vehicles, ranging from half-ton pickups to tractor-and-double-trailer jobs. Four farm tractors, three bulldozers, and one back-haul shovel, used at Trailer City, were donated. This giant transportation system was gathered from all over the United States. In most cases, the owners themselves supplied the fuel and upkeep expenses and volunteered their personal services as operators.

Personnel: 288 men and one woman. (A volunteer-service application read: "I own a 1953 Ford half-ton pickup which I would like to put to use. My wife will serve as my helper." Trucking Department Manager S. H. Plumhoff, not being the kind of man to interfere with family working arrangements, accepted the female truck driver "with pleasure.")

Scope of work: 61,102 articles for the cafeteria, sound, installations, and other departments were gathered from eighty United States circuits as distant as Texas and California and hauled to New York and back. Other items included twenty truckloads of refrigerators, steam kettles, ovens, and the like; 265,000 board feet of lumber for the seventy-eight buildings at Trailer City; 650 wiring poles; eight miles of plumbing pipe; forty-one miles of wiring; twenty truckloads of chairs, and two truckloads of greenery to decorate the stage.

"We handled everything from a delicate postage-weight scale to two baby-grand pianos, one upright piano, and a bass fiddle," enumerated Mr. Plumhoff.

"We even trucked in two mothers and their eight children, two trunks, three suitcases, and one tent," he chuckled. "These delegates got stranded at Grand Central Station. They had no way of getting out to Trailer City, forty miles away."

Witness Plumhoff concluded his report cheerfully. "It took us eight days to haul the equipment into Yankee Stadium. We have thirty-six hours to get it out."

"We made it," he added three days later.

Transportation of an eighth of a million people from

ninety-six countries to one point on earth at a specified time
is no small feat.

"We organized for it months in advance," Transportation Supervisor H. E. Miller explained.

"But how?" I asked.

"Jehovah's witnesses have international headquarters in
Brooklyn, New York. Then there are sixty-five additional
branch offices world wide. This was organization enough for
us to integrate ship and plane facilities and bring delegates
from all the continents."

At least one hundred thousand delegates were expected
from North America. "There were special trains from Seattle,
Los Angeles, Canada, and other points. More than three
hundred buses were chartered. The air lines were taxed to
the limit. But all these took care of only twenty per cent
or so of the delegates," Miller said.

"What about the other eighty per cent?"

"Well, in Alaska, Canada, the United States, and Mexico
there are four thousand one hundred and thirty-seven Kingdom Halls. Under the Society's direction in Brooklyn, these
were used as transportation centers, wherever necessary,"
Miller explained. "A month or so in advance the conventioners were organized into car groups."

"How many cars?"

"Oh, twenty-five thousand I would say. And fifteen hundred of them pulled trailers."

"So by all means of transportation you had from one
hundred and twenty-five to one hundred and fifty thousand
people coming at you from outside of New York?"

"That's about right."

"How did you manage to take care of them when they
arrived?"

"You had better ask Information Department," Miller
advised.

Tall, dapper New York Witness Jerry Molohan, with a
staff of three hundred special volunteers, handled the Information Department. "Only it was more than information
we gave out," Molohan avowed.

He explained what he meant by describing all the qualifications an Information Department worker ought to have had to fill the job perfectly. "First of all, he would have to be a native New Yorker with a taxi driver's knowledge of the city. He would need to know the languages of ninety-six countries. He would have to own a rugged car, his own gasoline station, and the stamina to stay on call twenty-four hours a day."

Information booths were posted on all incoming highways. From these the auto caravans were directed to individual destinations.

"What about the rest of the traffic?"

"We had information booths set up in all the bus, train, ship, and air terminals to greet them."

"What about the foreigners?"

"All plane and ship arrivals were met with car drivers and interpreters."

"What did you do with them?"

"First, we took them to nearby temporary residences, which were converted Kingdom Halls. There we fed them and gave them a chance to refresh themselves. They were assisted through the Customs too, of course. Finally, they were driven to their room assignments."

"All of this free of charge?"

"With the compliments of the American Witnesses."

"And you say each person's room assignment was waiting for him when he arrived?"

"The assignments were waiting at the reception halls."

"How did you arrange for the rooms?"

"Go see Ray Anderson," Molohan replied. "He will tell you how the rooms were arranged."

In three months' time Jehovah's witnesses listed rooming accommodations for 85,000 people (not counting Trailer City). Only about 15,000 delegates obtained their accommodations privately, at hotels or in other ways. "Most of the listings came through the Rooming Committee and were obtained the hard way," R. L. Anderson, the rooming supervisor recounted.

"How?" I inquired.

"By the biggest house-to-house and stair-climbing hunt for rooms in the city's history."

In his soft-spoken voice Anderson described how, on April 26, a vanguard of 509 house-to-house canvassers sallied forth to obtain the accommodations. "By July, an average of sixteen hundred were in the field every day," he related.

After spending 133,825 hours (fifteen years of time) on this assignment and incidentally leaving a third of a million pieces of literature with the people they called on, Jehovah's witnesses arranged accommodations, including Trailer City, for more people than live in Alaska.

New World Trailer City, near Plainfield, New Jersey, was marked off into streets and lots a month prior to the assembly. Sanitation facilities, water supply, and electricity were installed. Seventy-eight buildings, exceeding a half mile in length if placed end to end, were constructed. A crew of four hundred volunteers, mostly from surrounding New York and Jersey congregations, did the work.

"We prepared to receive a population of thirty-two thousand," George Couch, the Trailer City manager said.

"Had you received that many requests for accommodations?"

"We had. We thought that was a remarkable number. It was twice the number that occupied Trailer City at our other world assembly, in nineteen fifty."

"But you had more than thirty-two thousand?"

"Did we!" Couch laughed guardedly, almost appalled at the memory. "We had thirty-two thousand arrive a day before the convention opened."

An assistant, Witness L. M. Dugan, butted in. "People kept pouring in at the rate of twelve hundred an hour. They took up all the lots and they kept on coming."

"We saw blind spots there for a while—Dugan and I!" George admitted.

He had rushed Dugan over to lease some extra fields from the nearest farmers. "We didn't have time to survey them. lay out lots, or anything," he continued.

"How did you manage?"

Both men laughed. "We simply clipped the wire fences," Dugan said. "Then, with a big staff of attendants, we led the caravans out across the fields. We turned them off, right and left, onto unmarked plots, with street spaces between them. They all camped right where they stopped, and the installation crews followed through as fast as they could."

"That," said Couch, "was one of the fast-growing boom cities in history. There were forty-five thousand four hundred and ninety-two people living there the last day!" (About five thousand people visited the city the last day.)

Between fifteen thousand and twenty-three thousand volunteer workers—about one to every six people attending—were used to operate the New World Assembly. "The main core of this army of personnel has become something near to professional in their particular departments," John Donnenwirth, the Volunteer Service manager told me.

"How is that?" I asked.

"Because they have had so much previous experience."

Jehovah's witnesses, he explained, must be the "most convention-minded people in the world." "About every twenty local congregations comprise a circuit. Each circuit holds two assemblies a year, from three hundred to a few thousand attendance.

"About every twenty circuits comprise a district," he continued. "Each district holds an assembly once a year. For example, in nineteen fifty-two there were forty-six district assemblies in North America.

"Next come the branches," Donnenwirth went on. "There are branch or national assemblies the years we hold no world assemblies. In nineteen fifty-one, a string of national conventions was held in most of the European capitals, outside the Iron Curtain countries, where Jehovah's witnesses are banned. Climaxing the string was one in Washington, D. C., where fifty-seven thousand people overflowed Griffith Stadium."

Topping all the rest are the big world assemblies like the 1950 and 1953 conventions at Yankee Stadium.

"Now, with all this training in conducting assemblies," Donnenwirth continued, coming to his point, "each department is developing its own special group of workers. I mean workers who are growing more and more skilled in their particular line."

"How many departments are there?" I asked.

"Oh, twenty major ones or more—cafeteria, attendant, refreshment, cleaning, trucking, installations, sound, public relations, and so on."

"So each department is developing a class of specialists?"

"From the circuit level on up."

"These specialists," I inquired. "Are they professionals or craftsmen in that line, in everyday life? For instance, the convention plumbing department. Is that made up of professional plumbers?"

"As a rule, yes," Donnenwirth replied, nodding. "But it is not always so."

"No?"

"For one thing, there are people who follow trades or professions that don't fit into any department at a convention. For instance, suppose a ballet dancer came up and volunteered for service?"

"Did it happen?"

"It did."

"What did you do with the ballet dancer?"

"We assigned her to the Pioneer Registration Department."

Besides these innumerable "misfits," Donnenwirth added, there were Witnesses who wanted to escape from their specialized work in everyday life and do something altogether unrelated.

"The First Aid Department is staffed with Witness doctors, surgeons, chiropractors, osteopaths, and nurses. But there is one surgeon here working in the attendant department." (The Witnesses do not call them ushers, but "attendants.")

Shield Halvajian, besides being a regular minister of Jehovah's witnesses, is an interior decorator in Los Angeles,

California. "But Halvajian runs the cafeteria," Donnenwirth pointed out. "He is an expert cafeteria manager, whether on the circuit-assembly level or world-convention level."

Donnenwirth himself has specialized in running Volunteer Service departments for several years. He earns his living as an insurance-accounts executive in Akron, Ohio.

Something significant might be read into their experiences as assembly operators, Donnenwirth ventured to add. "We have developed something peculiar and unique among religious groups—or, for that matter, among any other groups."

"What is that?" He had me curious.

"Do you realize that we are organized and trained to set up living arrangements on any scale?"

"You mean from the circuit level to the world-assembly level?"

"Not only that, but on a permanent basis, if we wanted to."

The tall, angular Ohioan, whose eyes have a gift of flashing inflections along with his words, restated his meaning in question form.

"Look. Don't Jehovah's witnesses believe that Armageddon will devastate all present world systems of things within the present living generation?"

"Right."

"And that the Armageddon survivors will have to reorganize their living arrangements right out of the rubble?"

"You mean these assembly activities are training a corps of post-Armageddon reconstructors?"

"I would not go so strong as that," Donnenwirth confessed. "I'm just saying that almost anywhere on earth you might go you will find Jehovah's witnesses there. And you will find them trained and conditioned to set up community living arangements at the drop of a hat.

"Or maybe," Donnenwirth concluded, grinning, "I am just overenthusiastic about what these twenty-two thousand volunteer workers have done here at the New World Society Assembly."*

*1953 CONVENTION VOLUNTEER SERVICE STAFF OF 22,281

(General average at assemblies of all sizes is one volunteer worker
for every six conventioners.)

DEPARTMENT	NUMBER OF WORKERS
Attendant (Ushers)	4,383
Auditing	869
Book Rooms	376
Cafeteria	4,662
Cleaning	962
Engineering & Installation	679
Field Service	226
First Aid	195
Immersion	300
Information	230
Lost & Found and Check Room	110
Orchestra	84
Pioneer Registration	53
Public Address	34
Public Relations	45
Recording (Tape)	35
Refreshments	4,235
Rooming	189
Signs	20
Trailer City	4,105
Trucking & Equipment	315
Volunteer Service	174
TOTAL	22,281

This figure does not include a battery of interpreters who worked with
Public Relations.

The 189 Rooming workers cover only the office staff. For three months
there was an average of 1,600 canvassers going from house to house
seeking accommodations.

The Field Service Department operated through 39 Kingdom Halls
from the Coney Island section to the top of Yonkers. When the Rooming work ended the day before the Assembly the Halls were kept
open as field service centers for the conventioners. Tens of thousands
took part in daily ministerial work, inviting New Yorkers to the
Assembly, offering them Bible helps, standing on the streets handing
out invitations, or displaying the magazines *The Watchtower* and
Awake!

Orthodoxy in Reverse—"These men that have upset the inhabited earth are present here also," said the Jews, when Paul and Silas came to Thessalonica.—ACTS 17:6

CHAPTER TWO

ORTHODOXY IN REVERSE

MOST folks—church leaders especially—keep saying that something has got to be done about religion, that "religion as usual" has lost its savor. "Religion in our time has little 'kick' in it," declared Dr. Robert J. McCracken of New York's Riverside Church.

Everybody agrees that the Witnesses of Jehovah are doing something about religion. You could not produce a more revolutionary religion, even if you took the sum total of all the tenets of Christendom and turned them precisely

upside down. It is as if the Witnesses had hit upon the
formula that religion as we know it has everything in reverse. To get true worship straightened out (you could
almost accuse them of reasoning), you adopt the opposite
of what you hear in church.

For just that reason Jehovah's witnesses find themselves
in a peculiar position: while on the one hand, church leaders
declare unequivocally that something has got to be done
about modern religion (preachers are admitting that communism, for example, is beating Christendom "at her own
game of evangelizing the world"), on the other hand, you
could not do more toward revolutionizing Christianity than
Jehovah's witnesses have done during the past eighty-odd
years.

So look, for a moment, and ask yourself: Are Jehovah's
witnesses the kind of antidote that modern religion has been
needing? Are they the bitter pill the Doctor says to take?
Are they the landmark on the horizon *toward* or *away* from
which orthodoxy had better be hastening her careening ship?

Thriving on Universal Opposition

Latin-American Catholics label them an "off-brand
Protestant sect." Protestants on the island of Cyprus announce on street corners that they have no relation with
Jehovah's witnesses. The Orthodox Church in Greece brands
them a "Jewish sect." The Jews remonstrate to the Government. Pakistan Moslems abhor them as "Christians." Quebec
Canadians prosecute them as seditionists. Americans mob
them as Communists. Communists murder them as spies for
American imperialism.

Jehovah's witnesses quote a statement by Dr. W. L. Pettingill, pastor of the First Baptist Church of Broadway and
79th Street, New York. "The weakness of the church today,"
he declared, "is largely the result of the absence of persecution and suffering."

Lack of persecution and suffering may be, as Dr. Pettingill says, the weakness of modern orthodoxy. Does that imply that abundance of persecution and suffering has something to do with the strength of Jehovah's witnesses?

Churchbook membership in the United States has increased by sixty per cent during the past quarter century. During the same period Jehovah's witnesses multiplied by two thousand per cent.

During the pangs of world-wide depression, the second total war, and the wildfire rampage of communism among one third of the earth's people the Witnesses multiplied internationally by more than fifteen hundred per cent. For several years during that time they preached their good news underground in seventy out of eighty-two countries.

I do not believe the Louisville *Courier Journal* was exaggerating in 1950 when it tabbed Jehovah's witnesses "the fastest-growing religion in the world."

Appeal of the Nonconformists

A precise definition of Jehovah's witnesses is not easily arrived at. Think of a religion whose *members* do their own preaching. Think of a religious group that spends more on field preaching than it does on building church structures. Think of a religion with no paid clergy—no class distinctions of clergy and laity. Everybody, young and old, male and female, is enrolled in strenuous, regular ministerial education that turns out one thousand ministers—not members, but ministers—a week and organizes one new congregation somewhere in the world every day in the year.

And think of a half million preachers—the largest single body of united preachers in the world—whose pulpits, in more than one hundred and fifty countries, are the doorsteps, living rooms, curbstones, store counters, business desks, vacant lots, ball parks, stadiums, and civic auditoriums of the inhabited earth.

When you walk into a Kingdom Hall congregation of one hundred Witnesses, you won't be looking at one minister sermonizing ninety-nine lay members. You will be looking at one hundred preachers, Bible evangelists, Bible educators. Some may be only nine years old. Some of them may be ninety. But they know how to thumb a Bible. And the Bible is their textbook.

Just as the message the Witnesses preach cannot be served up in any orthodox shape, form, or fashion, neither will it support any orthodox system, supreme councils. No money drives. No collection plates. No crusades to save an "irreformable and doomed world." No attempt to "put God into business" or "God into politics" or "God into religion," as religious systems now stand.

Jehovah's witnesses tell you that this whole world system of things, held together by its three main components of commerce, politics, and religion, is "a goner." They urge and beckon you toward a New World System of Things.

This New World Society is no pie-in-the-sky dream to them. It is not coming tomorrow—it is here today. It is to them the realest reality on earth today. Tomorrow, if Armageddon struck all worldly systems from the planet as completely as the Flood washed out "the world that then was," there would still remain the New World Society intact, a going concern. They believe that. That is how real it is to them.

And it *does* exist.

Back in 1949, George R. Stewart published a fascinating book called *Earth Abides*. He described an imaginary plague that reduced the population of the planet to a few straggling survivors. These few banded together, here and there and started rehabilitating the planet as best they could. By the time the second generation was established they found themselves divided into fearful, jealous little families and clans. The story of nationalism, wars, misery, and confusion started all over again.

Jehovah's witnesses anticipate an early annihilation of all earth's population except the New World Society of perhaps a few million. But in the post-Armageddon New World they envision no confusion, disunity, divisions, or wars. The millennial reign of Christ will hold sway over earth. In fact, a preliminary reign, the "day of Jehovah's judgment," has already started, here "amid its enemies." Its aim is to draw together a "great crowd" from all races, kindreds, and tongues from out of the world's great tribulation.

The unity, purpose, devotion, and irrepressible advancement of Jehovah's witnesses proves well enough that this, to them, is the paramount fact of the universe. They are literally conditioning *now* for life in the New World.

*Their World-wide Mission— "And this good news of the kingdom will be preached in all the inhabited earth for the purpose of a witness to all the nations, and then the accomplished end will come."—*MATTHEW 24:14, *New World Translation of the Christian Greek Scriptures*

CHAPTER THREE

THEIR WORLD-WIDE MISSION

JEHOVAH'S WITNESSES have volunteered to carry out what to them is a divinely inspired mission to deliver a special message to all the inhabited earth. To that end they are organized and trained.

This peculiar good news the Witnesses have for all earthly residents is that of Kingdom Here. "Do you ever pray the Lord's prayer?" the Witnesses ask you.

"You mean the one we memorize in school?" you inquire.

"That is it," they reply. "You know how it goes—'Your kingdom come, your will be done on earth . . .' " and so on.

20

"Of course," you say, nodding.

"Jehovah's witnesses are not looking for the kingdom to come in the future. We consider it as having started to operate here toward the earth already."

"Since when?" you demand, startled.

"Since nineteen fourteen."

"But how," you insist, "do you get such an idea?"

They open their Bibles to show you prophecies such as Matthew, chapter twenty-four. "Here, for example, is Jesus' famous world's-end prophecy," they point out. "It reads like a blueprint of things happening since nineteen fourteen."

"Why nineteen fourteen?" you want to know.

"Notice that the disciples inquired of Jesus what would be the sign of his presence in kingdom power, and of the end of the old world 'system of things.' "

"Yes?"

"The sign is composed of dozens of separate occurrences, all coming within one generation. For example, he indicated, the world's time of the end or consummation period would be marked by the outbreak of world wars. There would be world food shortages, disease, pestilences, earthquakes, distress of nations, global perplexities. All these, once starting, would go on growing worse till the final end, Armageddon."

"And it started in nineteen fourteen?"

"Even *The New York Times* remarked," they reply, "that nineteen thirteen was the last normal year in human history." And they point out that World War II was worse than World War I, and that World War III will be an even greater disaster.

"You mean then," you reason, "that God is bringing increasing sorrows upon the world to make it aware of His Kingdom's establishment?"

"No," they reply quickly. "God is not responsible for this world distress. The Devil is. This is his world, the Bible says. Other Bible prophecies, such as Revelation, chapter twelve, show that the Devil knows he has reached the end of his wicked rule. He is now enraged. He is bent on ruining all future prospects of life on earth. He is determined to blind people to the only hope, the Kingdom."

The work of Jehovah's witnesses, then, counteracts Satan's mad drive to plunge the world into violent chaos. That work gives the people hope for life in a new world, under the heavenly kingdom. Those choosing the kingdom will survive the showdown fight at Armageddon, where Jehovah's forces under Christ achieve a smashing victory over Satan and his world, visible and invisible. The survivors will receive their reward either in heavenly glory or here on earth in a paradise of everlasting life.

The preaching of this good news of the Kingdom constitutes one of the more important aspects of the great composite "sign" that humanity has reached the "consummation of this system of things." Matthew 24:14, in The New World Translation, reads:

"And this good news of the kingdom will be preached in all the inhabited earth for the purpose of a witness to all the nations, and then the accomplished end will come."

Fulfilling that prophetic command is another law of "new world living" translated into literal action from the pages of the Bible by Jehovah's witnesses.

"But to put all the inhabited earth on official notice that God's kingdom has entered upon the earthly scene," you observe, "is a world-size job."

The Witnesses reply: "We are a world-wide organization. We think, speak, and act in terms of a world movement. We have accepted a world-wide mission."

"How can you accomplish it?"

"By a world-wide Bible educational program."

Education is their weapon. Their religion is intellectual, not emotional. In countries such as Mexico, and the Latin-American republics, and throughout Africa, their Kingdom Hall religious centers are also secular educational centers. There Witness ministers serve as school instructors. Tens of thousands of African adults have learned to read and write in these Kingdom Halls of Jehovah's witnesses.

For their global mission, assemblies like the 1953 world rally serve to furnish, among other things, more educational ammunition. At that convention new published releases included: a brand-new Bible translation (first eight books of

Hebrew Scriptures), a 416-page Bible handbook, a 384-page Bible study book called *New Heavens and a New Earth,* and seventy other new releases in twenty-eight languages.

Public sessions were held in twenty-one languages, including English, and a deaf-mute section took in all the English sessions through interpreters.

During the eight days of the assembly, 3,073,675 pieces of literature and printed matter (not including 5,100,000 handbills) were distributed to Greater New York's thirteen million people. But this was just a starter, an indicator of the global expansion the assembly touched off.

In the more than one hundred languages employed by them, Jehovah's witnesses can scarcely find words eloquent or expressive enough to impress on you and me and all the earth's inhabitants that this generation is one of unparalleled transition. Within the next few years this world's systems of things—religious, political, economic, and otherwise—will go down to dust in God's battle, Armageddon. The comparatively small society that will survive is now being shaped, conditioned, and matured for the world's final end. It is gaining a unity "that not even the shaking of the mountains into the seas can disrupt." It is growing faster, comparatively, than any other religion on earth.

That is the preachment believed implicitly by Jehovah's witnesses. It fires them to zeal. They live in an atmosphere of urgency that keeps growing. They drop every other hope, aspiration, and work in this world to devote their lives and resources and time and energies to preaching it.

"Living Now as a New World Society" was one of the key addresses delivered by the Watch Tower president, N. H. Knorr, at the 1953 world assembly. Positive evidence of a kingdom is its subjects, Knorr stressed. Jehovah's witnesses are subjects of God's kingdom government. That government now operates through the "absolute heavenly monarch Christ Jesus." The Kingdom is more real to Jehovah's people than the United Nations, or any Indian-summer peace the world may enjoy here in the evening of the "last days," Knorr stressed.

Jehovah's witnesses in world assembly, he concluded, were demonstrating things the world's United Nations could not demonstrate—the ability to draw together, live together, and worship together, void of age-old racial, national, religious, or political differences.

"Jehovah's witnesses are a thousand years before their time," one journalist commented.

To which a Witness responded: "Human society has grown six thousand years behind the times since Eden; that's all."

EXPANSION SINCE GILEAD SCHOOL WAS ESTABLISHED

In the table of continents given here you will see the advance of the New World Society since 1942. In that year the Watch Tower Bible and Tract Society was not sending out missionaries to all parts of the world. But in 1943 the Bible School of Gilead was opened by the Watch Tower Bible and Tract Society, and from then on the Society's world-wide missionary work began.

Place	Lands Witnessed To	Total Ministers	Hours Spent Preaching	Gilead Graduates Teaching
AFRICA				
1942	(11 lands)	10,070	2,200,163	None
1947	(17 lands)	24,896	6,298,189	20
1952	(32 lands)	72,228	15,460,243	84
1953	(34 lands)	81,793	16,979,027	80
ASIA				
1942	(6 lands)	406	93,223	None
1947	(8 lands)	475	140,661	17
1952	(19 lands)	2,274	504,301	164
1953	(19 lands)	2,698	597,050	173
EUROPE				
1942	(13 lands)	22,796	5,344,006	None
1947	(19 lands)	74,196	12,819,994	21
1952	(24 lands)	158,867	19,147,879	177
1953	(24 lands)	179,374	19,433,567	216
ISLANDS OF THE ATLANTIC, CARIBBEAN AND MEDITERRANEAN				
1942	(6 lands)	1,297	237,057	None
1947	(12 lands)	6,429	1,448,810	135
1952	(15 lands)	15,659	2,200,647	149
1953	(29 lands)	17,421	2,248,941	133

ISLANDS OF THE PACIFIC

1942	(3 lands)	4,275	701,037	None
1947	(6 lands)	7,385	1,390,228	13
1952	(12 lands)	26,690	3,590,037	51
1953	(13 lands)	31,980	4,214,497	49

NORTH AMERICA

1942	(7 lands)	75,589	19,668,961	None
1947	(12 lands)	91,740	20,787,495	163
1952	(12 lands)	168,752	25,810,384	493
1953	(12 lands)	193,542	26,734,105	674

SOUTH AMERICA

1942	(8 lands)	807	219,905	None
1947	(12 lands)	2,431	956,928	117
1952	(13 lands)	11,795	1,990,208	303
1953	(12 lands)	13,174	2,137,541	301

GRAND TOTALS OF THE WORLD

1942	(54 lands)	115,240	28,464,352	None
1947	(86 lands)	207,552	43,842,305	486
1952	(127 lands)	456,265	68,703,699	1,421
1953	(143 lands)	519,982	72,344,728	1,626

During the decade 1942-52 the number of Jehovah's witnesses doubled in North America, multiplied five times in Asia, more than six times in the Pacific Islands, about seven times in Europe and Africa, more than twelve times in the Atlantic Islands, and nearly fifteen times in South America.

*Across Nineteen Centuries— "Go in through the narrow gate, because broad and spacious is the road leading off into destruction, and many are the ones going in through it; whereas narrow is the gate and cramped the road leading off into life, and few are the ones finding it."—*MATTHEW *7:13, 14, New World Translation of the Christian Greek Scriptures*

CHAPTER FOUR

ACROSS NINETEEN CENTURIES

"*YOU* look around you and you see a person sitting near you who expects, when he dies, to go to heaven. Then you see other persons sitting close by who expect to keep living here on earth and never die a human death."

That is the way one of Jehovah's witnesses opened his talk in a Kingdom Hall one evening, in October, 1953.

"Think of it," he continued, "you are sitting in a congregation of people who believe that in this generation the greatest change of all time is about to take place. A change that will free the earth of death—death-dealing forces and systems of wickedness. That cataclysmic change is called Armageddon in the Bible. A remnant of humanity will pass alive through Armageddon. They will go on living in happiness forever. This will be a cleansed earth—a new earth. They will be living under the thousand-year reign of Christ."

Did that sound to us like the strangest religion we ever heard? the speaker asked. "When did another group of people —Christians, at that—teach such a thing?"

The Witness speaker paused.

"Ever since Jesus promised that the meek should inherit the earth; ever since Peter quoted Isaiah's prophecy about a new heaven and a new earth to come, Christians have hoped for that new world. Some have hoped for life in the heavenly realm of it. But if there is a new earthly existence promised, then not everybody would go to heaven. Still, the earthly prospects have not been given much thought since the days of Jesus. Not until Jehovah's witnesses began stressing the new earth during the last half century.

"And now, another thing. No matter whether Christians looked for heavenly or earthly life under the Kingdom, they had always, until now, cast it ahead, into the future. But this generation has been startled by a new message. The message that the Kingdom is here. New heavens and a new earth!"

Because they preach the doctrine of "Kingdom Here" instead of the doctrine of "Kingdom Come," Jehovah's witnesses, the minister reflected good-naturedly, are brushed off by the world with a shrug of the shoulders and a shake of the head. " 'A freak religion,' they call it. 'Don't you people claim any connection with Christians in the past?' they want to know. 'Did you just appear out of nowhere, without precedent, during the past eighty years or so? All other religions have traditional church fathers. Don't you Jehovah's witnesses have any?' "

Christianity a Story of Persecuted Minorities, Witnesses Say

"It brings up a challenging thought," agreed the Witness. "And the answer is yes. We do claim a heritage. A line of Christian predecessors stretching all the way back to Christ.

"It was at times an almost unbelievably thin thread of believers—a thread reddened by their own blood—stretching down the centuries only a perilous inch above the Pagan sea of darkness," said the Witness.

"To understand what I mean"—his face grew intent—"you will have to view the history of Christianity in an opposite light."

Opposite to the orthodox history, he meant.

"The world tells the history of Christianity like this: Jesus Christ founded and left a church organization. It continued as such until A.D. 325. Then at the Council of Nice, the Christian Church was established as the one universal, or catholic, church. The dogma and doctrines of the Church were assembled and codified. From that time on Christianity grew in power. Pagan Rome gave way to Christian Rome. The principal world was converted through the Holy Roman Empire to Christianity. Whole nations today profess the Christian faith. Collectively, these nations are called Christendom."

But Jehovah's witnesses view the history of Christianity as an exactly opposite story, he explained.

"Christ Jesus founded the true church, yes. He established twelve apostles as its pillars. These twelve had no apostolic successors. The last apostle to die was John, who wrote the Revelation. By the time of his death, about A.D. 100, some ninety-six schisms had appeared in the original church. The schisms widened and kept multiplying. Christian congregations, through their leaders, were compromising with Paganism. Emperor Constantine wanted to integrate the religions of his subjects. That would make it easier for him to rule the Empire.

"So, A.D. 325, Constantine called the religious leaders together at Nice, in Asia Minor. He wanted them to settle upon a body of religious doctrines that would wrap up Christianity and Paganism in one package. The church doctrines adopted at Nice were more Pagan than Christian. From that time on the world has been held together by a fusion religion. It is Christian in name only."

The world, said the Witness, had not been converted to Christianity. It was the other way around. The Witness' version of Christianity's history pictured the human race following in an almost solid body far below "that cramped and narrow way" of real Christianity. Christendom, as an organized system of religion, dropped body and soul into the "morass of fused apostasy and outright Paganism," especially from A.D. 325 onward, he felt.

Even Christians Veered from True Teachings

"Only a few, at all times, held above the quagmire of errant faith," he declared. "In some respects even the few were drawn underneath the Pagan waters of false religion. About the only thing they did not get buried under was the hierarchical authority of the nominal church. That they kicked against, sometimes at the cost of their lives."

For fifteen hundred years, down to the dawn of the twentieth century, there were martyred minorities, he continued. There were the Arians, the Waldenses, the Lollards, and the Hussites, to name a few. These groups stayed adamantly aloof from "priestcraft." But, cautioned the speaker, "Even these groups remained in shadowy light when it came to understanding many principal Bible doctrines."

I was learning from this speaker that Jehovah's witnesses' version of Christianity over the centuries opened your eyes to a better understanding of the viewpoint and attitude and character of this modern group. During a search through their theocratic library I found that they have compiled a prolific literature on Christianity's history. It is chock-full of profiles, biographies, and critical evaluations of the men and movements to whom they would have felt closest had they lived in those times.

I have pieced together, from their literature, a bird's-eye view of the history of Christianity the way Jehovah's wit-

nesses write it. You will note that in the entire nineteen-
century period there was not a time when the Witnesses feel
that they would have been clasped to the heart of the church
and the state. They always cast their lot with a dissident
group. What practices and doctrines Jehovah's witnesses have
salvaged from the "interim since Christ," they gleaned from
these minorities. It was only with these that the Witnesses
found anything at all in common.

What follows is condensed from material published over
a period of many years by the Watch Tower people. The
authorities they cite are not obscure and questionable
sources. Witness writers quote from theological authorities,
accepted historians, and standard encyclopedias. The quotations I make are from the Witnesses' publications. Some of
these quotations are made, in turn, by the Witnesses from
other sources. To save cluttering up the narrative with endless citations, however, I believe that this explanation will
suffice.

I

From Jesus to the Death of Paul

The apostle Paul, up to the time of his death, about the
year 65, was probably the most outstanding advocate of
Christianity, in the opinion of the Witnesses. This Roman
citizen and Benjaminite Hebrew was, by training, a highly
educated Pharisee. He eventually renounced "the traditions
of the fathers" to become the twelfth apostle, taking the
place of Judas Iscariot. Paul pioneered Christianity in the
continent of Europe. Centuries later, the Waldenses in the
Po valleys were said to have been originally founded by Paul.
Jehovah's witnesses doubt this tradition. The Waldenses,
they say, had veered "too far afield doctrinally" for their
religion to claim its origin from Paul.

One of the things the Witnesses admire about Paul, and
practice in their twentieth-century ministry, is his policy
of being financially self-supporting. The book of Acts, chap-

ter 18, verses 1-4, mentions an instance when Paul worked six days a week and preached the seventh.

He supervised a broad district of congregations. He sent out circuit supervisors, like Titus and Timothy, to cover portions of the district. These organizational features are copied by modern Witnesses of Jehovah.

II
From Paul to Arius

The last living link with the original Christian organization was the apostle John. He died about the year 100. John contributed more to the Greek Scriptures than any other writer except Paul. At John's death, apostasy had set in. The primitive Christian congregation was showing several distinct schisms.

By the beginning of the fourth century, the truly primitive-type Christians in the Roman Empire were few. They stood out as social misfits. They were marked as "refusing military service, obeisance to Caesar, political support, reverence to idols, or any semblance to religious interfaith with their contemporaries." They kowtowed to no orthodox method of worship, "Pagan or supposedly Christian." They were in fact, branded as "atheist." It was against these nonconformists that the most savage persecutions in Christianity's history were leveled.

When the beheading block and the bloody arena failed to wipe them out, Emperor Constantine struck upon the idea of "interfaith" as a solution. He called together the religious leaders of the Empire at Nice, in Asia Minor. That was in the year 325. The purpose of the conclave was to set down a body of religious doctrines that would suit everybody. There would be one universal, or catholic, code of religion. Ruling the Empire would be easier with the churches organized.

Not everybody was happy with the product. Arius, an aged elder, spoke up for the dissident segment of Christians.

He took issue with the Council on its adoption of such doctrines as the Trinity. The Council was settling, in the case of the Trinity, for the theory that the Father and Son were coeternal and coequal. But, said Arius: "The Father is a father; the Son is a son; therefore the Father must have existed before the Son; therefore once the Son was not; therefore he was made, like all creatures, of a substance that had not previously existed."

Arius got himself condemned for such arguments. The Trinity doctrine was set down to be as—quoting the *Catholic Encyclopedia*—"the central doctrine of the Christian religion." When Protestantism split off from the Church of Rome it retained the Trinity doctrine.

Great Apostasy Organization, A.D. 325

Constantine, the Pagan Caesar, condemned the writings of Arius. The aged dissident was banished into "one of the most inhospitable places in the world," the Balkan mountains.

"From the time the Nicene Creed was promulgated and accepted," conclude Jehovah's witnesses, "there was practically no more Bible study for more than twelve centuries."

During that interim the Bible "lay buried in the dead Latin tongue." Few people besides educated monks in monasteries could read it. The Church, say the Witnesses, veered all the way from Bible teachings. "A hierarchical system of Pagan origin" took the place of the "congregational system of Christian origin." The authority of man-made doctrines and traditions replaced the "God-breathed authority of the Scriptures." The Church was busy accumulating and absorbing, in the words of Cardinal Newman, "the use of temples, and these dedicated to particular saints; . . . incense, lamps and candles; votive offerings on recovering from illness; holy water; asylums; holy days and seasons, use of calendars, processions, blessings on the fields; sacerdotal vestments, the tonsure, the ring in marriage, turning to the East, images at a later date, perhaps the ecclesiastical chant, and the Kyrie

Eleison." All such things were placed above Scriptural teaching and were, as Cardinal Newman admits, "of pagan origin, and sanctified by their adoption into the Church." (*Essay on the Development of Christian Doctrine,* 1881, pp. 355-73.)

Having this "fellowship with idols," the system of religion developed in Christendom could not, by any stretch of the imagination, be identified with the "original Christian congregation of Bible educators founded by Jesus Christ," say Jehovah's witnesses.

III
From Arius to Peter Waldo

Peter Waldo was a wealthy merchant of Lyons, France. He arranged for the translation of the Gospels from Latin into French about 1160 (the other books of the Scriptures followed later). Waldo is cited by Jehovah's witnesses as a man who represented the minority Christians of his day. The Waldenses, say the Witnesses, were "the torchbearers for the cause of freedom" during "the gross darkness of the Middle Ages."

The name "Waldenses," by the way, is not derived from Waldo. It is an Anglicized form of the European word "Vaudois," which is drawn from a root meaning "valley." Waldenses refers to the geographical location of the people who lived in the valleys of the Po River and its tributaries. The Presbyterian Board of Publications published a study of the Waldenses in 1853. It states that the Waldenses were not founded by Peter Waldo. They had existed from time immemorial in the Piedmont valleys of northern Italy. The peculiar dialect of the people stemmed from a very primitive form of Latin. It marked them as being "separated and cut off from Roman influence before that empire broke up under the infiltration of Teutonic powers."

In the esteem of Jehovah's witnesses, the Waldenses were. and still are, one more among the "hundreds of Protestant sects that have sprouted." They stood by the Apostles Creed, which, say the Witnesses, includes "that notorious Pagan doctrine, the trinity." The Waldenses embraced from earliest times "the heathen doctrines of immortality of the soul and hell-fire damnation." So, the Witnesses conclude, the Waldensian claim to apostolic origin "falls flat, for these three principal doctrines did not originate with the apostles but are hand-me-downs from the Pagan philosophers, picked up and adopted by cultists after the apostles fell asleep."

Waldenses against Priestcraft

But the Waldenses did have their Christian virtues, the Witnesses say. "They have always believed the inspired Scriptures as the only source of divine truth." That way they disowned the added traditions of the church "fathers." And among other things:

"They have believed the office of Pope to be a creation of man. Papal pardons and simony they have considered a racket; nunneries and monkeries are inventions of Satan, celibacy of the clergy a snare of the Devil, and confession before a priest and death-bed repentance of no consequence. They never believed in the doctrine of the mass, but held that the Memorial bread and wine are only symbols. Image worship, worship of the cross, and temples they believe to be idolatry. Likewise the worship of Mary as 'Queen of Heaven.'"

In addition: "They have always believed that purgatory is a fable invented by men, that pilgrimages are only a means of emptying one's pockets, that holy water is no more valuable than rain water, that the so-called holy relics are nothing more than dead men's bones. They were also opposed to the shedding of human blood even in a so-called righteous war."

Personal Ministry

Another thing that rates the Waldenses high in the opin·

ion of Jehovah's witnesses was the way they carried on their ministry. "They were most energetic in preaching what they believed and in carrying on an activity in harmony with what they preached. Their missionary zeal and the method of their preaching were in the tradition of primitive Christianity. They trained and sent out missionaries two by two, usually a younger with a veteran."

Their itinerant ministers accepted food and clothing from the people to whom they preached. But for the most part "they worked with their hands to maintain themselves and their families," the Witnesses add approvingly. "Some were merchants, others were artisans of various trades, and some, like Luke, were practicing physicians. Almost all of them had training in farming and stock raising."

The Waldenses "placed great stress on reading and studying the Bible, even back in those days before printing from moveable type was invented and when copies of the Bible were very scarce. They memorized great portions of the Christian Greek Scriptures as well as passages from the Hebrew Scriptures. They also made handwritten copies of portions of the Bible and distributed these in the form of Bible tracts."

Translated Bible

In Peter Waldo's day the Waldenses produced the *Ancient Vaudois* version of the New Testament or Greek Scriptures. It was produced in what we know as the Provençal language, the common people's language. This translation predated any other complete version in English, German, French, Italian, or Spanish.

The missionary work of the Waldenses must have had quite an impact. J. A. Wylie, in his *History of the Waldenses,* says: "There was no kingdom of Southern and Central Europe to which these missionaries did not find their way, and where they did not leave traces of their visit in the disciples whom they made."

Persecution

Expansion brought persecution and suppression. Beginning about the end of the twelfth century, and for the next four hundred years, the Waldenses fell victims to the wrath and inquisition of the Roman Catholic Church. They were branded as "heretics." Pope Innocent IV consigned them to extinction, and his ruling was sustained by the most important council of the Middle Ages, the Twelfth Ecumenical Council of 1215. "Political vassals of Rome, dukes and governors, princes and kings, were sent forth to bear the Papal sword in the 'holy war.'" Armies numbering as many as 18,000 men marched to wipe out the Waldenses.

According to the Witnesses: "Some of the most horrifying pages of history are those recounting how these devout people were imprisoned in dungeons, burned at the stake, beheaded before their children, hurled over precipices. Their houses and villages were burned; their womenfolk were stripped naked and outrageously violated; their innocent children massacred."

The Waldenses and the Witnesses

Modern Witnesses of Jehovah have retained a number of features of Waldensian Christianity. The Witnesses translate and distribute Bibles. They rely only upon the Scriptures for divine authority. They study and preach the Bible as their sole message. To them Christianity is a religion you learn with your mind and practice in your personal ministry. Like the Waldenses, each Witness is a minister, a missionary. The Witnesses go forth by twos, one training the other, from house to house. And similarly, the two groups, ancient and modern, are targets of universal religious anathema.

IV
From Waldo to Wycliffe

Of the Waldenses the *Encyclopaedia Britannica* says:

'Persecution gave new vitality to their doctrines, which passed on to Wycliffe and Huss, and through these leaders produced the Reformation in Germany and England."

So across this bridge we advance a couple of centuries. Here the Witnesses pick up the history of Christianity in the days when the activities of the harassed minorities were symbolized, more or less, in the person of the Englishman, John Wycliffe.

A number of nonconformists were burned to death in England in the year 1428. The deposition of one of the victims reads: "*Item*—Nicolas Belward is one of the same sect and hath a New Testament . . . and taught the said William Wright [for] the space of one year and studied diligently upon the said New Testament."

John Wycliffe, a Roman Catholic clergyman, lived, in these troubled times, to translate the Bible from the Latin Vulgate into the English language, "for the benefit of the common man and to the great consternation of Catholicism."

Wycliffe was a prolific writer. In his day there were no English dictionaries, no spelling books, no grammars. He is known as the father of English prose, as Chaucer is known as the father of English poetry.

He was the foremost scholar and philosopher of England's foremost university, Oxford. Because he was also Oxford's foremost theologian—so keen a Bible student that he earned the title of "Gospel Doctor"—Wycliffe belongs in the Christian tradition claimed by Jehovah's witnesses.

Wycliffe Fights Priesthood

Wycliffe got into the thick of the fight that involved Papal benefices. These church offices carried with them, according to the account, "very lucrative incomes and political rank and were auctioned off by the Papal court at Avignon to the highest bidders."

Another bone of contention was the Papal tax. Somebody declared in Parliament that the Pope's tax was "taking five times as much from the people as the king's tax."

It seems that Wycliffe began to make a name for himself when he campaigned publicly against "the abuse of the monastic orders and, later, against the mendicant friars."

"These begging friars, of the Dominican and Franciscan orders," we are told, "had entered England comparatively recently but soon exceeded older orders in power and wealth. They roamed the countryside, mixed Bible stories with ridiculous legends and Greek fables, sold the Pope's indulgences, privileges and livings, and had great influence with the womenfolk.

"To swell their ranks," the chronicle continues, "they kidnapped youths from the universities, causing Bishop Fitzralph to complain to the Pope in 1357 that as a result of their depredations students at Oxford had dropped from 30,000 to 6,000, all because of parental fears that their sons would be kidnapped."

Wycliffe's Political Career

Wycliffe was a member of the House of Commons. He coupled together quite a train of Parliamentary proceedings against "the ever-increasing wealth of religious bodies, tax exemption for the friars, the right of sanctuary, . . . and the Pope's demand of . . . the annual vassal fee of 1,000 marks."

He held that each state enjoyed supreme jurisdiction over its own lands. The Pope, he argued, "had no right to levy taxes but merely to accept alms." Further, "it was sheer fatuity to send immense sums to the Papal court, rich as it was, when the country was so impoverished."

Among the seven Royal Commissioners sent to the Pope in 1374, to discuss grievances, Wycliffe was one. Being a Roman Catholic priest, he was later, in 1377, summoned before the church superiors. The outcome: "A dispute between one of Wycliffe's friends and the presiding bishop caused the hearing to end in a riot."

When a year later, he was again summoned—the Pope had issued five bulls excoriating him—the queen mother sent word forbidding any untoward action to be taken against him. A popular mob broke up the trial.

His Religious Career

Wycliffe's religious activities, which gradually crowded out his political career, endear him to Jehovah's witnesses. Religiously, they feel, he was a reformer in the right direction. "To spread his message as well as to counteract the baneful influences of the mendicant friars," the Witnesses relate, "he instructed, trained and sent forth itinerant preachers known as the Poor Priests. The example that Wycliffe set before these was that of the seventy evangelists sent out by Jesus."

The Poor Priests, says the account, "went forth in simple attire and preached to the people from the Bible texts they had, to the extent they understood them, in churchyards, market places and in the fields.

"Their message so delighted the common folk that they often emptied the churches. They spread so that an enemy of Wycliffe complained that every second Englishman was a Lollard, or follower of Wycliffe."

As to the origin of the Lollards the Witnesses say history is confused. "In the previous century," they note, "certain devout and semi-monastic societies in Germany and the Low Countries had been termed such because of their remarkable singing or 'lollen,' as it was called in Low German. The term was also used to designate heretic." Whatever its origin, the connotation of the term in Wycliffe's day was "unfavorable."

Lollard Doctrines

Doctrinally, the Witnesses say that the Lollards, like the Waldenses, did not possess "the truth" on such subjects as soul immortality. Yet in Wycliffe's time "they did present a decided step forward in contrast to the teachings and practices of the Catholic Church."

Here are some of the reasons given by Jehovah's witnesses for their opinion: "They condemned use of images,
pilgrimages, monastic orders, hierarchy of priests, and pray-
ers for the dead. To them Christ's sacrifice was sufficient."
No need for confessions, penances, indulgences and the mass,
argued the Lollards. "Condemned also were the great tempo-
ral possessions of the Church, political offices of the clergy,
and wars."

Wycliffe's attack on the doctrine of transubstantiation
(that the priest has the power to transmute the bread and
wine of the Mass to the actual flesh and blood of Christ)
brought him a third time before a Catholic court. The
verdict: He lost his post at Oxford.

Persecutions and Recantations

Richard II, the "Black Prince," turned the heat of
severest trial upon the Lollards. In 1395, Richard forced
the Chancellor of Oxford to publicly condemn Wycliffe's
"errors." Toward the close of his reign the Black Prince
became "the indefatigable pursuer of heretics." He forced
them to recant Lollardism. One church historian says:

"A [Lollard] was forced to swear to god . . . that 'from
this day forward I shall worship images, with praying and
offering unto them in the worship of the saints that they be
made after and also I shall no more despise pilgrimages.' "

Fiery heat was applied to the minority throughout the
reign of Henry IV. Lollardism, for a time, waned. Arch-
bishop Arundel caused a law to be passed that "none should
therefore preach, hold, teach . . . [anything] contrary to
the Catholic faith." Offenders were "burned alive in con-
spicuous places, for the terror of others."

Thereafter, we read, "recantations were the rule, and
willingness to embrace martyrdom the exception." The first
"heretic" to be burned at the stake in England was William
Sawtrey, a Lollard and a priest of London. Sawtrey was condemned "chiefly for denying the doctrine of transubstantiation and refusing to worship the cross."

Lollard Remnant Perseveres

That was enough for the rank and file of the "titled and distinguished gentry" who had courted Lollardism. But there remained a hard core of Lollards who "showed themselves to be of sterner stuff." English kings came and went, but the Lollards continued on. In 1428, a number were burned to death.

A hundred years later, Erasmus, "lacking the courage of a Wycliffe," advanced the doctrine to the Pope "of the uselessness of persecution." Said he: "Once the party of the Wycliffites was overcome by the power of the kings; but it was not overcome and not extinguished."

The Lollards and the Witnesses

Jehovah's witnesses believe that Lollardism during its period "came the closest thing to being Bible Christianity." The Witnesses have preserved and advanced numerous Lollard practices: Condemnation of hierarchical ecclesiasticism; personal and individual ministry; missionary work; translating, publishing, and distributing Bibles and Bible literature. Today in England the Witnesses have been called the modern Lollards.

The thread of Lollard Christianity, though badly frayed, was never snapped apart, the Witnesses find. It was saved by being transplanted from England to Bohemia. Queen Anne, wife of the Black Prince, came from there. Wycliffe's manuscripts eventually found haven there. It was in Bohemia that Lollardism found "an earnest advocate in John Huss, resulting in the Hussite movement, the forerunner of the Lutheran Reformation."

V
From Wycliffe to Luther

Martin Luther, say Jehovah's witnesses, is to be remembered not only as the man who first translated the Bible into

German, but as the successful challenger who courageously
defied the all-powerful domination of the popes of Rome.
What Wycliffe in the 14th century started in a small way
Luther in the 16th century rekindled in a big way. Previously the Roman Catholic Hierarchy, by means of persecution through its hideous Inquisition, had quickly brought
under control the few flames ignited by the Waldenses in
France, Wycliffe's Lollards in England and Hussites in
Bohemia (modern Czechoslovakia). But the reformation
flames of opposition Luther started in Germany soon became
a roaring forest fire in all Western Europe which over-
whelmed Papal Rome's corrupt, wicked ability to handle.

Overnight Luther found himself in the forefront of a rebellion of honest-hearted Western Europeans who were cry-
ing out for deliverance from the bondage of degraded priest
rule, credulity, superstition and fear. Unwittingly Luther
lit the match which finally set off the powder barrel of pent-
up, mounting, underground opposition to Catholicism. The
Papal Hierarchy's thousand-year golden "age of faith" (as
they term it) came to an abrupt end. No longer could Papal
Rome hoodwink all the people and bind them in mental
slavery to the Church in unquestioning obedience to its every
whim and dictate.

This destined 16th-century reaction to the long harsh
rule of the Catholic church, Jehovah's witnesses hold, was
actually what made possible the current four-hundred-year
era of freedom, progress, enlightenment, education, and
democracy of the Western world. The Witnesses claim in
fact that our modern age of amazing technological development would have been impossible if there had not been this
breakaway from the papal hierarchy's stranglehold of the
human intellect whereby they had kept Bible knowledge and
truth from the masses.

Luther's Religious Career

Martin Luther was born in 1483 at Eisleben in Prussian
Saxony. After a stormy religious career and untouched by

the murderous hands of Rome's agents, Luther died a natural death, February 18, 1546. A miner's son, he had had a stern upbringing. Luther's father was able financially to send him to the well-known University of Erfurt in 1501; in 1505 he graduated with a Master of Arts degree. At the desire of his father who was somewhat anticlerical, Luther entered Erfurt's law school in May, 1505. Two months later he suddenly renounced the world and entered the monastery of the Augustinian convent at Erfurt. When Luther's father heard that his son had taken monastic vows he became bitter. In reply to a friend who said that his son must have answered a call from heaven, Luther's father said: "Would to God, it were no spirit of the devil."

In 1507 Luther was consecrated to the Roman Catholic priesthood and later became associated with the teaching staff of the University of Wittenberg. As an Augustinian monk and priest he made a pilgrimage to Rome in 1510. The corruption, irreligion and vice Luther witnessed among the priests in Rome greatly disturbed him. Years later he said that he would not have missed "seeing Rome for a hundred thousand florins; for I might have felt some apprehension that I had done injustice to the Pope; but as we see, so we speak."

Luther "Bells The Cat"

Returning from Rome to Germany he pursued his studies in the Latin Bible which was available to him and also continued to teach theology at Wittenberg University. By the winter of 1512-1513 his inner struggle of conscience became such that he began to make an independent study of basic Catholic teachings. Finally on October 31, 1517, enraged at the Catholic church's campaign of selling indulgences which to him amounted to divine bribery, the selling of forgiveness of sins, Luther nailed his ninety-five protests on the church door of Wittenberg. This one act touched off what became known as the Protestant Reformation. Luther's many delighted friends, eagerly employing the then very new art of printing, quickly reproduced and widely circulated this stirring protest so that within two weeks all Germany was informed and the righteous moved to indignation and opposition. At last some one had come along with courage to "bell the cat," that is, to publicly expose the prowling, dangerous catlike Papal Hierarchy.

Shocked by this rebellion in Germany, the Pope of Rome finally issued a bull of excommunication against Luther in 1520, dismissing him from the Catholic church. Ignoring this action of the Pope, Luther continued as a priest to preach and teach. On December 10, 1520, Luther, in public, spectacularly consigned this papal written decree to the flames. He also released for wide publication his great reform treatises, the *Address to the German Nobility, The Babylonic Captivity of the Church,* and *The Freedom of a Christian Man.*

The next year, 1521, Roman Emperor Charles V called for an assembly at the city of Worms of high church dignitaries and German princes to hear Luther's defense against the Pope's orders. After a two-hour defense spoken in German, repeated for two hours in Latin, Luther concluded: "Unless I am convinced by the testimony of Scripture or by an evident reason—for I confide neither in the Pope nor in a council alone, since it is certain that they have often erred and contradicted themselves—I am held fast by the Scriptures adduced by me, and my conscience is taken captive by God's Word, and I neither can nor will revoke anything, seeing that it is not safe or right to act against conscience. God help me. Amen." Today, on a global scale, Jehovah's witnesses "maintain the same Biblical stand that did Luther so rightly."

Incidentally, in April, 1523, nine nuns escaped from the convent of Imptsch near Grimma, fled to Wittenberg, and appealed to Luther for protection. Among them was nun Catharina von Bora whom Luther married in 1525 in further defiance of the Catholic church. In time they came to have six children, three sons and three daughters.

Luther's Original Doctrinal Views

During years that followed Luther made the first translation of the entire Bible into German. He also made great progress in his Scriptural studies, "coming to some very accurate glimpses of Bible truth." Note the following quotations from Luther's early works, which were printed and widely distributed.

Jehovah

In an exposition of Jeremiah 23:1-8 Luther says: ". . . but this name Jehovah belongs exclusively to the true God." From *Ein epistel aus dem Propheten Jeremia, von Christus reich und Christlichen freyheit, gepredigt durch Mar. Lu ther,* Wittenberg, 1527.

Soul Mortal

"I permit the Pope to make articles of faith for himself and his faithful—such as 'the soul is the substantial form of the human body,' 'that the soul is immortal,' with all those monstrous opinions found in the Roman filth-pile of resolutions." From his *Defense,* prop. 27, *"Adversus Execrabilem Antichrist Bullam"* (Luther's Works, Vol. 2, folio 107, Wittenberg, 1562), first published in 1520. Also *Zion's Watch Tower,* 1905, p. 228.

What Is Death?

"Therefore the Scripture calls death a sleep. For as one falls asleep, he, when he awakes in the morning, knows nothing about how the falling asleep happened, nor about the sleep itself, nor the awakening, so shall also we on the last day arise with haste and not know either how we came into death or through death." *Kyrkopost,* 1 band., no. 29, par. 9, sid. 259. See also *Watch Tower* Reprint Vol. 1, p. 408.

Resurrection

"Hereof it must follow that they who lie in the grave-yard and sleep under the ground do not sleep as profound as we do on our beds. For it may happen that your sleep is so profound that you must be called ten times before you hear once. But the dead will hear at the first calling of Christ, and awake, as we here see of this young man and of Lazarus." *Evang. Luk.* 7. 11-17, par. 8.

State Between Death and Resurrection

"Let this be unto you an excellent alchemy and a master-piece that does not turn copper or lead into gold for you, but changes death into a sleep and your grave into a sweet room of rest, and all the time elapsing between Abel's death and the last day into a short little while. The Scripture gives this consolation everywhere." *Kyrkopost,* 1:a band., no. 109, par. 39-47, sid. 434-436.

Truth Sacrificed for a Compromise

Today Jehovah's witnesses publicize that neither Luther nor his present-day admirers "have held fast to these and many more original Scriptural teachings advocated by Luther. Regrettably those admirers of his have followed a course of watering down and compromise." For example:

By 1530 Luther's Greek scholastic friend Melanchthon had persuaded him to be party to a proposal now known as the Augsburg Confession. Melanchthon wrote up this creed-like document and presented it before the assembly at Augsburg of Emperor Charles V together with his princely and hierarchic co-rulers to effect a reconciliation between the vast number of followers of Luther and the Roman Catholic church. In this way Melanchthon and Luther hoped to bring about an internal cleansing of the Papal church by inducing her to reform some of her ways. "But the assembly flatly rejected this proposal. Luther's supporters were left holding

the bag of compromise which was full of half truths and re-
pudiations of some of Luther's earlier right views. Upon
this sacrifice of compromise, the Augsburg Confession, many
of the present-day separate Lutheran sects were founded."

VI

From Luther to Russell

Martin Luther represented a movement that did more
than throw off the ecclesiastical authority of Rome. Jehovah's
witnesses say that he planted the seeds of a doctrinal reformation as well, although the doctrinal reformation did not "get
to first base" until the 1870's. The signing of the Augsburg
Confession in April, 1530, and the Westminster Confession
in 1648, by the representative Protestant faiths sealed Protestantism's cohesion to the principal doctrines of the Roman
Catholic mother church—for example, the trinity, hell-fire,
and soul immortality. Protestantism, in short, adopted the
Nicene Creed.

Doctrinal Reformation Lacking

Real doctrinal reformation, going deeper than Luther,
than Wycliffe and the Lollards, than Waldo and the Waldenses, and digging back beyond Arius of the fourth century
into the "first-century primitive Christian teachings set out
by Jesus Christ and the apostles," was, say Jehovah's witnesses, to await the movement symbolized by a nineteenth-
century Bible student named Charles Taze Russell.

By Russell's day, of course, Rome had waned as a world
ruler. The Protestant Reformation was "degenerating" so
rapidly that "with every golden jubilee it celebrated the
appearance of fifty new schisms." Darwin had rocked the
smug complacency of orthodoxy with the anti-Bible doctrine of evolution. Although church-book memberships grew,
a lot of people were taking religion with a sack of salt. The
time was ripe for a re-evaluation of things that people had
just naturally taken as "unquestionable and unanswerable."

People were going to have to find in the Bible a new hope, a
new faith, a new outlook; or they were going to have to
ditch the Bible along with the fables of the Iliad, at least,
as far as being a live and divine force in religion.

Within another half century the iron fist of communism
would be knocking at Christendom's doors.

If the hand of Rome's priest-rule had been thrown off
and the field opened to a "buyer's market" for competitive
Protestant brands of religion, then it was naturally to be
expected that a "consumer's union" would, by and by, take
religion into the Bible laboratory and test it for "what it
was worth against what it was advertised as worth."

In other words, a doctrinal reformation, "an era of deep,
penetrating and continual Bible research," was impending.

Bible Students Launch Reforms

Jehovah's witnesses feel that when their immediate predecessors, the Bible Students, plunged into an "objective ex-
amination of Christendom's doctrines," they were taking the
biggest single step since the days of Jesus toward restoring
"doctrinal teachings originating in the Bible," teachings that
had been buried under "more than fifteen centuries of
Pagan sludge."

Here was a movement that would collide dramatically
with the whole body and soul of Christendom—Catholicism,
Protestantism, Judaism, as well as Islam. It was a work that
would "trace the teachings of Protestants back to the Catho-
lics and from the Catholics back to Pagan philosophers like
Socrates and Plato." It would probe beyond the Council of
Nice. It would reach into the vitals of "first-century primitive
Christianity." It would bring to light a religion that to
Christendom would appear new, strange, unorthodox, non-
conformist, and unwanted by the modern world.

The movement would, for the first time, "drive dissident
Protestantism back into the arms of Mother Rome" in a
unified front against the "doctrinal reformation."

Evolutionist atheism, sweeping across the minds of more

than half the people of Christendom, might leave mankind with no faith in orthodox religion, as Galileo with his theory that the earth was round knocked the props from under Christendom's "unquestionable" preachment that the earth was flat. The religious movement that dawned about the 1870's would discredit orthodox religion in general as thoroughly, or more so, than evolution. However, it would vindicate the Bible, not turn people away from the Bible, like evolution. Those who embraced it would become Bible students of the Waldensian-Lollard zeal.

While the Bible Students would not attract the general body of Christendom any more than did the original Christians, the Arians, the Waldenses, or the Lollards, their impact would be increasingly felt.

The man who stands in history as the symbol of the Bible Students is Charles Taze Russell. He was also the last living link with modern Witnesses of Jehovah. For that reason a separate chapter is devoted to his life and works.

C. T. Russell: Millennium's Prophet— "For then will I turn to the people a pure language, that they may all call upon the name of Jehovah, to serve him with one consent."— ZEPHANIAH 3:9, *American Standard Version*

CHAPTER FIVE

CHARLES T. RUSSELL— MILLENNIUM'S PROPHET

THE man who used to be mentioned most often in connection with Jehovah's witnesses was Charles Taze Russell. "Russellism" came to be a reproachful term for the doctrine of the Witnesses, or "Bible Students," as they were once known. "Russellites" was a name their enemies tacked upon them, for the same reason that the name "Lutheran" was given the adherents of the German reformer.

Pastor Russell, as he was called by both his associates and his enemies, was said to have "founded" the modern organization of Jehovah's witnesses. The Witnesses acknowledge that Mr. Russell organized the legal corporation known as the Watch Tower Bible & Tract Society, in 1884, and that he started the *Watch Tower* magazine, in 1879, which he edited and published for thirty-seven years thereafter.

And in proclaiming the "second coming, or presence, of Christ as due in 1914, with the subsequent establishment of God's Kingdom power toward the earth beginning at that date," Pastor Russell had no equal, they say. He was Millennium's foremost prophet. His successor, J. F. Rutherford, declared: "He did a greater work for the cause of Messiah's Kingdom than did any other man that ever lived on the earth." (*The Watch Tower*, December 1, 1916, p. 374.)

But as for founding the spiritual society of Jehovah's witnesses, the Witnesses do not agree that it was the doing of any man. That was, they affirm, one of the "fruits of the Kingdom itself." It was a result of "returning to pure Bible teaching." When hundreds and thousands of minds and hearts were drawn together by the "pure language" of the Scriptures, the Power that produced the Bible necessarily produced the society of modern Bible adherents. The spiritual society is produced by Jehovah's spirit, the Witnesses emphatically state.

To illustrate: Moses did not produce the theocratic nation of Israel. He was a leader used by Jehovah. In similar ways Pastor Russell was a leader, not of men. His was a leading voice in proclaiming that the time was at hand for the long-awaited Kingdom of heaven.

With the Kingdom's advent there must come a uniting and a cleansing work, a reformation in doctrine, a clarifying of the Bible's teachings. The product would be a new society of Christians. They would be brought around to a new conception of Christianity, or, rather, to a "return to the primitive, original teachings promulgated by Christ himself."

Thus do the Witnesses view the era that dawned with Pastor Russell during the 1880's. They regard him as the foremost human pioneer in a doctrinal reformation "more far-reaching and important to posterity than anything that had been done since the days of Jesus and the apostles."

Most Widely Syndicated Writer

"His writings," declared an enemy, "are said to have greater newspaper circulation every week than those of any other living man; a greater, doubtless, than the combined circulation of the writings of all the priests and preachers in North America; greater even than the works of Arthur Brisbane, Norman Hapgood, George Horace Lorimer, Dr. Frank Crane, Frederic Haskin, and a dozen others of the best-known editors and syndicate writers put together." (*The Continent.*)

Photo-Drama—First "Sound Movie"

His sermons went out to some four thousand papers; they were syndicated in fifteen hundred at a time. At the dawn of the twentieth century a generation before the coming of the sound "movie," Pastor Russell produced the Photo-Drama of Creation. It was "a story of the world, as told from the Bible." It was "set forth in an orderly manner" by combining colored stereopticon views and motion pictures. But what a production it was! It was eight hours long. There were four two-hour parts. Besides, the introduction, intermissions, and conclusion were garnished with twelve short talks in the voice of Pastor Russell.

As for the film itself, it was accompanied by synchronized phonograph records. The ninety-six four-minute explanations were the Pastor's. The voice was that of the then-renowned recording artist Harry Humphrey. The ninety-six four-minute explanations are still in print.

The Photo-Drama was the first sound motion picture ever presented to the public. It played in private homes, church houses, theaters, opera houses, and auditoriums all around the world. Nine million persons saw it. A few theater managers attempted to run the drama at regular shows where admission was paid, but the undertakings failed. So actually no admissions were ever charged to see it.

Millennialism Divides Christendom

For forty years prior to World War I the burden of Pastor Russell's preachment focused on the year 1914. That year "marked the date in Bible chronology for the appearance of the Kingdom of Heaven," he declared.

Millennial Dawnism and Russellism came to be synonymous terms. The doctrine gained prominence all over the world.

Church leaders found themselves divided over the Millennium issue. No insignificant number agreed with Pastor Russell. During the height of World War I a joint manifesto was published by a group of England's most noted clergymen, representing Baptists, Congregationalists, Presbyterians, Episcopalians and Methodists. The manifesto read:

> *First*—That the present crisis points to the close of the times of the Gentiles.
>
> *Second*—That the revelation of the Lord may be expected at any moment, when he will be manifested as evidently as to his disciples on the evening of his resurrection.
>
> *Third*—That the completed church will be translated, to be "forever with the Lord."
>
> *Fourth*—That Israel will be restored to its own land in unbelief and be afterwards converted by the appearance of Christ on its behalf.
>
> *Fifth*—That all human schemes of reconstruction must be subsidiary to the second Coming of our Lord, because all nations will be subject to his rule.
>
> *Sixth*—That under the reign of Christ there will be a further great effusion of the Holy Spirit on all flesh.
>
> *Seventh*—That the truths embodied in this statement are of the utmost practical value in determining Christian character and action with reference to the pressing problems of the hour.

The churches of Christendom abandoned the Millen-

nium doctrine following World War I. They adopted the
League of Nations as their "political expression of the Kingdom of God on earth." How the Witnesses clung to their
conviction that the Kingdom really did begin in 1914, and
how the New World Society grew, expanded, and reformed
"under Kingdom rule, amidst its enemies," from 1919 onward, is to them one of the most dramatic stories ever told.
To the world, it may be the most fantastic thing ever heard
of. Had Jehovah's witnesses disappeared along with their
proclamation of the Millennium after 1914, the world would
have said that Millennialism was just one more of those
human idiosyncracies that come and go. The fact that the
Millennium doctrine has fed and matured the fastest-growing
religious group in the world particularly since 1919 has led
orthodoxy to conclude that it is one of those fantasies that
came and stayed.

Opposition to Russell

Pastor Russell indeed was Millennium's foremost prophet.
wielding an influence around the globe. On other counts
he became the target of unified opposition from orthodox
Christendom. For the first time since Luther, the Bible Students noted, Catholics, Protestants, and even Jews re-
united "on a common ground," because of their mutual
antagonism toward Pastor Russell. "It is a well-known fact
that, for centuries, Catholics and Protestants have been dead-
ly enemies, and the Ecclesiastical Heavens have long been in
turmoil because of the mortal combat between them,"
bristled the Pastor's legal counselor, Judge Rutherford. "In
the controversy we are here examining, Catholics and Protestants have united."

No segment of the religious world was excluded from the
furor, lawyer Rutherford observed. "In the case here we see
Greek Catholics, Roman Catholics, Anglicans, Gentiles and
Jews, Presbyterians, Methodists, Baptists, Lutherans, Congre-
gationalists, etc., etc., not only in America, but in Canada, in
Europe and from the four corners of the earth, united for

the avowed purpose of overthrowing this one man," he wrote. The fight against Martin Luther "seems a pigmy compared with this one," Rutherford recorded.

If the Judge's language of 1915 sounds sulphurous to our ears today, it was as mild as an April breeze compared to the blast-furnace fulminations of the opposition. One of the gentler remarks from the enemy camps came from the Reverend William G. Moorehead, D.D., who wrote that Pastor Russell was "being used of the evil one to subvert the Truth of God."

Viewing the tempest, one neutral observer, Professor S. A. Ellis, a Southern educator and writer, declared: "I believe there is no one more bitterly persecuted, harshly condemned, woefully misrepresented and misunderstood than this fearless, conscientious man of God." The Professor added that "no infidel writer, such as Hume, Voltaire or Ingersoll, ever suffered such ruthless attacks as have been made against Pastor Russell."

Apparently Pastor Russell's gift for stirring up a hornets' nest every time he opened his mouth was not so much the preaching of the doctrine of Kingdom Come; it was, rather, the preaching of the things that attended the great "spiritual reformation issuing from the Millennium hope." In other words, it was the associated doctrinal controversies that started the fires. The Pastor committed, it would appear, three major acts against orthodoxy. These were of unpardonable proportions, and are here set forth.

First: Challenge to Orthodox Doctrines

Martin Luther challenged the Papal authority of the Roman Catholic Church. The Protestant revolt, spearheaded by men like Luther, threw off Rome's hierarchical authority but not the primary doctrines of Catholicism. By the Augsburg Confession, the Protestant churches adopted the Catholic Nicene Creed. Included in the Nicene Creed were cornerstone doctrines such as the trinity, immortality of the soul, and eternal torment. In short, the Protestant Reformation, starting about the sixteenth century, was a revolt against established church authority. It was not, essentially, a revolt against orthodox doctrine.

Pastor Russell went a step further. His was a revolt against orthodox church doctrine. Had church authority, under Rome, strayed so far out of line from the congregation system established by Jesus that a revolt from the prevailing hierarchy was necessary? Then what about church doctrine? If the hierarchical system of church rule were essentially a "Pagan innovation" seized upon by Constantine and his successors, what about the teachings of the church? How could church officials "go Pagan" in their manner of exercising authority and "still retain Christian teaching"? In fact, had they retained Christian doctrine, would not that of itself have kept them from "going Pagan" in their employment of ecclesiastical authority? So Pastor Russell and his associates reasoned.

No wonder, then, that Russell found himself ranged against the Pope. "For nearly three hundred years after Martin Luther's day there was a gradual development of Protestant denominational churches," commented Judge Rutherford, singling out the position of Pastor Russell. "Trouble would start in one denomination; a division would result; some would withdraw, and the seceders would organize a new denomination, each as 'Baptists,' 'Methodists,' 'Campbellites,' 'Congregationalists,' 'United Brethren,' 'River Brethren,' 'Christadelphians,' etc. Each sect, by its own authority, authorized certain persons to preach, and seemingly no one had any special objections to this until about 1840."

In 1840, Rutherford continued, something appeared which Pastor Russell would eventually find himself ranged head on against: As summarized in the Watch Tower publication, *Battle in Ecclesiastical Heavens,* 1915, pp. 9-10, it was this:

> The Bible teaches that THE Church is *one,* the Body of Christ, whereas the Protestant Systems, *each* *claiming* to be "The Church," number nearly two hun

dred. Because of this apparent inconsistency, they feared that all their organizations will be brought into disrepute, and therefore there should be some alliance between all of them; hence, in 1846, the "Evangelical Alliance" was formed. While allied, each sect formed its own Ordination Boards, which Boards exercised the power of ordaining or authorizing others to preach.

One of the rules resulting from this Alliance has been, and now is, that no one shall be allowed to preach unless he has received an ordination at the hands of one of these "Ordaining Boards" already existing. Anyone attempting to preach without being licensed or formally ordained by one of these "Ordaining Boards" is branded as a scab preacher.

This Alliance has become virtually a Preachers' Union, and an edict has gone forth that if anyone desires to preach he must get a union card (ordination); otherwise, he is irregular. Some of the independent thinkers have held aloof from this Alliance, claiming the right to worship God according to the dictates of their own conscience and to exercise the liberty of free speech.

The defendant herein, Pastor Russell, has refused to accept such man-made ordination, recognizing the Scriptural method provided by the Lord, and *none other*. He has refused to be forced into the Combine; hence the Combine seeks to force him to quit preaching.

Second: Renounces Clerical Profession as Means of Financial Gain

The clerical profession, like law or medicine, had always been viewed as a vocation that afforded its members more or less financial security, along with a high degree of respectability and prestige in the community. Pastor Russell renounced the orthodox viewpoint as "worldliness." Each living creature owed it, as a matter of simple gratitude, to school himself to the extent of his ability in the word and

law of his own Creator. Then he should want to share with
others whatever he learned, for the common good of all,
and to the honor and vindication of the Creator. Should
creatures make merchandise of the Word of Life? he asked.
Should you be paid for loving your neighbor as you love
yourself? Could you really be a Christian unless you "gave
to others freely as you freely received"? How many members
of the primitive Christian church were mere nonpreaching
members? Were not all teachers and preachers of the Word?
True, there were overseers of the flocks. Some were apostles,
some prophets, some evangelists, some pastors, some teachers. But why? "For the perfecting of the saints, for the work
of the ministry, for the edifying of the body of Christ."
(Ephesians 4:11, 12) In other words, all engaged in the
ministry. To be a Christian meant to be a minister. The
orthodox distinction between clergy and laity was "just
another mark of Christendom's apostasy." It was a shame to
professing Christians to accept life, a hope of salvation, and
the promises of their Creator of a better world, and then refuse the plain, simple expression of gratitude shown in
ministering the Word to others. Russell, reasoning this way,
would have none of the paid clergy.

He set the pattern by donating his personal wealth of
more than a quarter of a million dollars—no inconsiderable
fortune in his day—to the nonprofit Bible educational work
of proclaiming the Millennium's dawn and its attendant
doctrinal reform throughout the world. He spent forty thousand dollars to publish a booklet exposing "the hell-fire doctrine." "Pastor Russell," Rutherford remarked, "adopted a
kind of trade-mark on all his announcements—'Seats Free,
No Collections'—and the Alliance concluded that this was a
reflection on their constant begging for money, and therefore
another cause for anger."

Third: "Turns Hose on Hell"

Part of the "comforting food" served up by the Pastor
brought upon him the anathema of practically all of orthodox Christendom. It was the teaching that hell is not hot—

that it is a *condition* of death, not a *place* of torment. In the first place, he contended, the Bible does not teach that man possesses an "immortal soul" that can endure endless roasting in torment. In the second place, if God is the very personification of love, who sets before all men the choice between life or death—not life in heavenly bliss or life in hellish agony—how could God maintain a place of torture that not even the Devil would care to operate through tedious eternities? "Would you hold a puppy-dog's tail in the fire three minutes? Of course not, unless you were subhuman. Yet we are taught that God himself consigns creatures to everlasting torture in fire hotter than any we can imagine."

"If God is love, then he draws his creatures to him solely on the basis of love. He draws no one by fear. To love, the pure in heart respond. Fear can drive even the vilest criminal to obey, for purely selfish preservation. But God does not tolerate the wicked-hearted to gain life. Only those who respond to love gain his favor. There is no point, then, in trying to terrify people against their heart's desire, into righteousness. Scare religion, based on the eternal-torment teaching, would be the last thing God would resort to, to attract men to Him."

So the hell-fire doctrine, the Pastor contended, was one of the oldest and most formidable weapons of the clergy, both Pagan and Christian. By it they sought to hold their flocks in the church systems. "Hell-fire gone, the collections come slowly," soliloquized Russell's biographer, Rutherford.

The orthodox reaction to the "no-hell doctrine," as they called it, was that Pastor Russell had thrown down the one restraint that held people in check. Now the world was certain to go to the Devil. To which the Bible Students retorted: "Does not the Bible say the world already belongs to the Devil? That the whole world lies in the wicked one? And remains there till its final destruction from God's own hand? Where is there any proof, scripturally or in history, that the world was ever converted to Christianity?"

More than anything else, these three doctrinal issues— "Man-made Ordination," "the Paid Clergy," and "Hell-fire" —were responsible for Pastor Russell's becoming the "most hated and most feared one man to appear in orthodox Christendom since the first century A.D.," said Rutherford.

Russell's Wealth

Opposition to the Pastor, to a great extent, took the form of personal attack. The brunt of the assault was aimed at his financial manipulations.

Russell must have been a boy wonder in the business world. Before he was thirty years old he had expanded his father's clothing store in Allegheny, Pennsylvania, and in short order established four more. By the time he was thirty he sold out the chain for a quarter of a million dollars. That amount of money in the 1880's was equivalent to more than a million dollars in 1950.

At this point in young Russell's life the study of the Bible had so engrossed him that he resolved to forsake the commercial world and devote his time and means to educational work of a religious character. It was not, of course, a matter of entering the conventional ministry. His Presbyterian, and later his Congregationalist, background gave him a high moral outlook; but it proved to be weak soil for nurturing the revolutionary convictions that were growing in his mind. No existing form of religion was fertile enough for that.

Surrounding young Russell was a growing body of men and women devoted to a systematic study of the Bible, particularly in relation to the doctrine of Christ's second coming, or presence. Ministers of twenty-nine denominations were eventually represented in the group.

These pastors and their associates were of the opinion that due to the diversity of their teachings they were dividing the people into a growing number of irreconcilable schisms, for no good reason. "How many Bibles are there?" they asked themselves. "But one," they acknowledged. "How many Gods?" "But one." "How many true faiths?" "Necessarily but one." "Then what are we doing with twenty-nine faiths?" The Bible branded sectarianism as "marks of carnality," they noted.

They "faced up to the fact" that the root of their differences was a matter of disagreement over doctrines. "Does the Bible teach one doctrine twenty-nine different ways?" they asked themselves. They found the answer obvious. "One Bible. One God. One faith. One doctrine."

Surely there was some way to resolve the twenty-nine differences of opinion and "let God be true, though every man a liar." There was a way. It was simply to single out one doctrine, then search throughout the Bible for its teachings on that doctrine. Then by "laying our own preconceived and prejudiced differences on the mantel," and by "comparing spiritual things with spiritual," it was no insurmountable or unpalatable task to arrive at the "truth which makes us free."

What was good for resolving twenty-nine "confusions" ought to be as good for resolving 129 they felt. Especially, if their convictions that Bible chronologies focused on 1914 as the end of "gentile rule" and the time marked for the Kingdom's advent proved true. This was no time for sectarian wrangling. "It was high time for a doctrinal reform to sweep over Christendom."

The prospects of such a spiritual rebirth so fascinated Russell that he plunged his fortune and energies into the crusade. He labored under no delusions about "converting the world, any more than Noah converted the world of his day." But "to reach those who would hear" was worth the price of a global evangelical crusade the like of which had never been tried before.

In 1879 the magazine *Zion's Watch Tower and Herald of Christ's Presence* was launched, with Russell as editor and publisher. In 1884, Russell and his associates incorporated Zion's Watch Tower Tract Society (later, 1896, named Watch Tower Bible & Tract Society) of Pennsylvania. This they would use as a publishing and directive agency.

His enemies charged that all this was a scheme to form a publishing house as outlet for Russell's prolific literary output, and to net him a personal profit that would put his earnings in haberdashery in the shade.

To that his militant friend and legal counselor, Judge

Rutherford, replied: "When Pastor Russell closed out his business, many years ago, he had upward of a quarter million dollars. The greater portion of this he freely spent in the publication of Bible literature, which was distributed to the people without charge for the purpose of enlightening them concerning the harmonious plan of God as taught in the Scriptures." The balance of his wealth, continued the lawyer, "was transferred to the Watch Tower Bible & Tract Society by agreement with Mrs. Russell, who co-labored with him in his religious pursuits."

Rutherford cited the charter of the Society. It was a "non-stock corporation" that "pays no dividends, no salaries," and "no one has ever, as its books clearly show, reaped any financial benefit therefrom." In Russell's time, the Society received the bulk of its financial support from thousands of voting members, who were entitled to one vote for each ten-dollar contribution. During lawsuits launched against Russell and the Society, the books were audited in court. Although Russell donated more personally to the organization than any other individual, it was proved that neither he nor any other person ever appropriated any of the money for personal use.

Pastor Russell died penniless, in 1916, with no bank account, no personal property, and only a handful of personal effects. During the last forty years of his life he had received, along with fellow workers at the Society's headquarters, Bethel, his room and meals, traveling expenses, and ten dollars monthly for incidental expenses. This monthly allowance was increased to twenty dollars, but again dropped to ten dollars, during the presidency of his successor, Judge Rutherford, who died in 1942. Recently it was raised to fourteen dollars monthly.

Domestic Disagreements

In addition to financial woes, Pastor Russell suffered public criticism because of domestic difficulties. They were eventually ended through a legal separation by his wife.

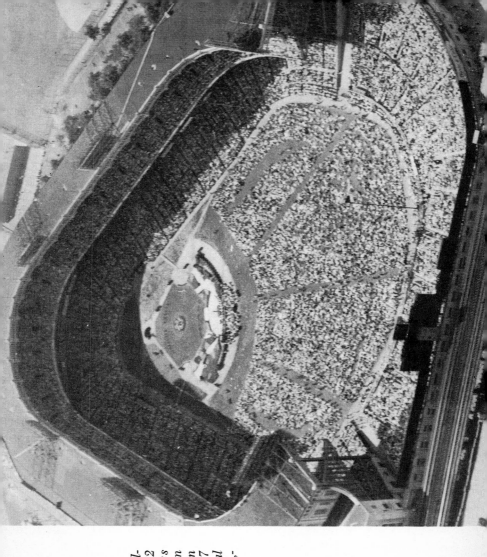

Yankee Stadium's all-time capacity — 91,562 Jehovah's witnesses packed Yankee Stadium July 26, 1953, and an o v e r f l o w of 74,267 swelled the grand total for the meeting to 165,-829.

Vice President Franz (left) and President Knorr overjoyed with release of the New World Translation of Hebrew Scriptures at Yankee Stadium assembly.

While others hear, deaf mutes "see" a lecture at Yankee Stadium. Inset shows sign for "society."

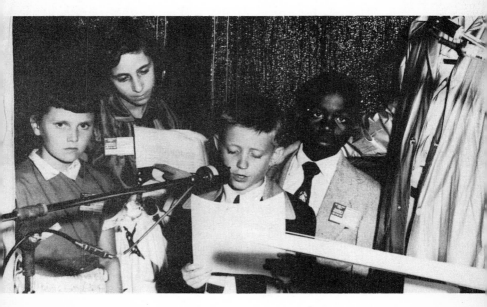

Youngsters in skit before 125,000 at assembly demonstrate results of ministerial training.

Happy conventioners display new preaching aid Make Sure of All Things, *released at Yankee Stadium assembly.*

Branch Servant Erich Frost headed German delegation at Yankee Stadium. Frost survived eight years in Nazi concentration camps. More than 10,000 were imprisoned; 2,000 died there. Since Nazi downfall over 50,000 German Witnesses have been added.

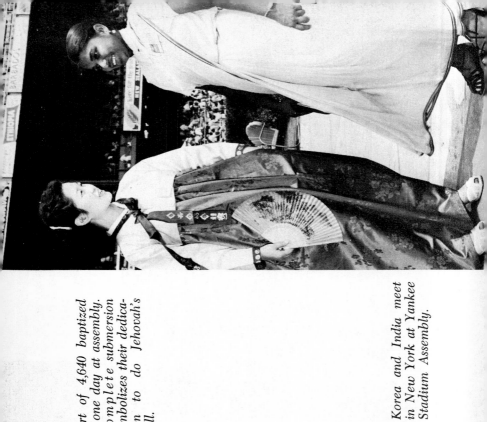

Korea and India meet in New York at Yankee Stadium Assembly.

Part of 4,640 baptized in one day at assembly. Complete submersion symbolizes their dedication to do Jehovah's will.

Trailer City near Dunellen, New Jersey, eased the rooming problem by accommodating 45,000 delegates. This city appeared in two days, lasted eight days, vanished in two days, to the astonishment of the countryside. It was the biggest city in the county.

Missionary uses interpreter to address 6,152 at Manila.

9,313 *Witnesses at San Fernando, Philippine Republic,*

Volunteer orchestra accompanied singers at San Fernando assembly.

under shelter constructed by volunteers, March, 1954.

Watch Tower headquarters at Magdeburg, Germany, seized by the Communists in 1950.

33,600 Witnesses at West Berlin Waldbuhne in 1949.

Branch office in Berne, Switzerland.

President Knorr addresses public meeting at Ramallah, Jordan.

5,000 in open-air assembly at Limbe, Nyasaland, 1952.

African Witnesses at Ndola Twapiya Kingdom Hall, Northern Rhodesia, before preaching activity begins.

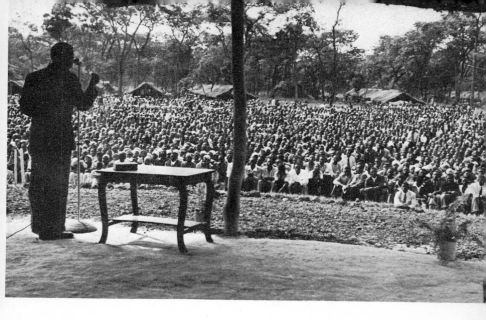

Kitwe assembly, Northern Rhodesia, 1952. 18,000 attended.

Administration offices specially built to serve Kitwe assembly.

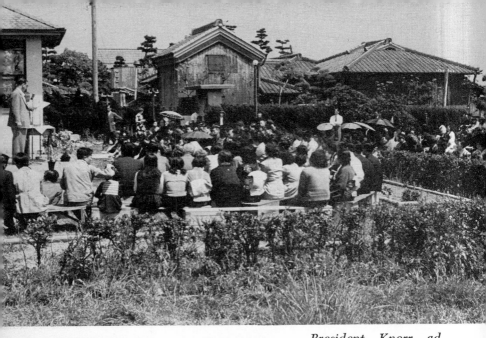

President Knorr addresses group near Kobe, Japan.

284 baptized at Seoul assembly, Korea, 1954.

Kanarese group of Watchtower *distributors in Bombay, India.*

One of the new Kingdom Halls at Kingston, Jamaica.

The WATCHTOWER AND AWAKE!

In 1954 more than 73 million magazines (43,467,909 *Watchtower* and 29,620,128 *Awake!*) were distributed throughout the world.

Total world circulation for the WATCHTOWER, 1,950,000 in 40 languages

AWAKE 1,300,000 " 13

AFRIKAANS
ONTWAAK!

GERMAN
ERWACHET!

HOLLANDISH
De WACHTTOREN

AFRIKAANS
WAGTORING

JAPANESE
ものみの塔

ZULU
INQABAYOKULINDA

MALAYALAM

ENGLISH
The WATCHTOWER

SWEDISH
VAKTTORNET

UKRAINIAN
ВАРТОВА БАШТА

IDO

FINNISH
Herätkää!

The WATCHTOWER

CINYANJA

CISHONA

GERMAN
Der WACHTTURM

PORTUGUESE
SENTINELA

ILO-NCHE

ATALAIA

GUJARATI
BANTAYAM

FRENCH
TOUR DE GARDE

SLOVAK
STRÁŽNA VEŽA

FRANCAIS

PANNACHIET

GREEK

GERMAN
Der WACHTTURM

SRPADNA VEŽ

EKOTIA

ARABIC

13

Mrs. Russell had been associated with him, prior to their marriage in 1879, in his religious work. For about thirteen years of their married life the Russells "lived happily." They had no children, but in 1889 a ten-year-old orphan girl was taken into their home and "treated as a member of the family."

In the late 1890's, the Russells began to disagree over the management of *The Watch Tower* magazine. "She became dissatisfied with his manner of conducting this journal and attempted to dictate the policy thereof," Rutherford recounted. "Being the head of the house," Rutherford firmly continued, "Pastor Russell would not submit to his wife's dictating the manner of conducting his business affairs."

After some five years of growing friction, Mrs. Russell decided to bring matters to a head. She selected and called together a committee of three to hear both sides of the controversy.

But the only point of contention between the Russells, two committee members testified, seemed to be "the management of the paper, or journal." Mrs. Russell's committee ruled against her.

The lady seemed to accept her defeat. The Russells "kissed and made up."

But the reconciliation lasted scarcely longer than it took the committee to break up and go home. That same year, 1897, Mrs. Russell "without notice . . . voluntarily separated herself from him . . . nearly eighteen years after their marriage."

For about six years thereafter she lived separately from the Pastor. Finally, in June, 1903, she filed in the Court of Common Pleas, at Pittsburgh, for legal separation. In April, 1906, nine years after Mrs. Russell left her husband, the trial was brought before the jury.

Miss Ball and the Jellyfish

While on the stand Mrs. Russell let slip a remark that there was more to her leaving her husband than a once-

patched-up squabble over the management of *The Watch
Tower* magazine. With due encouragement from counsel she
related a little fish story that was to grow into a whale of a
lot of ammunition for the Pastor's enemies for years beyond
his death.

The story Mrs. Russell told centered around a revelation
the Pastor allegedly made to the orphan girl whom the
Russells had reared. To quote Mrs. Russell, the Pastor had
remarked to the girl slyly: "I am like a jellyfish; I float
around here and there. I touch this one and that one, and if
she responds I take her to me, and if not I float on to others."

The jellyfish story created a sensation in the courtroom.
The Court asked if the complainant had brought the girl; a
Miss Ball, to verify the charge. Mrs. Russell had not. Did
she know where Miss Ball lived at the time? Mrs. Russell
did. When had the Pastor told the Ball girl about the jellyfish? In 1894. Had Mrs. Russell lived with her husband three
years after that, knowing about the jellyfish story? She had.

The next question focused on 1897, when Mrs. Russell
brought her husband before her committee that decided in
his favor. "Did you, at that time, reveal to the committee that
the Pastor was as promiscuous as a jellyfish?"

Mrs. Russell replied, "No."

Her own lawyer pinned her down. "You don't mean
that your husband was guilty of adultery?"

"No."

Russell, on the stand said he had never heard the fish
story until that moment, in the courtroom.

"About the girl that was in the family," Judge Collier
charged the jury. "That is beyond the grounds of the libel
and has nothing to do with the case because not being put
in it, and it was condoned or allowed to pass."

As the Russells had already been separated seven years
before legal recourse was sought—or almost ten years from
the time of the hearing—the court legalized the separation.
No absolute divorce was ever granted either party.

From then on the Pastor was never to hear the last of
the jellyfish. The Washington *Post* pounced upon the "scan-

dal." It charged the Pastor with "immorality." And it was served with a libel suit. The jury exonerated Russell of the libel. It awarded him one dollar damages.

Counsel Rutherford felt that the judge's instructions to the jury on behalf of the defendant, the *Post,* "were manifestly erroneous and prejudiced." He appealed the case to Superior Court. It reversed the judgment of the lower court. The case was remanded for retrial.

When the case came up again, Russell had advanced to the point of putting in part of his testimony when the *Post* offered a compromise. The newspaper accepted all the court costs. It paid the Pastor "a substantial sum of money." Thereafter it published his sermons.

Next on the list was the Chicago *Mission Friend.* It published an attack by a New Jersey clergyman, who painted the Pastor as quite a philanderer, citing the jellyfish episode as proof. In the suit that followed, the *Mission Friend* sought to compromise. "Pastor Russell, not desiring 'blood money,' but merely that his good name be vindicated, agreed to the compromise upon the following terms, which were carried out:

"The *Mission Friend* paid all the costs and published a retraction admitting that it had wrongfully published the Miss Ball or 'jellyfish' story concerning Pastor Russell; further stating that Pastor Russell is a Christian and a gentleman of the highest integrity and moral standing and entitled to the respect and esteem of all good people."

The Miracle Wheat Episode

The jellyfish "scandal" dematerialized into "the greatest fish story ever manufactured," as the Pastor's friends called it; but there was to be yet another incident no less bizarre.

That was the Miracle Wheat episode.

Pastor Russell's ill-wishers could not have hoped for more sensationally toned adventures than those that came his way. The Miracle Wheat story reminds me of the irrepressible Herodotus, who wrote that in Babylon "the blades of wheat and barley grow there to full four fingers in breadth; and though I know to what a height millet and sesame grow, I shall not mention it; for I am well assured that, to those who have never been in Babylonian country, what has been said concerning its production will appear to many incredible."

On November 23, 1907, a year after the Russell legal separation, the Assistant Agriculturalist of the United States Government, a man by the name of H. A. Miller, had no notion, I am sure, of vying with Herodotus. But on that day he filed a report on an astounding species of wheat. It seems to have originated spontaneously three years earlier, in 1904, in a Virginia truck garden belonging to a farmer named K. B. Stoner, of Fincastle.

Without the slightest forewarning or fanfare, a fantastic plant had put in its appearance in Mr. Stoner's garden. At first sight he mistook it "for a kind of grass known as parlor grass." It was fortunate—or maybe unfortunate—that he didn't pull it up right away. For, given a little more growth, the plant proved to be wheat. And what wheat! It had one hundred and forty-two stalks, each stalk bearing a head of fully matured wheat.

Modestly, Mr. Stoner confessed that he had never beheld the like of it. His acknowledgment that he had never before seen a stalk of wheat "bearing more than five heads" must have been the prize understatement for the year 1904.

This was something right out of Herodotus. It was a miracle. Mr. Stoner named the plant "Miracle Wheat."

For several seasons he kept sowing the grain and replanting, and each season he got a prodigious outburst of wheat stools that flabbergasted everybody in the country. Mr. Stoner's wheat, of course, made headlines.

"Mr. Stoner was amazed," announced one ultraconservative press report. "It seemed incredible. When a Frenchman in 1842 announced that he had discovered a species of wheat in the Mediterranean country which produced *four* heads to the plant, people said he was crazy. But here was a plant with 142 heads!"

At this point the objective news report injected a pardonable exclamation point. It continued: "That first year after discovering the plant he got 2,000 grains. In 1906 he got sixteen bushels, and has now raised the crop of wheat, all carefully preserved for seed, to 800 bushels."

The most remarkable thing about Miracle Wheat, the newspaper explained, was this: "Whereas there is produced in the wheat sections [of Virginia] an average at the best of seventeen bushels to an acre, the average yield of the Miracle Wheat during the last three years has been fifty-six bushels to the acre; and whereas from eight to ten pecks of seeds are required to plant an acre in Virginia, Mr. Stoner uses only two pecks; and in comparison to the yield of ordinary wheat in the neighborhood, which is eight bushels for each bushel of seed, Mr. Stoner gets about seventy-five bushels for one. An ordinary stalk of wheat covers about four inches of space. The Miracle Wheat covers twelve."

So you can see why Miracle Wheat got so much notoriety that eventually the United States Government sent its expert, Mr. Miller, to examine the product. In his report Miller stated: "The wheat, which came from an unknown source, has been grown in the nursery . . . and . . . under field conditions . . . giving excellent results. Milling tests have been made of the wheat, and its quality seems to be as good as, if not superior to, other varieties of winter wheat.

"The average height of the wheat," according to the report, "is four feet, four inches."

One paragraph of Mr. Miller's Government release ought to arouse one or two Congressional committees, even at this late date.

"It is said," the paragraph read, "that the Russian government has secured an option on the wheat, and will buy a consignment of 80,000,000 bushels when that quantity shall have been raised."

To be sure, Russia was, in 1908, a respectable pillar of Christendom, under divine rule of the Czar. Mr. Stoner was neither a Russian agent nor a member of Pastor Russell's religion. He was just a hapless Virginia farmer who by some unknown chance got visited by a miracle out of Herodotus.

And too, old-timers say, Miracle Wheat was gradually merged and blended into lower strains until it lost its identity before 1920. Russia evidently never got any of it. That it was the "real thing" nobody in the South disputes. Farmers had but one objection to Miracle Wheat. It grew a beard.

You will find that milling processors don't like the job of cleaning bearded wheat.

But how did Pastor Russell get involved with Miracle Wheat? Here is the story.

First, he published the press report, which you have just read above. He also included Mr. Miller's Government report. Mr. Russell ran the story as an item of perhaps unusual significance to the readers of *The Watch Tower.*

By the time the story appeared in the March 15, 1908, issue of his journal, it had, of course, appeared in the general press as the Government release had been published five months earlier, on November 28, 1907. The Pastor was publishing anything but a "scoop." The comment he tacked on, by way of an introduction to the press-release quotations, was not original, either. It voiced a general sentiment. "The public press is telling of the origin of 'Miracle Wheat' in answer to prayer," began the Pastor. He then gave his own opinion: "The description has the earmarks of truth to it."

What was probably original about the Pastor's story was his conclusion. He mused: "If this account is but one-half true it testifies afresh to God's ability to provide things needful for the 'times of restitution of all things which God hath spoken by the mouth of all the holy prophets since the world began.' " (Acts 3:21)

In other words, it was the Pastor's hope that Miracle Wheat might be a sign that the Millennium was at hand— even in a material, physical sense.

After the appearance of *The Watch Tower* article, some of the Bible Students took more interest in Miracle Wheat. During 1911, J. A. Bohnet, of Pittsburgh, Pennsylvania, and Samuel J. Fleming, of Wabash, Indiana, made up a joint donation of about thirty bushels of Miracle Wheat for the

Watch Tower Bible & Tract Society. They proposed that the wheat be sold by the Society for seed at one dollar a pound. Current market prices averaged $1.25 a pound. The donors specified that the proceeds, about $1,800, was to go to the Society to be used in its religious work.

The Society, of which Pastor Russell was president, appreciated the contribution. It sold the Miracle Wheat.

Then came March 22, 1911, and the Brooklyn *Daily Eagle,* a fire-breathing foe of *The Watch Tower,* commenced a series of articles and cartoons ridiculing the Pastor, his religion, and his wheat. On September 23 the *Eagle* published a caricature of the Pastor and beneath it this question: "If Pastor Russell can get a dollar a pound for Miracle Wheat, what could he have got for Miracle stocks and bonds as a director in the old Union Bank?"

Russell sued the *Eagle* for libel. The suit that followed was one of the most sensational trials in the annals of Kings County, New York. It revolved around the issue of "whether or not the wheat in question was superior to ordinary wheat."

The Pastor's religion came up for some red-hot castigations during the trial. Mr. Stoner came from Fincastle, Virginia, equipped with a "To Whom It May Concern" letter signed by the Honorable Claude A. Swanson, Governor of Virginia. He and seven others of the eleven wheat farmers who testified swore they had "never heard of Pastor Russell or his religious teachings prior to the trial."

While the issue was wheat, not religion, the jury, "being largely composed of men of strong religious prejudice, and at least one of them being an atheist," let the point of the battle escape them, the Pastor's lawyer, Judge Rutherford, charged. The Brooklyn *Eagle* won the case and Russell appealed to the Supreme Court's Appellate Division (168 App. Div. (2d) 121).

Pastor Russell's Scholarship

His marital troubles, sensationalized by the jellyfish story

and the Miracle Wheat episode, were not all the tribulations that jounced Pastor Russell's career. To go into all his ups and downs would fill a bigger book than this one has any right to be, and it would take more skill to make them interesting than I can muster. Each story sketched is essentially the story of them all. Whenever an issue came up that reflected upon the Pastor's integrity and the religion he stood for, he did his best to fight it down, for the sake of the good name of the work and the organization he served.

Opposers of Mr. Russell, while not disputing his mental brilliance, and even fearing his devastating sharpness on Scriptural matters, ventured nevertheless to scorn the idea that the Pastor was really a qualified Bible scholar. He could not read the Hebrew and Greek languages, they pointed out. They challenged him, in public debates, and demanded on the witness stand that he say whether or not he understood the old Bible languages. The Pastor said, of course, he did not. Neither did his enemies, as a rule, he added.

One charge made against Mr. Russell was that he perjured himself in court by saying he knew Greek. The trial in question was brought by the Pastor against a tract writer who, Mr. Russell felt, had slandered him. On March 17, 1913, before the Police Court of the City of Hamilton, Ontario, the Pastor gave this testimony:

Question: "You don't profess, then, to be schooled in the Latin language?"

Answer: "No, sir."

Question: "Or in Greek?"

Answer: "No, sir."

Then he was asked if he knew Greek letters, the Greek alphabet. He answered yes. His critics then twisted his statement that he knew Greek letters into the false and unwarranted allegation that he had said he knew the Greek language.

What he did have, the Pastor explained, was the school-boy ability to look up an English Bible word in a Hebrew or Greek lexicon. That way he could find out what the original Hebrew or Greek term was. Then he knew how to look up the Hebrew or Greek original in a dictionary that gave its definition in English. From that he could then look back in the Bible and compare the English word used in the translation with the English words used in the dictionary. Sometimes the English word in the King James or Catholic Bible translations did not agree with the English words defining Hebrew or Greek in the dictionary. So somebody was wrong—the Bible translators or the Bible dictionary makers.

For instance, he could look up in the Old Testament or Hebrew Scriptures, the words "hell," "grave," and "pit" in the Protestant and Catholic Bible versions. He would then find that all three words had but one original Hebrew origin, the transliteration *sheol*. So "hell" must mean the same as "grave" or "pit," or else the translators themselves did not know Hebrew.

Or he could look up the word "hell" in the New Testament or Greek Scriptures and find that in the original Greek there were three different Greek terms, "hades," "gehenna," and "tartarus," all translated by the one word "hell." According to the Greek dictionary, these three Greek words meant three different things. So why hide three different meanings under the one English word "hell"?

By the time you studied up every reference to "hell" throughout the Bible, in the light of facts such as these, you were liable to wind up with an idea or two that did not jibe with orthodox preachment.

In doing such research Russell employed the standard translations and versions produced by Catholics and Protestants. He used Bible dictionaries and concordances and other instruments prepared by Presbyterians, Methodists, Jews, and Christadelphians. There was nothing highly complicated about looking up words and sentences in books, he asserted. What was complicated was the fact that the churches had, by the 1880's, succeeded in splitting up into more than 200 denominational schisms. The process had, a half century later, grown to more than 265 schisms in the United States alone. The Bible students were concerned with a fundamental reformation, a "going back to the Bible" for the "original doctrinal truth," upon which to produce a "primitive Christianity" that would draw together from all other religions a people unified by a "cleaned and purified concept" of Christianity.

After more than seventy years of the most intensive Bible study, the group has found that the process must still go on, that there is still more to learn. In 1946, their standard Bible help, *Let God Be True*, was published to cover twenty-four foundational Bible doctrines. In 1952, they issued a revision of the book because, during the four-year interval, their understanding of some of the doctrines had been magnified by further Bible research.

This is an indication of the pace at which the reformation religion of Jehovah's witnesses is evolving. The foremost pioneer in the movement, Pastor Russell, touched to greater or lesser extent upon practically all the "New World" doctrines. He established the policy of the scientific researcher's approach. In doing so he ignored the orthodox concepts. He dug back as far as he could into the original-language meanings of the Bible. Not being a scholar of Hebrew and Greek, that laid him open to ridicule by orthodoxy.

Being concerned most of all with the doctrine of Christ's return, Russell and his associates found that the "clearing up" of the Millennium doctrine involved a consequent revaluation of all other doctrines. For instance, at Christ's second coming, Paul indicated, there would be a resurrection of those of Christ's body members who had "fallen asleep" in death. So an understanding of resurrection was required. But what was the resurrection? Was it something that took place at the death of the physical body? If so, how could the soul be still sleeping in death awaiting Christ's coming? If, as orthodoxy taught, the soul is immortal and cannot die, how could it be resurrected? On the other hand, if the Bible teaches a resurrection of souls sleeping in death, what about the "immortal soul" doctrine? Too, if the Bible teaches the destruction of wicked souls in Gehenna, what about the teaching of conscious torment of souls that are not destroyed at all? And so on.

In the preface of his books Pastor Russell made it a rule to quote Proverbs 4:18, "The path of the just is as the shining light, that shineth more and more unto the perfect day." In 1950, the Watchtower Society began to release its first original Bible translation produced by the New World Bible Translation Committee of scholars among Jehovah's witnesses. No wonder, then, that Russell's forty years of investigation only pioneered a work still pursued by the Watchtower Society.

The End

On Monday afternoon, October 16, 1916, at five o'clock, Pastor Russell said good-by to the Bethel Home family of workers at Brooklyn. He had put in a hard autumn of lecture tours. He was sixty-four years old. He was serving as pastor to the congregations of New York, Washington, D.C., Pittsburgh, Chicago, Los Angeles, other cities in the United States, London, England, and places in Europe, Africa, Asia, Australia.

He was now embarking on a cross-country circuit extending to Los Angeles and back. His traveling companion, Menta Sturgeon, insisted that this last tour was more than the aging man could stand. But the Pastor would not hear of canceling the trip.

He had been suffering for thirty years from cystitis. The case had developed to an incurable stage. He knew it. He would rather go ahead with his regular routine till death came, than to sit still and die anyway. That was the way he seemed to feel about the matter.

By now, Russell's six volumes, *Studies in the Scriptures*, were circulating in sixteen million copies throughout the earth, in thirty-four languages. The Watch Tower Bible & Tract Society of Pennsylvania, whose charter he personally wrote, now had a sister corporation, the Peoples Pulpit Association (after February, 1939, named Watchtower Bible and Tract Society, Inc.) of the state of New York. There were numerous other sister corporations and branch offices in

Great Britain, Germany, Finland, Norway, Sweden, Denmark, Switzerland, France, South Africa and other countries. For thirty-seven years he had edited and published the semimonthly journal, *The Watch Tower*. It was "the only publication on earth that has ever announced the presence of our Lord." His sermons, which it published, were, by 1916, carried in fifteen hundred newspapers, world wide.

By Tuesday, his second day on the train, Pastor Russell found himself failing fast. His companion, Mr. Sturgeon, noted that, as usual on trips, Mr. Russell "was awake every hour of the night, and thought pretty much day and night." Wednesday turned into a wearisome ordeal, starting off with a detour caused by a train wreck. A layover in Kalamazoo with nothing to eat and a six-hour delay in reaching Chicago caused the Pastor to miss his speaking assignment. He also missed the train to Springfield. In the Chicago station a woman writer taxed him for material for a book she was writing about his work. "People on the train knew him— brakemen, porters, conductors and passengers," Sturgeon remarked. "In the stations, hotels, on the streets, everywhere, he was recognized. Many a time people came to me on the train and inquired, 'Is that not Pastor Russell?' and would say, 'I knew him by his picture in the paper,' or 'I heard him lecture at such and such a place.' Sometimes they would inquire, just after he had walked through the train, 'Who is that distinguished gentleman with you?'"

On this trip, for the first time, he had to cancel speaking engagements. He was feeling too low to meet the one at Springfield. At Kansas City, he had to run to catch a train. "How different this trip was from anything that had ever preceded it!" lamented Sturgeon later. At Wichita, the Pastor lost his valise, which fell off the running board of the car that was carrying him to his engagement. With the valise went his notes. He arrived in Dallas for a three-day convention, which was staged amid the hurly-burly of a state fair. The ordeal left him "tired, and his head was aching."

Sturgeon related that by the time they arrived in Galveston, the next morning, the Pastor "was not well by any means." And "it was at this meeting he did something we never knew him to do before. He wrote on a piece of paper his text and one verse of a song, and told the friends that he had done so that he might make no mistake."

The Pastor, Sturgeon, and nine friends dined together that day, October 22, at the Hotel Galvez. "This proved to be the last meal that Brother Russell ate," Sturgeon said. Thereafter it was to be "a little fruit juice, a swallow or two of a soft-boiled egg, or something like that."

Following his last luncheon, the Pastor gave a public discourse in a Galveston auditorium, then immediately boarded a train to Houston and delivered a two-and-one-half-hour talk there. That meant a total of six hours on the platform for the day, not counting hours of listening to private problems and giving advice. Then he boarded a train for San Antonio and traveled all night.

Next morning he began a day's grind of correspondence and business matters pertaining to the Society's interests. That night Russell mounted his last platform.

Three times during this talk he had to leave the podium, for five-, seven-, and ten-minute intervals, during which his secretary, Sturgeon, filled in.

That night they boarded a train for Los Angeles. Sturgeon, for the first time, removed the Pastor's shoes for him. He massaged the failing man's hand.

"That is the greatest creed-smashing hand I ever saw," Sturgeon told the Pastor.

"I do not think it will smash any more creeds," Russell replied.

Later in the night the Pastor asked weakly, "What shall we do?"

"You seem to know your case better than anyone else," Sturgeon answered helplessly. "You have thought of everything that can be done. Have I done everything that you can think of that I ought to do?"

"You have," the ailing man gasped. "I do not know what I would do without you."

By now, the Pastor was suffering mortal agonies. Sturgeon

urged him to try to make it back to Brooklyn. "You are getting weaker all the time. Your vitality is being drained while you are eating nothing to replenish it."

No one could help him at Brooklyn or anywhere else, the Pastor said stoically.

A bridge on the Southern Pacific had burned out and a layover of a whole day at Del Rio in hot weather, alongside a trainload of soldiers, did not help his pains.

On Sunday the twenty-ninth, Russell talked to the Los Angeles congregation, seated in a chair. That night he and Sturgeon boarded a Sante Fe train for the long voyage to Brooklyn. But Pastor Russell never left the drawing room of the car *Roseisle*. Not alive, that is.

Tulsa, Topeka, Lincoln, were to be stops. Tuesday, the thirty-first, Menta Sturgeon sent a wire to Brooklyn saying that before October closed the Pastor would be gone. "After embalming will come home with his remains."

A physician was called aboard at Panhandle, Texas. He diagnosed the case, recognized the symptoms, gave Sturgeon his name, and "was off before the train got under way."

Not many minutes later, near one o'clock, Tuesday afternoon, October 31, 1916, Pastor Russell breathed his last.

In the eyes of the man who had admired him greatly, Judge Rutherford, the Pastor was the greatest preacher this side of the apostle Paul. "He did a greater work for the cause of Messiah's Kingdom than did any other man that ever lived," Rutherford summed it up.

The religion that Russell professed and advanced has grown ever since the 1870's. By 1950, it was publicly acclaimed to be "the fastest-growing religion in the world."

THE TEACHINGS OF CHARLES T. RUSSELL

The greatest prophet of Christ's Second Presence to appear during the nineteenth century was said to be Charles Taze Russell.

For forty years he preached that the year 1914 would mark the "end of the gentile times" and the beginning of a world judgment that would reach its climax in the Bible Armageddon and the establishment of the thousand-year reign of Christ.

While Millennialism was Russell's main theme, he led the way in a full-scale doctrinal reform of Christendom's teachings, which paved the way for the theology of the twentieth century's Witnesses of Jehovah. Here is a summary of Russell's main beliefs.

Soul and Death

He taught, supporting his teachings by constant citation of Scripture authority, that man does not *possess* an immortal soul, but that he *is* a soul and is mortal; that the wages of sin is death, not eternal torment; that death came upon man as the just penalty for the violation of God's law; that death means the destruction of man.

Ransom

That God, in His goodness, has provided the great ransom price whereby man may be delivered from the bondage of sin and death; that God's beloved Son Jesus became a man and grew to manhood's estate, was put to death as a man and raised again from the dead a spirit being, possessing the divine nature; that by his death and resurrection Christ Jesus provided and produced the ransom price for man's deliverance and restoration; that Jesus Christ, by the grace of God, tasted death for every man.

Resurrection

That every man in God's due time must, therefore, have a fair trial for life, and to this end there shall be a resurrection of all the dead.

Christ's Second Coming

That Jesus Christ ascended into heaven and must come the second time.

Christ's Body Members

That the period of time elapsing between the first and second comings of the Lord is devoted to the election of the members of the body of Christ, taken from among men.

Requirements to Receive Election

That the requirements for election to that exalted position are a full faith in the shed blood of Jesus as the ransom price, a full dedication to do the Father's will, and a faithful continuance in obedience to the Father's will even unto death; that all who are thus dedicated and begotten of the holy Spirit and are overcomers shall have part in the chief resurrection, and be exalted to positions in the heavenly kingdom of God and participate with Christ Jesus in his Millennial reign for the blessing of all the families of the earth.

Thousand-Year Reign

That during the thousand-year reign of Christ all the dead shall be awakened and given a fair and impartial trial for life or death; that under that reign the willfully disobedient shall be everlastingly destroyed, while those obedient to the righteous rule of Christ shall be fully restored to human perfection of body, mind, and character.

Paradise Restored

That during this Millennial reign the earth shall be brought to a state of Edenic paradise and made fit as a place of habitation for perfect man; that man, fully restored to perfection, will inhabit the earth forever.

The positive side of Pastor Russell's message may be said to be twofold—that to the church and that to the world. (Isaiah 52:7) To the church it was a message of the ransom and of the second presence of our Lord (which he understood had been begun in 1874). To the world it was a message of the ransom and of human restoration, to follow the events of this age.

The negative side of his message was one of criticism and even denunciation of the "hypocrisy and sham of tare religionists," and particularly the systems that they support.

To him the church was still but an obscure traveler along the highway of nations. So far from mixing in and "leavening" the whole lump of earthly institutions with quasi-religious politics, she was intended of her Lord to remain separate from the world and to be engaged in the preliminary affairs of his kingdom.

J. F. Rutherford—"The Kingdom Is Here!"—
"While he was sitting upon the mount of
Olives, the disciples approached him privately,
saying: "Tell us, When will these things be,
and what will be the sign of your presence and
of the consummation of the system of things?"
And this good news of the kingdom will be
preached in all the inhabited earth for the pur-
pose of a witness to all the nations, and then
the accomplished end will come."—MATTHEW
24:3,14, *New World Translation of the Chris-*
tian Greek Scriptures

CHAPTER SIX

J. F. RUTHERFORD—
"THE KINGDOM IS HERE!"

"WHO will be our pastor?"

The question rang out when Charles T. Russell died.
It resounded through the ranks of International Bible
Students around the world.

"I will not be your pastor," replied Joseph F. Rutherford.

This was the man who had been appointed to Pastor
Russell's place as president of the Watch Tower Bible &
Tract Society of Pennsylvania, of the Peoples Pulpit Asso-

ciation of New York, and the British corporation, International Bible Students Association.

But Mr. Rutherford, a lawyer of twenty-five years' rough-and-tumble experience, did not feel that he had stepped into Mr. Russell's shoes; not in the role of pastor. No one would ever replace Russell in that role, he insisted. "In view of this, and in deference to his memory, it is my opinion that no one should be elected, henceforth, pastor of any ecclesia."

Then how would he—Rutherford—serve the congregations?

"If you feel that because I am president of the Society my name should be connected with your ecclesia," Rutherford replied, "then designate me as counselor."

He had served Pastor Russell many years as counselor, he reminded them. "I will be glad to continue in this capacity to the friends in general." He wanted to serve the organization as a whole "in the capacity of counselor, advisor, and helper." But not as pastor.

From that time onward a change began to take place in the character and attitude of the Bible Students. It was gradual but you could detect it. For the first time they began to perceive that the "organization" was more important than individual "personalities."

Character Development vs. Organizational Growth

Until 1916, the Bible Students had clung to the man Russell. He was the rallying point. There was not as yet any "society" of people that understood how to rally around anything else than a man.

More than once Russell cautioned the Bible Students that he was not above error. He made no claim that everything he preached or wrote was absolute, infallible truth. Proverbs 4:18 was his motto: "The path of the just is as the shining light, that shineth more and more unto the perfect day." He saw in himself just one more Bible Student. To him the Bible was a Book of Life whose teachings had

lain submerged for centuries under religious errors and
Pagan falsehoods. No man could see all the light in a
twinkling. It would take years and years for the light to
shine "more and more unto the perfect day." He had not
anticipated living to see the "full restoration" of Bible truths
to the Christian body.

But after forty years of listening to his sermons and
studying under his tutelage, the Bible Students found themselves too shocked, too stunned by the loss of him to know
in what direction to go. At any rate, many of them felt that
way. They seemed to think that "further revelation" had
died out with the Pastor. An editorial writer, through
The Watch Tower, had to assure the faithful, in 1917, that
the sermons still being run in the magazine were the Pastor's
sermons. He had left an almost "inexhaustible" lot of sermons and they were printed for a long, long time. Other
material was being published in the journal, of course, but
the principal sermons were the Pastor's.

So one of the first barriers Counselor Rutherford had to
demolish was the "creature worship" complex. The congregations doted on "character development."

Rutherford felt that the best antidote for "character
development" would be "organization development." The
Bible Students had been looking upon Russell as the "servant" who Jesus foretold would be "appointed to lead the
faithful into the truth at the Kingdom's advent." The Pastor himself had indicated, however, that it was the publishing organization that was more probably the "servant." For
forty years, using *The Watch Tower* as its mouthpiece, the
organization had calculated Bible chronologies to point to
1914 as the end of uninterrupted "Gentile rule." Kingdom
rule, at that date, was to interfere drastically with the Devil's systems of things. The Kingdom was to begin ruling
"in the midst of its enemies." Many of the Bible Students
seemed to have overlooked that. They failed to consider
that there would be a preliminary period, climaxed by Armageddon, before the unhindered thousand-year reign of Christ
began.

Rutherford pointed out that that meant a lot of work still had to be done. The people of the whole world had to be "set on notice" that "the Kingdom is here." It was time to fulfill the command: "This gospel of the kingdom shall be preached in all the world for a witness to all the nations, and then shall the end come." That text, Matthew 24:14, is probably the most quoted Scripture used by Jehovah's witnesses, even now.

"So we must advertise the Kingdom!" challenged Judge Rutherford.

This didn't appeal too well to a big segment of listeners. For forty years they had looked toward 1914. Many of them thought that about October of that year the Lord would come down and swoop them off to heavenly glory. He failed to come that way. Now they did not relish the task of having to pick up the work again and go on with it harder than ever. If the Kingdom was going to cost that much they were not too sure it was worth the price. Interest and enthusiasm were cooling off by the time Rutherford took the helm.

Rutherford pointed out that the Pastor himself had looked ahead to this "great judgment work." The Pastor himself had foreseen that every one of the "consecrated" must have a share "in the witness." Rutherford quoted Russell's words: *"He will give all His people a share."*

In fact, he reminded them, there was a project of unfinished work that Mr. Russell had been building up to when he died. It was bigger, more important, than anything the Pastor had done before. It was to have climaxed his career.

The Seventh Volume

The project involved the production of one last volume, the seventh. It was to top off the six preceeding *Studies in the Scriptures*. The first six had only laid the groundwork for the seventh. The seventh was to deliver the spiritual deathblow to Christendom.

For some time, a full, precise definition of the world, as

Scripturally pictured under the name "Babylon," had been maturing in Pastor Russell's mind. This was to be the message of the Seventh Volume. It would disclose that "the church nominal, Catholic, Protestant," and other divisions, in association with the civil powers, constituted Babylon— "an abomination in the sight of the Lord." The Seventh Volume was to deliver a judgment upon the world that would annihilate the popular idea that this is God's world and the Devil is just trying to mess it up. Rather, the truth was to be made plain precisely in reverse: that this is the Devil's world, unconverted and irreformable, and God is now interfering with its wicked course by bringing forth his Kingdom rule by Christ.

Consequently, in the midst of all the Devil's world the good news must be preached, to the chagrin of Satan, and for the sake of all who would heed the warning before Armageddon rid the universe of the old systems of things.

The prophet Elijah had prophesied fearlessly against sinful Israel till the day of his death. Then Elisha caught up Elijah's mantle. Elisha asked for a "double portion" of the spirit that had rested upon Elijah. Pastor Russell personally, the Bible Students thought, had done a work parallel to that of Elijah. He had notified Christendom for forty years that she was coming to her day of judgment at the Kingdom's establishment, in 1914.

Now it was time for the "Elisha work"—with twice the spirit!

Who would catch up "Elijah's Mantle"? It would not be himself, Rutherford declared. It would be the organization— all the Lord's people must join in declaring "The Judgment Day of Jehovah."

In what better way could the organization start than by bringing out the Seventh Volume? "Up to the very day of his death Brother Russell was bending every effort to prepare for the smiting of Babylon," Rutherford reminded. The aging Pastor had worked up some of the material. It now had to be completed. Babylon must fall irreparably, in the hearts and minds of all who saw the facts. The Seventh Volume would open their eyes to the facts.

Two prominent Bible Students, Clayton J. Woodworth and George H. Fisher, were invited to "write up manuscript and complete what had been written by Brother Russell." The product that came from their pens was published. The title page bore the names of the three corporations as publishers and sponsors.

And so, at last on July 17, 1917, the seventh and concluding volume of *Studies in the Scriptures* was released.

World's Biggest Best-Seller

The title of the book was *The Finished Mystery*. It turned out to be the most phenomenal seller of its day. "When the book was first published," recounted *The Watch Tower* in December, 1917, "it was thought that less than 100,000 volumes would be required. But by October the 850,000 edition was in the printing."

Editions in Swedish and French were already off the presses in Europe. Translations into German, Polish, Greek, and other languages were being rapidly completed. The Seventh Volume was also running serially in *The Watch Tower,* in several languages. "The sale of the Seventh Volume is unparalleled by the sale of any other book known, in the same length of time, excepting the Bible," the Society was happy to report six months after it was first published.

It was a triumph for the organization. "The arm of the Lord is not shortened; He can pour out His spirit upon any of His servants to accomplish His purpose." This summarized the sentiment in the letter columns of *The Watch Tower* thereafter.

"The work shall go on!" Rutherford emphasized.

The Seventh Volume proved up to the keenest expectation of the Bible Students in "exposing Babylon." It "put the world on judgment." Kingdom Here was the only hope. That fact must be made known. All who would not turn away from the age-old systems of things, held together by religious-political-commercial ties, would go down with the world systems at the battle of the great day of God Almighty.

The old world smarted under this indictment. It smarted violently. The Seventh Volume figured head-high when the United States Federal Government brought Rutherford and seven others up for trial on sedition charges, in 1918.

Internal Rebellion

Before that, however, the new president had to face another Himalayan obstacle placed squarely in his path. This was a plague of rebellion within the headquarters ranks in Brooklyn.

The theme of *The Watch Tower* for a long time had been "harvest sifting." The Bible Students were keyed up for a break within the ranks. "The love of many shall wax cold" was one of the prophecies to mark the sign of the Kingdom's presence. Pastor Russell's death, it seemed, was the signal that started a wholesale fight for supremacy within the Board of Directors.

Just before he died, Mr. Russell had arranged to reorganize the headquarters, or Bethel, personnel. Setting down some of the highest officials, including the vice-president, and raising up some from the lower ranks was part of his plan. The demoted members might have swallowed their pride had the Pastor lived to make the change. When Rutherford carried out the arrangements, they could not swallow it. Within five months after he came to the presidency, four of the seven directors challenged his power. The bone of contention was Alexander Hugh Macmillan. In his last days at Brooklyn, Pastor Russell had voiced a lot of confidence in Macmillan. He had not appointed him—nor had anyone appointed him—a director. But Rutherford, upon becoming president, did appoint Macmillan assistant, or aide, to the president.

Four directors wanted a reorganization. In the first place,

they wanted whatever Rutherford did to be subject to the Board's approval. The Board, they argued, was the supreme authority. The president was its figurehead. As things stood, the president was the administration. He was not consulting them. He was letting them know what he was doing only after it was done. He was putting them in the position of advisers on legal corporate matters.

Rutherford made no bones about "going ahead." The Pastor before him had worked that way. The Pastor made decisions. The Pastor issued administrative orders without the Board's prior sanction. They had not challenged the Pastor. But Rutherford was not Pastor Russell.

Appoints New Board Members

When they sought to hem Rutherford in, the four directors found the experience similar to four corks bobbing against Gibraltar. Rutherford was a man of fearsome personal power Against his forceful personality, few people were able to stand. He was also shrewd. But they had asked for it, and he showed the unhappy complainers a thing or two they had not dreamed of.

First, he pointed out a provision of the charter of the Peoples Pulpit Association. This was the New York corporation that corresponded in character to the Pennsylvania corporation, the Watch Tower Bible & Tract Society. So that the Society could carry on its operations in New York State, all the property and transactions of the Pennsylvania corporation had been turned over to the New York corporation. And the provision in the New York corporation charter read:

> The said corporation shall have as officers the following: A President, who shall be elected by the Board of Directors at the first meeting thereof, and shall hold his office for life, and whose duty shall be to preside at the meetings of the corporation or of the Board of Directors

and have the general supervision and control and management of the business and affairs of said corporation.[1]

That made the four dissident directors unhappy. They tried to force a Board meeting. Then Rutherford, with his lawyer's knowledge of things, rolled out a live bomb.

What you have not noticed, he said, in effect, is that you four Brothers are members of the Pennsylvania corporation. The charter of that corporation says you have to be elected in the state of Pennsylvania. Were you elected there?

No, they answered.

You were elected in the state of New York. If you want to get technical about it, then technically you are not legal members of the corporation, in the first place.

Well, why was not a legal election held? they demanded.

The Pastor, for some years, allowed the elections to be

---

[1] That the president of the Society thereafter continued to exercise such unrestricted freedom may be seen by the following account of N. H. Knorr's actions in relation to bringing forth a new Bible translation. The quotation is from *The Watchtower* of September 15, 1950, pp. 315, 316:

"Particularly since 1946 the president of the Watch Tower Bible & Tract Society has been in quest of such a translation of the Christian Greek Scriptures. On September 3, 1949, at 8 a.m., at the Brooklyn headquarters (Bethel) the Society's president convened a joint meeting of the boards of directors of the Pennsylvania and New York corporations, only one director being absent. After the meeting was opened with prayer the president announced to these eight fellow directors the existence of a 'New World Bible Translation Committee' and that it had completed a translation of the Christian Greek Scriptures. This it had turned over to the possession and control of the Watch Tower Bible & Tract Society, Pennsylvania corporation, just the preceding day. He read the committee's document by which it assigned the translation manuscript to the Society in recognition of the Society's unsectarian work of spreading the sacred Word of God and of promoting the knowledge and understanding of its teaching among the people of every nation, kindred, people and language, and in order that the translation might be a new means toward the expanding of its Christian educational activities throughout the world.

"The president himself had read the manuscript of the entire translation, and on request he read to the meeting several entire chapters to let the directors see the nature of the translation. This reading was followed by favorable comments by all the directors present. One of the Pennsylvania corporation directors then moved the Society's acceptance of the gift. This was seconded. The motion was unanimously adopted by all the directors of the corporation, and thus the translation became legally the property of the Society's Pennsylvania corporation. But it had to be printed at the plant of the New York corporation here in Brooklyn, N. Y. On September 29, 1949, the president turned over the first of the manuscript to the Brooklyn factory force to start working on it."

held in New York State. No one ever caused any trouble before, he replied. We got along peaceably until you four started to rebel.

There were only three members of the Board—Pierson, Van Amburgh, and Rutherford himself—who had been duly elected in Pennsylvania, he pointed out. Then he delivered the death blow.

Now another provision in the Charter states that when the corporation members fail to elect a new member within thirty days, the President has the authority to appoint a member to the Board, he pointed out.

You four not being legal members, and it having been long past thirty days since any legal appointments have been made, I'll tell you what I have done, he went on. In Pennsylvania I have appointed four legally constituted members to the Board of Directors. They replace you, he concluded.

On July 17, 1917, the same day for the release of the Seventh Volume, Rutherford announced his appointments of Dr. W. E. Spill, J. A. Bohnet, George H. Fisher, and the controversial A. Hugh Macmillan to the Board. They replaced the four complainers, R. H. Hirsh, J. D. Wright, A. I. Ritchie, and I. F. Hoskins.

At the Brooklyn Bethel, the ousted Board members and some other "unhappy complainers" were invited to "get out." They got. Before the "harvest sifting" was over at Bethel, thirty-one members were expelled.

Rutherford then put his action to a vote of confidence. All the congregations were invited to take part. On December 13, 1917, 813 American congregations registered the following tally:

Candidate	Director	Pres.	Vice-Pres.	Sec'y-Treas.
J. F. Rutherford	10,990	10,869	14	3
W. E. Van Amburgh	10,909	14	418	10,700
G. H. Fisher	10,333	4	395	30
J. A. Bohnet	10,323	1	126	4
A. H. Macmillan	10,204	2	1,856	102
W. E. Spill	9,880	—	183	1

Candidate	Director	Pres.	Vice-Pres.	Sec'y-Treas.
A. N. Pierson	8,888	49	5,722	13
C. J. Woodworth	1,776	28	328	2
M. Sturgeon	680	376	73	36
A. I. Ritchie	543	10	223	21
R. H. Hirsh	469	1	2	25
I. F. Hoskins	459	—	—	3
J. D. Wright	444	2	4	5
H. C. Rockwell	342	1	13	209
R. J. Martin	293	17	73	7
W. F. Hudgings	181	—	30	14
A. E. Burgess	143	—	9	11
P. S. L. Johnson	126	20	25	19
E. W. Brenneisen	100	1	4	3
89 others receiving less than 100 votes	1,036	26	182	94
Total Votes Cast....		11,421	9,680	11,302

It should be noted that the first seven names made up the new Board, including Rutherford's four appointments. The four ousted members placed tenth, eleventh, twelfth, and thirteenth.

The Sedition Trial

"Joseph F. Rutherford and six of the other seven Russellites, convicted of violation of the Espionage Act, were sentenced to twenty years each in the Atlanta pen yesterday by Judge Howe, in the United States District Court in Brooklyn."

This appeared in the New York *Tribune* on June 22, 1918.

A deferred sentence, the story said, was passed upon the eighth defendant, Giovanni de Cecca. "His companions," it continued, "each with a pink carnation in his lapel, marched out of court to start their sentence."

Along with the general press, the *Tribune* quoted some remarks from Judge H. B. Howe's opinion.

" 'If they had taken guns and swords,' he said, 'and joined the German army the harm they could have done would have been insignificant compared with the result of their propaganda.' "

The propaganda "advocated and spread throughout the

nation as well as among our Allies," Judge Howe declared, was in fact more dangerous and harmful than a "division of the German army." He did not speculate on the effect of the same propaganda spread throughout the enemy nations. There, the Bible Students were outlawed and imprisoned too. But as far as America was concerned he was going to make an example of this case. Others could beware.

"The sentence is that the defendants, Joseph F. Rutherford, William E. Van Amburgh, Robert J. Martin, Fred H. Robison, George H. Fisher, Clayton J. Woodworth, and A. Hugh Macmillan, serve a term of twenty years in the Federal Penitentiary at Atlanta, Georgia, on each of the four counts of the indictment, but that the sentences commence and run concurrently."

The *Tribune* observed that the defendants pleaded "not guilty" to all four charges. "They retained the self-possession that has characterized their conduct throughout the entire trial. As the judge's words fell on their ears not a shade of emotion crossed their faces."

Rutherford was quoted while on his way from the court to the jail: "This is the happiest day of my life."

"Why?" a reporter asked.

"To serve earthly punishment for the sake of one's religious belief is one of the greatest privileges a man could have," he answered.

The New York *Post* of the same date interpreted Judge Howe's severe sentence in a sarcastic vein. "It was necessary, he said, to make an example of those who sincerely taught their religion, which, like that of the Mennonites and the Quakers, and many another sect, forbids the taking up of arms. They were guilty plainly of having urged men to follow what they considered the teaching of the Lord and to apply literally the commandment 'Thou shalt not kill.'

"So," the *Post* went on, "the jury could do nothing less than find them guilty of having violated the statutes of the country, whatever may be the correctness or incorrectness of their [the statutes'] attitude toward the moral and religious law."

It frowned: "We trust that teachers of religion everywhere will take notice of this judge's opinion that teaching any religion save that which is absolutely in accord with state's laws is a grave crime, which is intensified if, being a minister of the Gospel, you should still happen to be sincere."

Judge Howe's sentences were, in severity, "all about double that imposed by the Kaiser upon Socialists who have been trying to upset his wicked regime, and three times longer than many sentences imposed upon would-be regicides," the *Post* concluded.

Specifically, the four charges for which they received twenty years each read: "The offense of unlawfully, feloniously and wilfully causing and attempting to cause insubordination, disloyalty and refusal of duty in the military and naval forces of the United States of America, in, through and by personal solicitations, letters, public speeches, distribution and public circulation throughout the United States of America of a certain book called 'Volume Seven— SCRIPTURE STUDIES—The Finished Mystery'—and distributing and publicly circulating throughout the United States certain articles presented in pamphlets called 'BIBLE STUDENTS MONTHLY,' 'THE WATCH TOWER,' 'KINGDOM NEWS' and other pamphlets not named, et cetera;

"The offense of unlawfully, feloniously, and wilfully obstructing the recruiting and enlistment service of the United States when the United States was at war."

These eight men composed not only the Board of Directors but also the Society's Editorial Board. In their not-guilty pleas they asserted that they had not interfered with the war. They had been expecting it ever since 1885. That year *The Watch Tower* foretold its outbreak in 1914. War would constitute one of "the signs of the Kingdom's advent."

World war, as they later saw and said, was a visible proof that Satan had been "ousted from any further intimidation of the heavenly hosts." Confined now to the earth's vicinity, he knew that "he hath but a short time." So he was stirring up the nations in a mad rage. He was bent on driving them all to suicide. He would stoop to any depth to prevent the Kingdom's being preached and the "sheep" gathered.

The Bible foretold the war. The Bible Students warned of its coming. Would they, of all people, try to interfere with the fulfillment of a God-given prophecy?

If *The Finished Mystery* and *The Watch Tower* criticized the nominal churches, they added, that was because "it is necessary to point to the false position which churchianity holds in relation to earth's affairs."

"Our business," they insisted, "is to announce Christ's Kingdom." Nominal religion would not do that. Churches in general were too busy taking sides between the political powers. They were engrossed in agitating members of their own denomination in one nation to fight a fratricidal war against their members in other nations. Instead of holding forth the long-awaited Kingdom as mankind's hope, the churches were holding up whoever should win the war as the one to put their trust in. Unless the Bible Students proclaimed the Kingdom's advent, then who else would?

Conscientious Objectors

The Federal Court was a long way from being persuaded by such arguments. This trial was, in fact, only the most outstanding of many others that were sweeping the nation. Bible Students were being arrested everywhere. Their stand as conscientious objectors had been outlined and published in *The Watch Tower*, August 1, 1917, under the title, "Application for Exemption." It suggested that an applicant file an affidavit. The affidavit might state that, as a member of the International Bible Students Association, "you are fully consecrated to the Lord, and that you follow the teachings of Jesus and the Apostles as set forth and explained in the Bible and in the publications of the International Bible Students Association and the Watch Tower Bible & Tract Society; that you are in harmony with and believe the teachings of said Association, which forbids its members to participate in war in any form, and that your

religious convictions are against war or participation therein
in any form, in accordance with the creed or principles of
said International Bible Students Association; that the teachings of said International Bible Students Association, in
harmony with those of Jesus and the Apostles, are briefly
epitomized in the following: 'Thou shalt not kill.' (Romans
13:9) 'All they that take the sword shall perish by the sword.'
(Matthew 26:52) . . ."

As for the stand Jehovah's witnesses took on military
service during World War II, see the article in the Appendix from the Watchtower publication, *Defending and Legally Establishing the Good News.*

When Rutherford and his companions were marched
off to the penitentiary, the headquarters organization closed
down. The whole body of the faithful was stunned, puzzled.
Church leaders who had smarted under the stinging indict-
ments of *The Finished Mystery* shed no tears when it looked
as if, after forty years, "Russellism" had reached its end.

The "Higher Powers" Issue

There remained a hard core of the faithful—about four
thousand, worldwide, but the body as a whole had succumbed to "fear of man." Rutherford never afterward tired
of reminding them of that.

The trouble in those days, the Bible Students perceived,
was that they were still "tainted" with too many "old-world
religious notions." For instance, they were still holding to
the orthodox view that the "higher powers" described in
Romans 13:1 meant the political nations of the world.

Since this was Satan's world, how would Jehovah be
authorizing its powers for it, they commenced to wonder. In
time, they grew convinced that the Higher Powers are
"Jehovah God and His Son-King, Christ Jesus." As for the
powers of this world? "All the nations are as nothing before
him; they are accounted by him as less than nothing, and
vanity." (Isaiah 40:17, *American Standard Version*)

Incidentally, the Evangelical Church in Germany, after
World War II, took a similar stand.

Somehow *The Watch Tower* kept coming out—it hadn't missed an issue since its birth, in 1879. Those who stood faithful, even though they were bewildered, kept telling themselves and the world that in spite of everything "the Kingdom is here." This was a period of "trial by fire." It was judgment that began with "the house of God itself," and extended to all mankind.

Scarcely had the incarceration of Rutherford and his six fellow prisoners in Atlanta begun than they came up with the idea for a new magazine. It would be a companion to *The Watch Tower*. It would be a "journal of fact, hope and courage." It would serve as a clearing house for all kinds of material. Particularly it would publish reports on current happenings that helped compose the great composite "sign" of the "beginning of sorrows" upon the world: wars, food shortages, disease and pestilence, earthquakes, distress of nations, world perplexity, as well as courageous news about the Kingdom. Jesus' world's-end prophecy in Matthew 24 gives a comprehensive outline of the editorial scope of the projected publication.

They decided to call the new journal *The Golden Age*. Later it was renamed *Consolation*. Again, in 1946 the name was changed to *Awake!* Born in a prison cell in Atlanta penitentiary, by 1954 it had reached a circulation of 1,200,000.

Exoneration

While their appeal was pending before the Federal Circuit Court, Mr. Rutherford and his companions were refused bail and held in prison for nine months. This was illegal.

On March 26, 1919, bail was granted. They were released under heavy bond. Soon thereafter the Appeals Court declared their conviction erroneous. It reversed the sentence against them.

The Government, for months, sought a new trial, but in vain. In May, 1920, upon an order of the Attorney General, it announced in open court, at Brooklyn, that its case against all the parties had been withdrawn.

(According to the records of the Clerk of the Supreme Court of the United States, Rutherford was admitted to practice before that court on May 24, 1909. Thirty years later—or twenty years after his exoneration from the charges —the nine justices of the court listened to Rutherford's argument in the case of *Schneider* v. *Irvington* (308 U.S. 147). It ruled 8 to 1 in favor of his client, Clara Schneider, one of Jehovah's witnesses.)

The year 1919 was one of immense rejoicing. Hope sprang up in the hearts of the Bible Students around the world. Their revival astounded a lot of religious leaders, who had viewed the Bible Students as "dead as corpses lying in the street."

The Bible Students held a reunion assembly in 1919 at Cedar Point, Ohio, and another at the same place in 1922, which 20,000 people attended.

The "remnant" felt reassured, then, that they had undergone a "temple cleansing." The trial by fire had purified the organization internally. They were chastened. They had learned a lot, the hard way. Creature worship, character development, fear of man, selfish ambition, and the like had been blinding them. They had not seen that their self-righteousness was "as filthy rags." The Lord had chastened his own.

Organizing for the Work

Now there was work to do, Kingdom work. The churches of Christendom had just proved themselves to be Babylon indeed. They had publicly denounced the doctrine of Jehovah's Kingdom by Christ as now ruling amid its enemies. This the churches had done in choosing a "counterfeit kingdom." Their choice had been the newly formed League of Nations.

The Bible Students were not against some sensible political arrangement among nations to keep operating in peace for the duration. But when the Federal Council of the Churches of Christ in America came out, in 1919, and labeled the proposed League the "political expression of the

Kingdom of God on earth," the Bible Students never forgave nominal religion.

If the door of repentance slammed shut on Catholicism with Martin Luther, then Christendom passed up its last chance when it sought its kingdom in man's political League of Nations. So the Bible Students were convinced.

"The claims of religion must be countermanded by the Kingdom proclamation," Rutherford declared furiously. "Jehovah is not going to materialize angels and send them down here to proclaim the Kingdom. He is going to use 'frail earthen vessels.' He is going to use his faithful human witnesses."

From now on this must be our cry: "Advertise, advertise, advertise the Kingdom!" he proclaimed at the height of the 1922 Cedar Point convention. Everyone who "appreciates the truth" must get out and preach it.

And here Rutherford hit upon what was to be the most important development among the rank and file. That was the doctrine of personal, individual ministry, to be shared by everyone in the faith.

Individual Ministry

Up to 1917, public speaking had been done by the Society's traveling ministers, called Pilgrims. That year there were ninety-three Pilgrims in the United States. They traveled 617,186 miles, visited 6,672 towns, held 1,956 public meetings, and 3,287 semipublic meetings, before a total audience of 850,734 people.

The field ministry was until then principally the work of specially appointed colporteurs. Their service was, primarily, distributing the Society's publications by personal call. In 1917, there were 461 colporteurs, compared with 372 in 1916, when many "were compelled to engage in secular business in order to provide themselves with the necessities of life." (Contributions for the Watch Tower publications were never at any time sufficient to sustain the distributors.)

The 461 regular colporteurs in 1917 were assisted by a

corps of "special," or part-time colporteurs. Three hundred and fifty-five classes (there were in the United States about 868 classes, or congregations, in all) were organized so that all those who wanted to could help carry on the special colporteur work.

"By this means," the Annual Report for that year set forth, "the county where the class is located is divided into smaller sections, and every one of the consecrated who desires to have a part in the work is assigned to a small district until he has finished, and then assigned to another district until the territory is entirely covered."

Such was the early setup of the house-to-house ministry. It resembled the ministry of the Waldenses and Lollards of previous centuries. To what extent it was developed in 1917 may be surmised from the Report, which stated: "Some of the classes have as many as 100 engaged in the colporteur work, many of whom have never before had any experience; . . . If we count ten members as the average of a class doing this colporteur work, we have 3,550 special colporteurs and 461 regular colporteurs, which at this time would aggregate 4,011."

During the year the workers distributed literature as follows:

Studies (English and foreign)	574,838
Drama Scenarios (bound books)	87,567
Mannas and other books	95,898
Booklets (English and foreign)	191,719
The Watch Tower (24 issues)	1,211,000
German Watch Tower (12 issues)	25,000
Polish Watch Tower	19,000

These totals did not include the British, French, Swiss, and Australian branches, which were similarly active.

But in 1918 the ax had fallen. The work came to a stop, practically. That year the world total workers dropped to 3,868. The big job in 1919, and from there on, was to revive the witness work.

Reconstruction meant personal ministry. Rutherford

found that not everybody wanted to get out and be a worker. Many of the Bible Students wanted their religion served up to them from the pulpit as in other churches—they were satisfied to sit back and listen. Or, as another put it, "They wanted the truth, but they did not want to share it." So a big sifting took place.

But amazingly enough, the skeletal ranks of the faithful that took up the personal ministry were rapidly filled with new faces. The Bible Students were finding "a lot of people who wanted a religion that gave them a big personal responsibility in the ministry." The doctrine of "each Christian a minister" became the central, dynamic, working credo of the group.

The Phonograph

In the beginning years, the publishers did little more than call from house to house, presenting the Society's publications. During the 1930's, the trade-mark of the Bible Students became a small portable phonograph.

The bearers cranked their machines and played them on every doorstep where they could get people to listen. The message was a five-minute recording by Rutherford. Each one stressed some special Bible theme. At the conclusion, the listener was usually informed that he could examine the theme more fully by reading the book or magazine that the publisher would now show him. Then the colporteurs, or "publishers," as they became known, would show the literature. Not much had to be said.

Personal Testimony

By the time of the Judge's death, however, in 1942, the famous talking machine had practically vanished. Publishers were learning to speak their own messages. They usually had them printed on "Testimony Cards," in case they needed them. In weekly service-meeting sessions, they practiced good presentations.

In 1943, the Theocratic Ministry School was inaugurated throughout all the congregations. It has run continuously ever since. Men who are old enough to get up and talk to an audience are drilled by student talks in all the arts of effective public speaking. Women listen and learn and practice the principles when presenting the message at the door (women do not preside from the platform among the group). By the middle of the twentieth century, the organization had produced, through its ministry school and service meetings, a body of presentable public speakers numbering hundreds of thousands, who were capable of holding their own by any standards.

Home Bible Studies

Before Judge Rutherford died, the public ministry had been broadened extensively in terms of personal responsibility. In the 1930's the "backcall" phase was developed. It was considered not enough just to call and leave literature with somebody. Had not Paul called back on those whom he personally introduced to Christianity? Did not Jesus himself travel in circuits? So now modern ministers must call back. People needed help with their Bibles and Bible literature. It was true that public Bible studies and Bible talks were held every week by each congregation. But not everyone who was interested in the Bible attended the public classes. Some people preferred home study and needed personal attention.

Judge Rutherford's last book, *Children,* came out in 1941. It contained numbered paragraphs and a question booklet. In later books the questions were printed at the bottom of the pages. A goal of at least one home Bible study for each field minister was set as the standard quota for the group, world wide. By 1952, 426,704 ministers were conducting 279,622 studies.

Home Bible study became the most important phase of the public ministry of the group, next to the house-to-house witnessing.

The New Name

At a convention in 1931, Judge Rutherford announced that it was the Society's opinion that the growing organization of Christians should clear the mists as to their identity. It was time they had a distinctive name. A name which, as *The Watch Tower* commented, "Nobody under the sun wants except those who are wholly and unreservedly devoted to Jehovah."

For many years the world had not known exactly what to call this body of adherents to what it deemed a "new religion." To complicate things, there had branched off several bodies of dissidents. These still clung to Pastor Russell's teachings as constituting the "complete revelation." Their literature was a patchwork of quotations from his writings, cast in one light or another, to bring out what they felt was a fuller sense of his meanings. It was something like the way Christian Scientists treat the works of Mary Baker Eddy.

But these disaffected groups were calling themselves by names that confused the average person, who could not always distinguish them from the Bible Students. "Russellites" was the popular name for the Bible Students. But they themselves felt that it was the wrong name for them. They vowed they were not following Russell or any other man. On the other hand, some groups felt it an honor to be called by Russell's name. Still another body called itself the "Associated Bible Students." This group opposed the International Bible Students Association.

It was time a clear-cut distinction was made as to who was who. The Bible Students did want to keep on using instruments like the Watch Tower Bible & Tract Society, the Peoples Pulpit Association, and the International Bible Students Association. But, they objected, "We refuse to bear the name of a corporation or the name of any man."

"By the grace of the Lord Jesus Christ and of our heavenly Father," Rutherford declared "we joyfully receive and bear the name which the mouth of Jehovah God has named and given us, to wit, Jehovah's witnesses."

The Watch Tower for October 1, 1931, gave some reasons for their acceptance of the new name, "Jehovah's witnesses":

> 1. Jesus Christ calls himself "the faithful and true witness." (Revelation 3:14) Mark 5:7 calls Jesus "the Son of the Most High God," and Psalm 83:18 says that the name of "the Most High" is Jehovah. Jesus stated, in John 17:6, that he had made his Father's name known to his disciples. At Revelation 3:14 Jesus called himself "the faithful and true witness." Jesus must necessarily be Jehovah's Witness, his Chief Witness. Imitators and followers of Jesus, to be Christians, would have to be Jehovah's witnesses.
> 2. The Bible declares Jehovah's purpose to "take out a people for His name." His name-people must publicly praise him, be His witnesses. (Acts 15:14; 1 Peter 2:9,10)
> 3. "Ye are my witnesses, saith Jehovah." (Isaiah 43:10, *American Standard Version*)

After 1931, the term "Russellite" was heard less. Hitler, when he outlawed the organization and threw ten thousand adherents into his concentration camps, in 1933, called them "Earnest Bible Students." When they emerged from Nazi ghettos, in 1945, they were known there as well as everywhere else as Jehovah's witnesses.

Within less than twenty years the name Jehovah's witnesses crowded out every other name for these people throughout the world.

Theocratic Rule

As the movement grew, it became more and more "organization" conscious, and less and less "personality" conscious. "Character development" dried up on the vine. The purpose of the Witnesses was, put bluntly, "Never mind about your sweet, pious character. Get out and preach the Gospel. Then your character will take care of itself."

But with organizational consciousness came a deep and fundamental reorganization within the local bodies. In 1938, the London congregation of Jehovah's witnesses made a revolutionary request of headquarters. It asked to have its local overseers appointed by the Society.

Until then, local officers or "elective elders," had been appointed by congregational voting, a democratic means. But a question was ripening in the minds of the faithful. "If the Kingdom is here," went the query, "and we are under Kingdom rule, then is the Lord directing our congregational organization? Or are we? Is the Kingdom a Theocracy or God-rule? Or is it a democracy or people-rule? Does the Kingdom operate from the bottom up or from the top down?"

Pastor Russell, through publishing agencies such as the Watch Tower Society, had started an all-out doctrinal reform in Christendom. The Witnesses felt that it was a work divinely directed. It was to prepare a people for the incoming Kingdom Government. Since Russell's time the reformation had continued to swell. A whole new and complete body of Bible teaching was accumulating. The light was shining brighter and brighter toward the perfect day of understanding.

So they were confident that the society of Jehovah's Christian witnesses was "the Lord's organization." Speaking for that great spiritual society or body of worshipers was the central organization that employed its legal publishing agencies. The work was carried on in the name of these agencies, such as the Watch Tower Bible & Tract Society. These agencies were merely man-made corporations. They were formed to meet the demands of the civil state. They therefore could not constitute the *real* Society. Yet if this arrangement was receiving Jehovah's blessing, why should not the Society, through the agency of these corporations, directly supervise the congregations on a local level?

In other words, the London Congregation renounced "democratic" rule. It asked for "Theocratic" procedure within its congregation. It asked for the Society to appoint its local

officers or servants. These appointments it would accept as
an act of "Theocratic rule."

Authority from the top down, instead of from the bottom
up, would then prevail. Jehovah, they felt, was directing the
"Kingdom interests" through his appointed King, Christ
Jesus. In turn, Christ was developing the Kingdom work on
earth through the spiritual Society of Witnesses. The Witnesses were using the Watch Tower organizations as their
legal mouthpiece and directive and unifying agency. Appointments should come through this visible Society, therefore, to proceed properly from the "Higher Powers."

When the Society received the London Congregation's request, it complied. It appointed overseers for various posts
for the congregation.

The news was then forwarded to all congregations.
Would they receive similar appointments from headquarters?

The congregations approved—all, that is, except some of
the "elective elders," who hedged at the thought of losing
their positions. Some of them might be poor "publishers."
The Society might appoint servants on the basis of their
public-ministry record. That would leave some of the elders
sitting out in the cold. The central organization, representing the international Society of Jehovah's witnesses, then
appointed servants for all the congregations throughout the
world. Theocratic rule was inaugurated.

How the Witnesses Explain It

I hope this term, "the Society," is not confusing. Many
people get at the matter by asking: "What connection is
there between Jehovah's witnesses and the Watch Tower
Bible & Tract Society?"

To that the Witnesses answer: "Jehovah's witnesses are
an international society of Christians. They are held together by one identical worship of Jehovah as the Almighty
God, and his Son, Christ Jesus, as their King. The Watch

Tower organizations are merely legal instruments used by the Witnesses. The world-wide body of Jehovah's witnesses are represented by a central directive council using these legal corporations to direct their ministry, their Bible educational work, and to publish literature for them.

"If you were one of Jehovah's witnesses and you received an appointment or a directive written on a Watch Tower Society letterhead, you would recognize the letterhead as representing the legal corporation. But the authority speaking through that letterhead would represent the central directing body of the spiritual Society of Jehovah's witnesses.

"If you think that is still too complicated, look at it this way: Let's assume that the civil power has dissolved the legal corporation. It has banned the Watch Tower Society. This has happened in all totalitarian countries. Well, then, there is no longer a legal society. But there still remains the spiritual Society. It may no longer have a central legal mouthpiece to speak through. But the real spiritual Society remains. It is held intact by a power that the civil authorities cannot touch.

"The proof of this has lived right through the onslaughts of the Fascists, the Nazis, and the Communists. All of them have outlawed our legal societies. None of them has destroyed our spiritual Society."

The proof? Jehovah's witnesses kept growing in numbers —underground, in some cases, more rapidly than aboveground. They remain unified in the one worship. Whenever they can, they emerge aboveground in a country and reorganize their legal societies. Then they immediately turn to the central ruling body for directions and supervision.

"The world headquarters, representing the international Society of Jehovah's witnesses has been, since 1909, in Brooklyn, New York. From there the representative officials supervise the world-wide society in the same way the ruling body of the original Christian church presided in Jerusalem and directed the Church's affairs throughout the world."

Districts and Circuits

The Society, extending the Theocratic structure from and after 1938, developed a system of districts in each branch. The United States, for example, was divided into six districts. It sent out a district servant to supervise each district. Each district was subdivided into about twenty circuits. A circuit servant was sent around to serve each congregation twice a year. There were about twenty congregations in each circuit. This arrangement was applied world wide.

Since 1938, with the adoption of Theocratic organization extending all the way down to the congregational level, Jehovah's witnesses have made their most amazing increase. In the ten years that followed that date new ministers were being baptized and entering the field at the rate of a thousand a week. The Witnesses attributed the increase to the Theocratic system of things. "The Kingdom is here. Theocracy reigns!" declared Judge Rutherford feelingly at his last major public appearance, in 1941, at the St. Louis, Missouri, convention.

During his twenty-five years in the presidency, Judge Rutherford turned out twenty-two books, many booklets and tracts, and a never-ceasing stream of material for *The Watch Tower* and *Golden Age* (later *Consolation*). This literature, along with Bibles, was distributed world wide to the astounding sum of about half a billion pieces. The publishing program expanded with "double the spirit" of the Pastor Russell era.

The Judge's career as chief spokesman for Jehovah's witnesses was born in a period of revolt within the group. During his second year, the organization crumbled under wartime interdicts. He found himself facing a penitentiary sentence, which, if served consecutively, would total eighty years. The Deliverance was followed by a torrid reconstruction period that saw a great body of the group fall away. From his first day in office, Rutherford faced a fight. All he knew was how to fight.

His career ended in fighting. From 1929 onward, he saw his German, Italian, and Japanese brothers thrown into slave-labor camps or put to death mercilessly. Beginning with 1938, the aging barrister-minister, supported by a young Texas lawyer named Hayden Covington, carried the first of a string of forty-six major court battles to the Supreme Court (Covington fought the majority of them after the Judge's death). In 1940, he saw the American Witnesses mobbed in forty-four states of the Union. In 1941, he saw them banned in Australia. But this time, during the second world war, the organization did not buckle under pressure. It did not even flinch. The Witnesses stuck together, and the organization expanded underground whenever it had to get along that way.

When he died, on January 8, 1942, the Judge, like the Pastor before him, died with his workboots on and a grim determination to go out as he came in—fighting.

The greatest triumph of Judge Rutherford's career was to see the organization expand, coalesce, and keep on through everything, despite the devastating attacks on it of the Fascists, the Nazis, and democratic mobocracies. His death occurred thirty days after the Japanese attack on Pearl Harbor, a shock that hurtled the democratic camp of Christendom into total war. To the Witnesses, the Judge's death came as a shock, too. But this time there was no despair; no chill came over the faithful.

Now they were an organization, a Society—an "indestructible nation" within themselves. The feeling of dependence on any one person had long since gone out of their system.

Covington was there to pick up the legal branch of the Judge's fight. In regard to doctrinal material, for years Rutherford had leaned heavily on the keen Bible brain of Fred Franz. Nathan Knorr had managed the business of the legal corporations for so long that by unanimous quiet consent he almost automatically slipped into the presidency.

This time there was no inside strife, no dogfights for supremacy. Rugged, bold, blunt though Rutherford had had to be, during his career, he died happy in the thought that activities would not cease after he was gone, that, in fact, they would increase, theocratically.

So the last great "name personality" in the history of modern Witnesses of Jehovah passed quietly from the scene. His career was born amidst deflections. It reached its climax as the work was caught in the fiery furnace of global persecution. But it was sparked from start to finish by his battle-cry, "The Kingdom is here!"

Defending and Legally Establishing the Good News— "As for you, look out for yourselves," warned Jesus. "People will deliver you up to local courts and you will be beaten in synagogues and be put on the stand before governors and kings for my sake for the purpose of a witness to them."—MARK 13:19, *New World Translation of the Christian Greek Scriptures*

CHAPTER SEVEN

DEFENDING AND LEGALLY ESTABLISHING THE GOOD NEWS

(See Appendix for Legal Summaries of Cases won by Jehovah's Witnesses)

"*SELDOM,* if ever, in the past, has one individual or group been able to shape the course, over a period of time, of any phase of our vast body of constitutional law. But it *can* happen, and it *has* happened, here."

The Bill of Rights Review, published by the American Bar Association, was describing a religious group battling its way, during a period of global war, through forty-six cases in the United States Supreme Court and one hundred and fifty state supreme court cases.

"The group is Jehovah's witnesses," continued the *Review*. "Through almost constant litigation this organization has made possible an ever-increasing list of precedents concerning the application of the Fourteenth Amendment to freedom of speech and worship."

Growing segments of patriotic Americans were becoming exasperated with the Witnesses. They were chasing them out of town with a bucket of tar in one hand and a bag of feathers in the other. From 1940 to 1944, more than 2,500 American mobs violently assaulted them. The Witnesses fought back legally. They defended to the limit every encroachment upon their preaching methods. These methods they claimed were copied literally from the Bible.

And, as the *Review* noted in 1942, the Witnesses were winning case after case. "A great victory in behalf of all the citizens," their legal counsel assured them. "You are writing your faith into the laws of the land."

Since that report was published, Jehovah's witnesses have projected the application of American principles of freedom, with qualified success, in other lands. The high courts of Australia, New Zealand, the Philippines, Canada, and the Scandinavian countries, for example, have been influenced by precedents set in more than 190 state and federal supreme court rulings in the United States. A growing family of civil-rights decisions brought to life in those countries bear the unmistakable features of American precedents.

However, warned Hayden C. Covington, the Witnesses' crack constitutional lawyer, "Other countries have not been so liberal to the Witnesses. Their judges do not have the power that American judges enjoy. Judges in other lands cannot say that a law is of no value. Jehovah's witnesses have asked that the law be read so that their preaching work is not touched by the law. In Switzerland, Norway, Luxembourg, and Canada they have succeeded. But," he concluded warily, in August, 1953, "an important case from Quebec now hangs in the balance."

Pastor Charles Taze Russell, President 1884 to 1916.
See Appendix page 209 for biography.

Judge Joseph Franklin Rutherford, President 1916 to 1942.
See Appendix page 213 for biography.

Nathan Homer Knorr, President since 1942.
See Appendix page 210 for biography.

Hayden Cooper Covington, Legal Counsel for Jehovah's witnesses. See Appendix page 212 for biography.

Thomas James Sullivan, Superintendent of Ministers and Evangelists in the United States.

Bethel, world headquarters for Jehovah's witnesses, 124 Columbia Heights, Brooklyn 1, New York.

Installing another magazine press.

Making ink for presses.

*Registered offices of Watch Tower Bible and Tract Society,
Pittsburgh, Pa.*

Watchtower Bible School of Gilead, South Lansing, N. Y., missionary training center.

Covington, a Texan with a flair for metaphors that stand up and walk, was surveying the world scene as it reacted to the activities and preaching of Jehovah's witnesses. What he saw he reported to 125,000 Witnesses and interested persons during the world assembly at Yankee Stadium, July 19-26, 1953. The picture looked pretty dark, and freedom shone but feebly, he reported.

In the United States

It was during or shortly after World War II that Jehovah's witnesses in the United States won the bulk of their court victories. And these cases "cast the application of Constitutional freedoms in a new light," a light that, in spite of the darkness, penetrated other lands.

"From nineteen thirty-five to nineteen fifty," Covington said, in a personal interview, "the Witnesses in the United States suffered ten thousand arrests."

During the war, 8,000 draft-age Witnesses applied to their draft boards as ministers. Roughly half the number were granted the ministerial 4-D classification. The other half preferred to suffer federal imprisonment rather than renounce their ministerial claim to exemption.

"What about American mobs?" I asked.

That was when Covington mentioned the 2,500 mobbings of the Witnesses, from 1940 to 1944. "In forty-four states," he itemized, "they were beaten, kidnapped, tarred and feathered, throttled on castor oil, tied together and chased through the streets, castrated, maimed, hanged, shot, and otherwise consigned to mayhem."

"On what charges?"

"Fascism and Nazism mostly—minorities always wear the paint, in every country, of the national enemies."

Not that the big, restless lawyer was trying to paint the Witnesses in martyr hues. His wry grin showed he detested that kind of sentimentality.

"Of course, everybody knew better than to call us Fascists," he went on without rancor. "The Mussolini Fascists liquidated our organization back in the twenties. Hitler personally outlawed Jehovah's witnesses in nineteen thirty-three. He had ten thousand of them thrown into his slave camps."

Abruptly, Covington came back to the American scene. He said that the Witnesses were justified in feeling that the lawmakers, on municipal and state levels, deliberately laid every legal snare they could think of to foil them. It was part of Jehovah's witnesses' creed, though, to fight off anything that interfered with their religion.

When an issue like that shapes up, you can always count on fireworks. The war years were a period that even tried the souls of the black-robed judges themselves—and issues divided some of them from their colleagues as far as the poles are apart. "Jehovah's witnesses," trembled J. Gordon Flannery, county judge of Dutchess county, New York, "may not realize that their actions may make it necessary for the preservation of our republic *to change the Amendments to the Constitution providing for freedom of religion, of speech and of the press."*

A Bill of Rights or no Bill of Rights—the issue came right down to that, Covington said.

Judge Flannery found out that others in the judiciary disagreed with him as much as it was possible to disagree.

"The claim, asserted widely, that Jehovah's witnesses through boundless courage and unending perseverance have won more United States Supreme Court victories for the Bill of Rights than any other single group seems to have ample support in the record of cases before the Supreme Court last term, in which freedom of speech and religious freedom were at issue," commented A. L. Wirin, American Civil Liberties Union counsel, in *The Open Forum,* August 21, 1943.

About the same time, Edward F. Waite, retired judge of the district court of Minnesota, published a summary of thirty-one cases won by the Witnesses. He showed how these had produced a strengthening or enlarging of the civil liberties of all Americans. "It is plain that present constitutional guarantees of personal liberty," Judge Waite observed, "are far broader than they were before the spring of nineteen thirty-eight, and that most of this enlargement is to be found in the thirty-one Jehovah's witnesses cases."

The United States, Jehovah's witnesses feel, may be the only nation in history that has fought a successful war on foreign soil for the protection of freedom at home, while, at the same time, strengthening and securing its freedoms on the home front, thanks to a beleagured minority that tested its Constitutional integrity to the hilt.

"People in general just don't seem to comprehend it. But the legal machinery—at the municipal and state levels —was set up to convert the country to totalitarianism," Covington reflected.

And probably not very many, he added, will ever seriously consider the idea that, because this group was the only segment to meet the whole body of "mischief framed by law" and fight it out, Jehovah's witnesses won a monumental battle for "freedom on the home front."

Any way you look at the issue, before the smoke of the war years cleared away, 28 different kinds of laws in hundreds of towns had been quashed, and 190 appeals were taken to higher courts. Twice the Witnesses caused the Supreme Court to reverse itself. They won not less than 150 state supreme court decisions and the majority of 40 United States Supreme Court decisions.

"Every important principle of law contended for by Jehovah's witnesses was eventually maintained by the courts," Covington said.

How important were these hard-won principles?

Scraping Legal Barnacles from the Constitution

"As in other countries," the Witness counselor explained, "American lawmakers and law-enforcement officers did not seem to notice what had accumulated—a weight of barnacle-like statutes and ordinances, hustled through legislatures in the war atmosphere. These virtually nullified the Bill of

Rights and wallowed the Constitution in an undemocratic sea.

"These laws added up to proscribing the preaching of Jehovah's witnesses. The Witnesses felt they were commanded by Jehovah God to preach. They must obey God rather than men. So they contested legally, full scale, all the way through, the application of these laws. Their action served like a sieve to strain out insidious by-laws that were cluttering up freedom of worship, speech, and press. Not only for them. But for everybody alike—whether it was realized or not."

To appreciate the Witnesses' view you would have to visualize how the antifreedom laws would have affected the original Bible characters. "The Christian ministry, the way Jesus Christ and the apostles practiced it, would' have been banned in the United States if those laws had not been challenged and defeated," Covington asserted.

"Was it that bad?" I probed.

"Those Bible characters—Jesus, Peter, John, as well as some of the prophets—preached their good news from house to house, in public places, on the streets. Jehovah's witnesses have copied those Bible methods literally," he explained. "But the Witnesses ran up against a barrage of petty laws that said you could not preach that way."

He began to illustrate: "The apostle Peter and the prophet Jeremiah spoke out against big religious majorities and ruling powers. If they had done such a thing in this country ten years ago, they would have landed where Jehovah's witnesses landed—in jail.

(The United States Supreme Court in *Cantwell v. Connecticut; Murdock v. Pennsylvania; Martin v. City of Struthers,* etc., declared the right of one religion to speak critically of another faith.)

What if the Bible stalwarts had been here and had adopted modern printing methods to publish and' circulate the Bible books and epistles they wrote? What if they had accepted contributions for them, as clergymen accept contributions for orally read or recited sermons in church? They would have broken the law.

"The law said you had to have a peddler's license or pay a tax to distribute Bible sermons in print," Covington pointed out.

The prophet Amos and Jesus Christ might have wound up in jail together on several counts. For one thing, giving free public talks in public parks, schools, or auditoriums, where the citizenry conduct patriotic rallies, civic programs, charity drives, and sports shows would have made them liable.

"And look what would have happened to the three Hebrews of Bible fame who refused to do obeisance to the image of the Babylonian state authority," Covington went on. "They would have been compelled by law to do obeisance to the emblem of the American state. Just as Hitler forced Germans to *heil* him and salute the swastika. Just as Communists enforce the salute to the hammer and sickle."

Sunday blue laws and Green River ordinances (forbidding uninvited calls at homes) like the laws of the Pharisees, would have outlawed Jesus from preaching on Sundays and holidays in his primitive manner. The young boy Samuel would have been forbidden by child labor laws from ministering at the temple.

Other freedoms won in court fights by Jehovah's witnesses since 1938 include the legality of doorbell ringing, door-to-door preaching; street preaching, free of license or tax; calling in privately owned or government-owned towns, and in apartments without permission of the landlord; the use of sound amplifiers "at reasonable volume"; recognition of the unseditious and unsubversive nature of the doctrine; the right of parents to retain custody of children reared in the faith; legal recognition of the religious society as an accredited religion; the right to ministerial status in spite of secular employment; protection from persistent arrests under invalidated ordinances and laws; the right to advertise meetings by placards worn by street marchers or on automobiles; the right of self-defense when attacked personally; and freedom from jury service.

It was a host of such innocent-appearing statutes that almost converted the United States of the war years into a semblance of the police state. That fact might have been realized too late by other groups and minorities, Covington declared.

In Canada

In 1948, fifteen thousand Witnesses spent two months going from house to house throughout the length and breadth of Canada. They were gathering a petition of 625,510 names—the biggest petition in that country's history.

Early in 1949, they laid it before the Canadian Parliament. It was a petition for a *written* Bill of Rights, American style.

"We have exhausted every legal means to win freedom for our religion, and freedom for yours," they told the people. "This is a last resort."

The Canadian Parliament was impressed by the 625,510 names. There was talk of really producing a Bill of Rights. Then suddenly, in October, 1953, Canadians woke up to find that they already had one.

Here is how it came about. Jehovah's witnesses in Quebec had waged a thirty-year war for survival against powerfully entrenched Catholic authorities. The Church party had beaten away unrelentingly at what they wishfully described as "a pesty fly buzzing about a bald head." The authorities tried to vanquish the "fly" with a double fly-swatter, the two charges being that the witnesses were seditious and that they broadsided people with "licentious" propaganda without a peddler's license.

Similar charges against the Witnesses had been dismissed in other democratic countries; for instance, *Taylor* v. *Mississippi*, decided before the Supreme Court of the United States, in 1943; the decision of the High Court of Australia, in *Adelaide Company of Jehovah's Witnesses, Inc.,* v. *The Commonwealth*, which, in 1943 vindicated them of sedition charges; the Supreme Court of South Africa, in *The Magistrate, Bulawayo* v. *Kabungo,* in 1938, when it was ruled that the literature of Jehovah's witnesses did not violate the Sedition Act of Southern Rhodesia.

But Jehovah's witnesses were informed that they were not in South Africa. They were not in Australia. They were not even in the United States. They were in the City and Province of Quebec.

By 1950, the "bald-headed gent" had landed more than twelve hundred thwacks, in the form of pending court cases, smack upon the "fly." After twelve hundred swattings the ordinary minority fly usually flies off into infinitesimal particles, but this beastie kept buzzing back. It obstinately kept on stinging the swatter by simply ignoring the legal swats. It kept on "preaching the good news." Fifteen hundred cases piled up in Quebec courts.

A national sensation was touched off when Premier Duplessis determined to make the crusade against Jehovah's witnesses a personal fight. But he withdrew somewhat abashed when the court ruled against him, in a suit filed by one of Jehovah's witnesses, and charged him with damages to the amount of $8,123.

Thus, in 1950, half of the double fly-swatter—the sedition charge—fell apart.

The Supreme Court of Canada ruled, in *Boucher v. The King,* that an unpopular religious minority is not necessarily seditious because it disagrees with a prevailing majority. At last Quebec was brought in line with a United States Court ruling in the 1940's that quashed sedition charges made by Harlan County, Kentucky. (There Harlan officials had seriously prosecuted Jehovah's witnesses "for advocating a government by one Jehovah God.")

December 9, 1952. For seven days the case of *Saumur v. City of Quebec and Attorney General of Quebec* had orally been argued by lawyers before the high court. Then it was tendered to the Supreme Court of Canada.

This was the license-permit issue—the other half of the fly-swatter.

All the way up through the lower courts the Witnesses had lost battle after battle. The City and Province of Quebec were resting their defense upon the legality of a city by-law. It prohibited distribution of printed matter without a license. Jehovah's witnesses were challenging the by-law with a hundred-year-old statute that had never been appealed to before.

This old statute is identical, in purpose, with the First Amendment to the United States Constitution. Apparently it had been taken almost verbatim from some of the American state constitutions. The state of New York in particular embodies, word for word, the same guarantee, namely, "the free exercise and enjoyment of religious profession and worship without discrimination or preference, so the same be not made an excuse for acts of licentiousness, or a justification of practices inconsistent with peace and safety of the province."

"If Canadians want American-style democracy, as shown by their copying American state constitutions, then let's resurrect the statute. Let's raise it out of its century-old grave. Let's put it into force," Jehovah's witnesses argued.

On October 6, 1953, Canadian news services and radio broadcasts proclaimed the answer. The Canadian Supreme Court had decided. Five to four, they ruled for Jehovah's witnesses.

The sedition stigma was wiped away. Canada seemed to be electrified by the news. Headlines in Ottawa, Toronto, Montreal, and other sections read: "Freedom of Religion Upheld." "Jehovah's Witnesses Win Fight Over Quebec Order." "Witnesses Of Jehovah Win Decision Affecting Some 800 Cases In Quebec."

Canadian columnist Judith Robinson headed her column "Equal Rights for All." She said: "Few decisions in the history of Canadian justice can have been more important."

Exactly twenty years after it became law, Quebec City's censorship by-law was ruled out. It had read: "It is forbidden to distribute in the streets of Quebec any book, pamphlet, booklet, circular, tract whatever without having previously obtained for so doing the written permission of the Chief of Police."

Exactly one hundred years after Canada adopted a Bill of Religious Rights, Jehovah's witnesses dug it out of musty, forgotten statute books, dusted it off, and made their appeal on the strength of its constitutionality. The statute had been adopted at the confederation of the first four provinces. "At the time of its enactment in 1852 there had been a tremendous religious controversy between the Catholics and the Protestants. The statute had been designed to put an end to the fears of each side that the other would destroy it," wrote the Canadian correspondent of *Awake!*.

Apparently the statute had been forgotten. It had not been printed in the statute books of Ontario for forty years. In Quebec it had been reprinted but never used. The law provides as follows:

> WHEREAS the recognition of legal equality among all Religious Denominations is an admitted principle of Colonial Legislation; be it therefore declared . . . That the free exercise and enjoyment of Religious Profession and Worship, without discrimination or preference, so as the same be not made an excuse of acts of licentiousness, or a justification of practices inconsistent with the peace and safety of the Province is by the constitution and laws of this Province allowed to all Her Majesty's subjects within the same.

An Irish Roman Catholic, Mr. Justice Kerwin, concurring in the majority ruling, wrote: "It appears from the material filed on behalf of the appellant that Jehovah's Witnesses not only do not consider themselves as belonging to a religion but vehemently attack anything that may ordinarily be so termed but in my view they are entitled to "the free exercise and enjoyment of [their] Religious Profession and Worship."

Arrests and prosecutions of Jehovah's witnesses in Quebec had numbered more than fifteen hundred. Eight hundred cases were pending the outcome of the Saumur case. For the first time in thirty years, Jehovah's witnesses breathed an air of official freedom in Canada.

And without realizing it for one hundred years, Canadians awoke to the fact that, after all, they had a written Bill of Religious Freedom.

Where the Courts Are Closed

In many countries, law courts are not open to Jehovah's witnesses. So the Witnesses swarm up like clouds of international locusts and harass authorities by petition barrages. Hitler banned Jehovah's witnesses in 1933. He reaped a harvest of telegraphed protests so immense it had to be delivered by vanload. (By 1945 he had 10,000 Witnesses incarcerated of which number 2,000 died, 2,000 emerged disabled, and 6,000 returned to preaching.)

When the Tito government, in 1949, sentenced the Witness branch servant to death, so many appeals from all over the world were telegraphed that even the Communists were jolted. They commuted the death sentence to long-term imprisonment.

Legal Counsel Covington said that the organization has been "banned, proscribed, exiled, or executed in every country where totalitarianism has appeared."

Portugal, Spain, Russia, and Turkey did not recognize them prior to the war. They still do not.

Following the Allied victories in 1945, the Soviet conquerors tolerated a revival of aboveground organization of the Witnesses in East Germany, Poland, Rumania, and other satellite countries. Since 1948 the picture changed.

"You say Russia herself has never recognized the group?"

"Neither before nor after the war."

"Does this mean there are no Witnesses in Soviet Russia?"

"The Society has reports of more than ten thousand there."

"How did they get there?"

"When Russia absorbed Poland and other border countries," Covington explained, "several thousand Witnesses of those nationalities found themselves within the Greater Soviet."

"Was that their only means of entrance?"

"No. Many Russian war prisoners came in contact with Jehovah's witnesses in German concentration camps. A lot of them accepted the religion of the Witnesses in those camps."

Consequent shufflings of populations scattered the ten thousand or more Witnesses throughout the Soviet domain. European delegates to the 1953 international assembly of Jehovah's witnesses, at Yankee Stadium, brought news of underground operations of the Witnesses, even in Siberia.

Meanwhile, after consolidating their power in the satellite countries, the Communists began to close down the Witnesses, Covington went on. "By nineteen fifty, Jehovah's witnesses were not being 'integrated.' They were being absolutely outlawed in all Communistic countries."

Litigation in 22 Countries

"Are the Witnesses still fighting court battles, now, in nineteen fifty-three?" I asked the counselor.

"Civil-rights litigation, similar to the cases in the nineteen forties in the United States, is being tried in at least twenty-two countries," he responded. Greece, the Gold Coast, Switzerland, Syria, the Philippines, Portuguese East Africa, the Netherlands, Singapore, Luxembourg, Mexico, Lebanon, Norway, Sweden, Argentina, Brazil, the Dominican Republic, and Cyprus were among the countries he named.

In some countries, he said, it is effective to cite American, Canadian, African, and Australian precedents won by the Witnesses. In other countries it is no help. On the whole, the pattern of civil liberties fought for and won in the United States by Jehovah's witnesses is fought for in other countries. Jehovah's witnesses are making a practical contribution toward world freedom that few suspect them of, Covington commented.

"What about court cases in the United States?" I asked. "Are there still many being tried?"

"Not so many," he replied. "Since nineteen fifty they have been draft cases, mostly."

"Are American Witnesses still going to prison on draft charges?"

"Some, yes. Draft boards and appeal boards refuse to recognize the claim of ministerial status of quite a number of Witnesses, even yet."

"Are the Witnesses winning any draft cases in court now?"

"More now than during the Second World War. The federal courts, in several instances, have borne down hard on local boards and appeal boards for capricious and arbitrary refusal to permit registrants who are Witnesses a fair opportunity to state their case, or denial of their exempt status, as ministers."

Precedent for Litigation

"If Jehovah's witnesses feel that their mission, above everything else, is their Christian ministry, a thing apart from the world," I asked Covington, "why do they, on the other hand, appeal to the law courts of the world to uphold their freedom?"

"A familiar question," Covington nodded, a congenial boom in his voice. "The answer is that the Witnesses claim for this procedure the same thing they claim for their ministry—a Bible precedent."

"Who established it?"

"The apostle Paul, for one. Twice he appealed his own case to Caesar. The first time he won his freedom."

"What was his motive? To preserve his freedom to preach?"

"Not only that. Christians understood that they would be brought before kings and rulers to testify about the faith. Paul at one time almost convinced King Agrippa that Christianity was the true religion. While at Rome for his trial, Paul told the Philippians he was 'defending and legally establishing' the reality and virtue of the good news."

"Is that what Jehovah's witnesses feel they are doing—'defending and legally establishing the good news'?"

"That is the whole thing in a nutshell," Mr. Covington said smilingly. "Jehovah's witnesses have won recognition as a religious society. An established faith. They have written their faith into the laws of the land."

(For summaries of international legal cases and legal status of Jehovah's witnesses, see section "Their Day in Court" in Appendix.)

A Nation without a Country— " . . . but they saw them afar off and hailed them and publicly declared that they were strangers and temporary residents in the land. For those who say such things give evidence that they are earnestly seeking a place of their own," said Paul, of the pre-Christian men and women who looked forward to the Kingdom of God.—HEBREWS 11:13,14. New World Translation of the Christian Greek Scriptures

---

CHAPTER EIGHT

A NATION WITHOUT A COUNTRY

I KNOW you have heard of the story of *The Man without a Country*. And perhaps of other stateless people that no country will claim. But have you ever heard of a whole *nation* without a country of its own?

No, I do not mean the Jews, before their return to Palestine. After all, the Jews—most Jews—did their best to identify themselves with whatever nation they happened to live in. They voted and fought and suffered and died along with the Gentiles and Pagans for the nationalism or political bloc of which they were a part.

What I am talking about is a new nation of "spiritual Jews." These claim Christ as their leader. He is, to them, the Chief Son and Worshiper of Jehovah, the God of the Hebrews.

These people have found in their religion a tie stronger than nationalism, a tie stronger than any nameable ism in the world. Scattered among all the nations, they nevertheless cling to each other as if the nations did not exist. If all of Jehovah's witnesses lived together geographically, in a colony or on some island of their own, this might be easier to conceive. As things are, they make a strange picture.

But maybe they appear no stranger to the world than the world looks to them.

"What is the strongest tie in the world?" a Witness might ask you.

I don't know what you would say. Maybe God. Maybe God and country. Maybe something else.

But the Witness would answer the question this way: "Worship of Jehovah is to me the strongest tie. That, to me, is the religion of Christ, the Son of Jehovah. It is Bible Christianity. When two people are joined in that religion, nothing will split them apart. Nothing will set them fighting and killing each other."

Why Do Christians Fight Each Other?

"What happens when one Christian nation moves upon another, and the two nations start a war?" the Witness asks.

"First-century Christians were faced with that kind of conflict," the Witness replies. "A Roman army destroyed Jerusalem in the year seventy. Up till then, there had been Christians in Jerusalem. And there were Christians in the Empire. But this political war did not set the Christians fighting each other.

"Imagine the apostle Paul being conscripted in Rome to march against Jerusalem. At the same time, picture the ruling body of the church, that was still in Jerusalem, joining in the fight against Paul and the Romans.

"What happened," he continues, "was that the Christians in Jerusalem fled in the interim between the appearance of the first Roman army, in the year sixty-six, and the arrival of the second army that slaughtered more than a million Jews, in the year seventy.

"This was not a matter of cowardice. It had nothing to do with pacifism. The Christians merely heeded the prophecy of Jesus, thirty-six years earlier, that Jerusalem was doomed and that they should flee to the mountains.

"Either the Christian religion is strong enough to hold its adherents together or it is not. In the case of the first Christians, it was strong enough. Why has it weakened now?"

You might ask the Witness what he means by that.

He will reply that people have become confused to the point where they identify religion and nationalism as the same thing, "The people in one nation look around their land. 'God founded this nation,' they say. On the other side of the border the people of another nation look around their land. 'God founded our nation,' they say, in like manner. Now if it is the same God and the same religion, how do the two nations stand with God when they fall out and fight each other? Is it any different than when two people fall out and fight in church?"

I heard a Witness of Jehovah one time talk about the American War between the States. "The North made God out to be on the Union side. The South had Him in the Confederate camp. Lincoln warned that God was not on either side—they got themselves into the mess. Had the Confederates won they would have claimed God did it. But since the North won, God was said to have saved the Union. Don't you think it is more likely that Lincoln was right—they got themselves into it and would have to get themselves out?"

What Jehovah's witnesses do not understand is this: Why is it that membership in the same church or group of churches, as in Christendom, has not kept a community or a nation from internal fighting? And why do nations of the same faith fight each other?

"Here is a generation that has tasted two world wars," a
Witness once told me. "These wars threw two hundred and
forty million Roman Catholics at each other. Virtually all
Protestants and Jews were involved in one way or another.
It took the Christian nations, not the Pagans, to show what
global war can be like. It was a Christian nation that
dropped the A-bomb on a Pagan nation. It is the Christian
nations that are preparing the H-bomb and germ warfare
and the Devil knows what else for more war. Why?"

The Witnesses don't say these things in a sneering tone.
They only mean to point out that religion, even when called
Christian, is a tie neither strong nor binding enough to
keep peace and love alive among nations. They say this
should not be so. They say there is no excuse for it. They
demonstrate in their own case that their religion is strong
enough to keep one national body of Witnesses from joining
in a war against another national body of Witnesses.

This is not a really remarkable display of integrity, they
assert. The world shows just as much integrity in its nationalism.

Conscientious Objectors but not Pacifists

At the same time, Jehovah's witnesses disclaim any trace
of pacifism.

"Conscientious objectors, yes," they agree. "But not paci-
fists."

How can you be one and not the other, you may wonder.

"Easily," they reply.

"You explain it," you say.

"Very well. Let's take yourself. Are you a pacifist?"

If you answer no, a Witness will tell you that nevertheless
you are a conscientious objector. "I'll prove it to you," he
offers.

This you've got to see, you reply.

"Do you have any moral scruples?" the witness asks.

You want to know what he thinks you are, anyway, you
retort.

"You mean you have scruples against something?" he asks. "Now what is that but your conscience objecting to a thing you believe is wrong?"

You can't deny it.

"To the degree to which you have a sense of moral integrity you are a conscientious objector to what your moral teaching has convinced you is wrong."

"Of course," you agree. "But there is more than one way—"

"Let's say you are a political envoy. You are in a foreign country. That foreign government seizes you. It conscripts you. Now you are in its army. You may have to fight your own native country. Do you conscientiously object?"

"Of course."

"Do you tell that foreign power that it can't get away with such a thing?"

"You bet."

"Would that make you a pacifist?"

"Not on your life."

"There you are," the Witness concludes. "A conscientious objector, yes; a pacifist, no."

Theocracy's Ambassadors

Jehovah's witnesses see themselves in a position like that. They are ministers and ambassadors of Jehovah's Kingdom by Christ, they declare. That Kingdom is a going concern— here—now. Their mission is to represent the Kingdom among all nations. Their role is to see that the good news is preached adequately, officially, among all nations for the benefit of all nations and individuals. It is a peaceful mission, but not a pacifistic mission.

"If you think it is war we are opposed to," a Witness will remind you, "then remember this. Who is preaching the biggest war of all? Jehovah's witnesses. We preach Armageddon. It will fall upon this generation. When it is over, there will be but one nation left—Jehovah's nation of worshipers."

It is a community of people, all right. It is growing as-
tonishingly fast into a New World Society. Drawn together
by an irresistible force, they are literally caught up into a so·
ciety unto themselves, like iron filings licked up into a
cluster by a magnet passed over a dusty floor.

These people make good citizens in every nation. Especially do they obey the civil laws. They live clean lives. They
pay their taxes. But they proclaim allegiance to, or vote the
political ticket of none of the nations—not even when the
son of two of Jehovah's witnesses, General Eisenhower, runs
for and wins "the biggest office in the world"—the presidency
of the United States.[1]

Kingdom's Reality the Issue

In Quebec, Canada, and in Harlan County, Kentucky,
Bible missionaries quoted the Lord's Prayer—"*Your* Kingdom come, *Your* will be done on earth as in heaven." They
declared they believed the Kingdom was here. The time for
God's will to be done.

What happened? Court trials.

The dignified, black-robed judge listened gravely to the
evidence. The Harlan County defendants were found guilty.
The crime was sedition. They were advocating a government "by one Jehovah God." That was the reading of the
indictment. In Quebec, the trials were carried right up to
the very highest court in the land before the sedition charges
were quashed.

That is the atmosphere Jehovah's witnesses live in. The
point is that Jehovah's witnesses see in the Lord's Kingdom
Prayer, and its attendant scriptural teachings, a Govern-

---

[1]When Dwight D. Eisenhower left Abilene for West Point, in June, 1911,
he must have taken with him memories of the efforts both his father and
mother made to persuade him, during the fourteen years up to 1911, to read
The Watch Tower. They had been regularly receiving and using it in their
home Bible studies since 1896, when Ike was six years old.

Another handbook in the Eisenhower home of Ike's youth was Charles T.
Russell's first "Millennial Dawn" volume, *The Divine Plan of the Ages*, written
in 1886. On Ike's parents, see Appendix, page 189.

ment. To them the Kingdom is no mere wispy realm of heavenly reward. No, the Witnesses contend, a *Kingdom*—any kingdom, America's or the Kremlin's or Franco's or Elizabeth's—is something that cannot exist without a *Government.* That is what holds it together. No government; no kingdom, they contend.

And a government—particularly the Heavenly Theocracy —is a place where people do something more useful than "shout hallelujah choruses."

I remember an incident that sharpens the point. It involved two women in rural Tennessee. The elder of the two had been studying with Jehovah's witnesses for a year. She decided she had had enough. The younger woman, a Witness, determined to make one final call.

"You people talk all the time about living on earth under the Kingdom," objected the old lady. "I am not going to live on earth. I am going to heaven."

"We know that the Bible holds out the heavenly hope for some," agreed the Witness. "But we don't want to overlook the earthly promise, just because of the heavenly one. After all, doesn't Peter say Christians look for new heavens and a new earth, wherein righteousness is to dwell?"

"But I am going to heaven," insisted the old lady.

"Well, I am glad for you," the younger woman replied. "But I am also concerned about you. I wonder what effect your going to heaven may have on me."

"What do you mean?" The old lady looked honestly astonished.

"I have been reading about you who go to heaven," explained the younger woman. "Revelation chapter one verse six describes your class as being kings and priests and reigning with Christ. Is that right?"

"Of course."

"When you get to be a king or ruler, what are you going to reign over?"

The older woman looked at her caller in silence.

"That is what disturbs me," the Witness went on. "Revelation chapter five verse ten states that you heavenly kings and priests are going to reign over the earth. Personally, if I get life I expect it will be in the earthly arrangement. If you are going to be up there in heaven, ruling over me, and you don't know what it's all about, I wonder how I am going to fare down here?"

These Witnesses talk about the Kingdom in just such tangible terms—an actual Kingdom ruling power, ushering in a complete New World.

It is no in-the-by-and-by conception in their minds. To them this heavenly Theocracy began ruling toward earth, in its premillennium, Day-of-Jehovah stage, in 1914.

So real is it to them that they profess allegiance to it above that of the nations in which they live. They claim the same world neutrality that Paul attributed to the pre-Christian "cloud of witnesses," such as sojourners Abraham, Isaac, and Jacob, who declared that they were "strangers and temporary residents in the land." The modern Witnesses of Jehovah claim ministerial and ambassadorial status among the nations as representatives and harbingers of the New World Government. They see it as their role to stand neutral among nations.

"But where is it—this Kingdom?" you ask, in bafflement. "I see no Theocracy. Do you mean that Jehovah's witnesses have set themselves up to take over the earth?"

True, if the Witnesses pointed to some man, such as the late Judge Rutherford, or his successor, N. H. Knorr, or to a religious presidium, such as the board of directors of the Watch Tower Society; if they proclaim, "There is the New World Government," they would be bringing this belief down to familiar ground. They would be proclaiming a visible, earthly theocracy. Nothing new. It would be as old, for example, as the Roman Catholic hierarchy. The only way I can approach an explanation is against a backdrop of familiar things.

Example of Visible Theocracy

We can conceive of the Roman Catholic hierarchy as it

conceives of itself. In its own eyes that hierarchy, headed by
its pope as the "successor" of Jesus Christ's apostle Peter,
constitutes actual ruling power over the entire earth. Early
in this century, in Ireland, a Roman Catholic Jesuit author,
with approval of the Bishop of Clonfert, wrote:

> He brings a message to the Caesar, and this is what
> his message means: "Caesar, thy work is done. . . . I
> will wield thy sceptre. Take down thine eagles from
> the Capitol. In their stead I will set up the Cross. Upon
> thy palace I will build my Vatican. . . . Caesar, thou
> mayest go. Rome is mine, for I am Peter." What was
> Rome's answer? Rome owned the earth. . . . Rome
> declared war against Peter. . . . The world was Pagan,
> then. . . . But, the Christian revelation being true, and
> good, and beautiful, conquered.[1]

Catholic philosopher Will Durant, in his *Story of Phi-
losophy* (New Revised Ed., Garden City, N. Y., 1933, p. 50)
gives some background on the history of the church organization.

> Much of the politics of Catholicism was derived from
> Plato's "royal lies," or influenced by them: the ideas of
> heaven, purgatory, and hell, in their medieval form,
> are traceable to the last book of the *Republic;* the cos-
> mology of scholasticism comes largely from the *Timaeus;*
> the doctrine of realism (the objective reality of general
> ideas) was an interpretation of the doctrine of Ideas;
> even the educational "quadrivium" (arithmetic, ge-
> ometry, astronomy and music) was modeled on the cur-
> riculum outlined in Plato. With this body of doctrine
> the people of Europe were ruled with hardly any resort
> to force; and they accepted this rule so readily that for
> a thousand years they contributed plentiful material
> support to their rulers, and asked no voice in the gov-

---

[1]Robert Kane, S.J., *From Peter to Leo*, Part 1, pp. 14, 15, 25 (Dublin,
Catholic Truth Society of Ireland).

ernment. Nor was this acquiescence confined to the general population; merchants and soldiers, feudal chieftains and civil powers all bent the knee to Rome. It was an aristocracy of no mean political sagacity; it built probably the most marvelous and powerful organization which the world has ever known.

The point here is not what the world was—or was not converted to. The point is that a hierarchical order of things called the Holy Roman Empire actually was established. It ruled over Christendom. It prospered. The pope crowned the heads of state, in the name of Christ and His Kingdom. Now *that* we can visualize. We know it happened.

And we know that this great spiritual city still claims the right to rule over the kings of the earth—more than a third of a million ministerial advocates or ambassadors (Catholic priests) represent its authority among four hundred million Catholics scattered throughout the world. According to the authoritative Catholic publication *The Liberal Illusion* (pp. 37-8):

Jesus Christ is the King of the world. He speaks to the world through His Priest (the pope), and the decrees of this Priest, being an expression of the royal rights of Jesus Christ, are eternal. They apply not to one time alone, but to all times; not to one society alone, but to all societies; not to some men, but to all men. The children of the King are kings. They form an absolutely superior society, whose duty it is to take possession of the earth and reign over it for the purpose of baptising all men and of raising them to that selfsame supernatural life, that selfsame royalty and that selfsame glory for which Christ has destined them.

Jehovah's Kingdom Invisible

You do not have to bat an eye to comprehend the reality and character of that kingdom. It is tangible. It is visible.

You simply point to the Supreme Pontiff, to the College of Cardinals and the priests and say: *There it is.*

But this Kingdom proclaimed by Jehovah's witnesses has no such visible counterpart. And the invisible nature of their King causes no worry to Jehovah's witnesses.

The contrast, however, is just that sharp. The Witnesses deny that Christ is King of this world. They claim He was put to death on the torture stake for declaring "My Kingdom is not of this world," while his own people cried, "We have no king but Caesar." This same "unreformed and murderous spirit" prevails to the world's end, the Witnesses contend. They point to Paul's prophecy that "in the last days" men would "profess a form of Godliness, while denying the power thereof." Christ's advent in Kingdom Power finds the world totally deceived by its god, Satan the Devil, the Dragon, the Serpent. Christ "thrashes the nations with an iron rod" to their utter annihilation at Armageddon.

This is their view of things. This is the touchiest issue in the world. It involves nationalism, patriotism, neutrality. Jehovah's witnesses have landed squarely in the middle of it.

But why discuss it? It is a message that brooks no indifference. Millions are influenced by it. During World War II Jehovah's witnesses accounted for the largest body of noncomformists in Christendom. They will account for more nonconformists from here on until either the world or Jehovah's witnesses literally vacate the planet.

That is as plain as I can state it. But it is not exaggerated —not by a syllable. Not forever, the Witnesses are the first to point out, will the nations tolerate this "Nation Without a Country" in their midst. On charges of "antigovernment," "sedition," and the like, the world will eventually and more or less unitedly move to "break their bonds asunder and cast them from us."

"Were they a more formidable group, tolerance of them would be less absolute, for they clash with a sentiment that is more universal in America than loyalty to a church, the sentiment of patriotism," warns the Catholic magazine, *The Liguorian* in its March, 1953, issue. It adds:

One feels also that if the Witnesses should ever grow large in number and begin to permeate a large segment of society with their anti-government tactics, restrictive measures would be sanctioned. For, in this country, while religious observance is not a universal practice, patriotism is; and, as Finley Peter Dunne once said: "The supreme court also reads the election returns."

This appeal to patriotic sentiment is not, of course, peculiar to America. It was aped by the Nazis. And the Communists. The only difference is that the totalitarians act first.

Before the windup, say Jehovah's witnesses, the nations will all move to obliterate this New World Society. And they will do it—unless something from out of this old world intervenes.

The Witnesses are banking on that something.

Armageddon.

> *Jehovah's Witnesses and the Bible— "If any-
> one thinks he has acquired knowledge of
> something, he does not yet know it just as he
> ought to know it."—I Corinthians 8:2, New
> World Translation of the Christian Greek
> Scriptures*

CHAPTER NINE

JEHOVAH'S WITNESSES
AND THE BIBLE

THE way Jehovah's witnesses go about studying the Bible
has a lot to do with what they believe and how they teach.
I have yet to see a better explanation of their method than
the one set down in an old copy of *The Watch Tower* dated
July 15, 1913. Pastor Russell, in a section entitled "Words of
Caution," summed up the working principles that guide the
organization. The first principle he listed was "No Claim to
Inspiration."

No Claim to Inspiration

"This may be as good an opportunity as any for a few words of caution," he began. "We are all in danger of going to extremes, and all should remember the Apostle's words, 'Let your moderation be known unto all.' At one place we found that a spirit of antagonism had been aroused by means of immoderate statements on the part of a few.

"They had suggested that Brother Russell and his writings were divinely inspired, as were the Apostles of old. What a great mistake! When asked if such were our opinion, we promptly assured the dear friends to the contrary.

Only Twelve "Special Mouthpieces"

"The view we have always presented, and still hold," he explained, "is that the Lord Jesus appointed only twelve Apostles, Paul being the one to take Judas' place.

"The words of these would be so supervised by Divine Power that whatsoever they would declare binding on earth, the Church would know would be bound in Heaven, and whatsoever they would declare on earth to be loosed or not binding, they might know would not be obligatory in the sight of Heaven.

"In other words, those twelve Apostles were the special mouthpieces of the Lord to His Church.

"They still speak to us. We need no others; we expect no others."

Message in Line with Apostles

Mr. Russell continued: "The most we have ever claimed for our own presentations, written or oral, is that they are in line with the words of the Apostles, that they harmonize with them—that we keep so close to the words of the Apostles and the words of our Lord that our message may be said to be their Message, except in respect to the particular words used and the arrangement of them."

Assembling Bible Texts in Topical Form

Then the Pastor laid his finger on the precise aim of the organization. That aim was neither to "add to" nor "take from" the Bible.

"In the *Studies in the Scriptures* we have classified the various presentations of Jesus, the Apostles and the Prophets into different studies or topics; and this is what we meant when we declared in an old *Watch Tower* that, on this account, whoever reads the *Studies in the Scriptures* is really reading the Bible in an arranged form—topically."

Down to the present this basic approach of Jehovah's witnesses has not deviated. They have kept at the work of making what is, to them, the proper classification of more and more of the Scriptures under whatever theme or doctrine the texts seem to belong. You might say they are working, year in, year out, to codify the whole Bible.

For instance: In one of their books, *The Kingdom Is at Hand,* all the texts from the Bible are drawn together in the form of a story of the Kingdom, from the time it was foretold, through periods when it was foreshadowed in miniature, to when its King first appeared, and on to its full establishment and accomplishments. In another book, *Let God Be True,* the second edition, twenty-six doctrines are covered. One chapter is devoted to each doctrine. Within the chapter are compacted the outstanding Bible texts from Genesis to Revelation, explaining that one doctrine.

And in their books and magazines Jehovah's witnesses index the Scriptures and subjects copiously. With a library of their works one of them can go into the Bible to just about any desired extent on almost any imaginable subject. Have you ever watched a smart housewife thumb her indexed cookbook? She can find the recipe for any menu she wants. So a Witness has at his command the means to find the Scriptural recipe for any problem in life.

Public Speakers Trained to Outline Bible

Public speakers of Jehovah's witnesses are trained in

weekly class studies and drills. The basic textbook, published in 1945, is called *Theocratic Aid to Kingdom Publishers*. In it there is a lesson on "Need of an Outline." It shows the minister how to make up his talk by outlining associated Scriptures. He learns to follow the method used by the Society in preparing their literature.

Theocratic Aid tells him: "The Bible does not generally discuss doctrines under a topically outlined arrangement, but merely touches upon them in running style as they come into the account.

"Texts bearing upon a particular subject are scattered throughout, not placed under one heading where a complete discussion is given. Such special treatment of fundamental doctrine was not needed back there at the time of writing, because all understood those things."

Religious confusions have beclouded the teachings so that a modern minister faces a hard task of "running to and fro" through the Bible to "draw together topically outlined discussions on doctrines," *Theocratic Aid* concludes.

Their Fight with Evolution

If hundreds of brands of religious confusions left any part of the Bible unmuddled, pseudo-science rushed in in a flying tackle to finish the job, the Witnesses believe. They point out Evolution as Culprit Number One. The theory, having been togged up in sacred-cow trappings, may be posed as unquestionable scientific dogma to awe some minds; but to the Witnesses, all its links are still missing.

The Witnesses believe that Fundamentalist religionists have done their bit to pave the way for the wildfire spread of Evolutionist doctrine. "Fundamentalists, with their doctrines of a literal six-day creation and the like, have made the Bible appear more ridiculous than anyone else. Evolution, for all its missing links, is at least an alternative. When Galileo produced the telescope of threefold magnifying power and exploded the Church's 'infallible' doctrine of a flat earth, millions of people commenced to wonder how much more of the Church's 'truth' was a bubble." People welcomed something new, something "based on scientific fact." Evolution came along. It donned the trappings of science. It bedazzled the popular mind, the Witnesses feel.

They feel that the people got hoodwinked by Evolution because the popular mind mistook apostate religious teaching for Bible truth. When millions of people began to heave the Bible out the window, some segments of religious higher critics hastened forward with the apology that while the Bible is a good moral book to go by, after all it is a depository, like other ancient literature, of some beautiful and some ugly fables collected by the Jews. Its story of a direct creation by an all-wise, all-powerful Creator, for example, was one of those nice fantasies like Santa Claus, that mature, intelligent, modern persons would naturally have to grow out of.

But, continue the Witnesses, as actual scientific knowledge increased, one evolutionist theory after another had to be dropped like hot potatoes. Meanwhile, thanks to archaeological discoveries, one Bible "myth" after another was being identified as historical fact. Sometimes the Higher Critics were left out in the cold, going and coming, to find that the Bible which they discarded was being vindicated while the evolutionist theories they espoused were being discarded. The Witnesses suspect that the Higher Critics in their way, like the Fundamentalists in theirs, have helped Evolutionists to a field day in discrediting the Bible. All the while, everybody has grown more confused.

As for themselves, the Witnesses would like neither to bury their heads in the sand of blind Fundamentalism; nor to be awed speechless by the deep-chested tones of Evolutionist theory. At their research library in New York, Witness scholars have dug deep and long into the study of Evolution versus the Bible. In 1950 they voiced a masterful rebuttal.

It was at their 1950 International Convention at Yankee Stadium, at a Session attended by 75,000, that their booklet, *Evolution versus the New World,* was released. Colin Quackenbush of the Society's editorial staff delivered the bulk of the document in the form of a major discourse. Shortly there-after *Evolution* figured in an incident which the press played up as a national sensation—the conversion of mystery writer Mickey Spillane.

Clearing up the Evolutionist controversy, the Witnesses held, was one of the biggest steps toward establishing the authenticity of the Bible. If it was that important to them, I felt that I should take particular pains to quote them clearly on the issue. Mr. Quackenbush was the first to speak out publicly, in a comprehensive and scholarly attack on Evolution. So I turned to him.

Ensconced in an airy office on the eighth floor of the Bethel headquarters at 124 Columbia Heights in Brooklyn, Witness Quackenbush, I found, does his deep digging into subjects like Evolution and the Bible at a big flat-topped desk that dominates the room. Behind him a large window looks out upon the Brooklyn Bridge and a part of the New York waterfront. In front of him are portraits of the Sierra Nevada Mountains, where he loves to hike two weeks out of the year.

What had Evolution done toward undermining faith in the Bible? In his mild, soft-spoken manner, scholar Quackenbush had this to say:

"Evolutionists hold that direct creation is unthinkable. So they invent theories of their own to explain the origin of life."

"Invent, would you say?"

"After all," he replied, "a theory is an invention, isn't it?"

Would he like to point out some Evolutionist inventions?

"At one time Evolutionists taught that fleas, worms, and mice and low forms of life sprang up spontaneously."

"From what?" I asked.

"From inanimate matter."

But that theory, he said, was exploded by an Italian named Redi. "Then came the microscope and Pasteur's work to further devastate the *spontaneous generation theory.*"

"But haven't Evolutionists since discovered the true origin of life?"

Not to his way of thinking. "They have expounded

theories about one-celled life in a mud puddle evolving to the stature of a man."

Could it not be proven that man has acquired some characteristics?

"Well, that theory teaches that environment causes certain minute changes to occur in size, shape, and color," he said, gathering his thoughts on the matter. "These traits were supposed to have been passed on and developed by succeeding generations. After millions of years, according to this theory of *acquired characteristics*, new families have appeared."

"Don't you accept the theory?"

"Genetics," he answered, "threw it out the same back door with *spontaneous generation*. Genetics has proved that acquired characteristics simply cannot be inherited. Darwin himself called the theory nonsense."

Which brought us to Darwin. What did this witness of Jehovah think of Darwin?

"His idea of *natural selection* won't work either."

"Why not?"

"It teaches that in the struggle for existence needed and useful variations are made. Variations that prove useless and weak perish. In other words, 'survival of the strongest and fittest.' Well, how could an eye, or ear, or heart develop according to that theory?"

It was his way of saying that an eye, an ear, or a heart would be useless until developed. But the theory ruled that useless variations were discarded. "No wonder Evolutionists themselves now toss out this folly of Darwin's."

Mutations was one of the more recent theories to backfire, I was told. "Fossil records reveal no evidence that small changes have evolved new families. On the other hand, big changes produce freaks. Mutations, in other words, are harmful, not helpful."

My informant had a way of laying one argument down against the other in sharp, crisp contrasts. In the conflict between Evolution and the Bible, he said, geology threw its weight more behind the Bible. "Geology discovers that very complex forms of life appeared suddenly. No unaccountable billion-year periods or missing links appear at their beginning, to indicate an evolutionary chain."

Earliest findings show animal life in the same great variety of families that we have today, he continued. This agrees with the Bible teaching in Genesis 1:20, 24, which Mr. Quackenbush quoted: "And God said, Let the waters swarm with swarms of living creatures, and let birds fly above the earth. . . . And God said, Let the earth bring forth living creatures after their kind, cattle and creeping things, and beasts of the earth after their kind: and it was so."[1]

Ancient archaeology revealed that, as for man, his civilization as far back as could be unearthed, was of a high level. No cave men or "gibbering gibbons" were to be found. By Evolutionist theory, man's life span should now be at its longest. Archaeologists discover that the ancients lived longer —vindicating the Bible. Evolutionists taught that original speech started with grunts and growls. But the oldest languages were actually the most complex. "According to the Bible, Genesis 2:19, 20," said my informant, "the first man had perfect command of language. He could coin new words so fast that he gave all the birds and beasts their names as they passed before him. Can you name a tenth of them?"

Evolution might teach that all life originated with one blob of protoplasm. But true science discovers that various forms of life appeared suddenly and complete and in distinctive families, first the marine forms, then fowl life, then the land creatures. This agrees with the Bible order of creation in Genesis, chapter one. Mr. Quackenbush also quoted I Corinthians 15:39: "Not all flesh is the same flesh but there is one of mankind and there is another flesh of cattle, and another flesh of birds, and another of fish."

But the big question that stops Evolutionists is this: Why is there such a vast gulf between the mental powers and

---

[1]The quotations made here and in Chapter 10 are taken from various Bible versions.

capacities of man and animals? Why are there no inter-
mediate stages between man and beast? The only answer
to it is in the Bible, concluded Mr. Quackenbush, and
quoted Genesis 1:26, 27: "Let us make man in our own
image, after our likeness: and let them have dominion over
the fish of the sea, and over the birds of the heavens and
over the cattle and over all the earth, and over every creeping thing."

"What does this mean," I interjected, "this being made
in God's image and likeness?"

"Among other things," he replied, "it means having
tremendous powers of perception and the ability to reason,
weigh arguments, use logic, decide between right and
wrong."

Only man has a conscience, I was informed. Only man
can display conscious justice. Only man has the impulse to
worship the Divine Being. "What set of mutations, what
chain of natural selection, what acquired characteristics
could ever evolve out of the lower stationary forms of life
such a creature as man?"

The Bible Authentic

By these arguments and many others Jehovah's witnesses
hold with a clear and satisfied conscience that the Bible is
authentic, reliable, and the only safe handbook of life. They
study it and use it until they know how to find the principle,
the proverb, the dramatic type or example that fits the need
or the problem of the moment. When they converse with you
from it they do so simply, unpretentiously, like Mr. Quackenbush, with no attendant glow of out-of-this-worldness or
sanctimoniousness or swallowing of the voice in the chest.
They do indeed respect the Bible as the work of a Divine
Authority. It is to them the Book of the Creator in which
He tells His creatures about creation, about Himself, about
His rules of life—rules that are simple and practical.

"Why should anyone think it incredible that the Builder

of the complex atom and Creator of the boundless cosmic universe could produce a simple thing like a book?" they want to know. "All God had to do was to inspire dedicated and devoted men with His holy spirit. These men, in turn, could surely write down what the Author dictated."

And this, the Witnesses find, is the way the Bible was produced. "Nearly forty different men were used to write it. Rarely did these individuals know each other. They lived over a period of 1,600 years. Yet their writings are in perfect harmony. Through all their writings is woven one single blending theme."

What is that Theme? What had Jehovah's witnesses discovered in the Bible that made them different? For the answer to this I was directed to a genial gentleman who presides over a big bustling office department on the ninth floor of Jehovah's witnesses' publishing plant at 117 Adams Street in Brooklyn.

One glance at his chipper countenance told me that his biography was correct—Thomas James Sullivan had been born some sixty-six years ago in County Kerry, Ireland.

*Doctrines of the New World— "Before them
the land lies like an Eden paradise, behind
them it is a desolate desert."—JOEL 2:3, Mof-
fatt Translation*

CHAPTER TEN

DOCTRINES OF THE NEW WORLD

THOMAS JAMES SULLIVAN was the logical one to brief
me on the doctrines that have produced the "New World
Society of Jehovah's Witnesses." His position in the organi-
ation carries a qualifying title: Director and Superintendent
of Ministers and Evangelists.

He came to work fulltime at the Witnesses' world headquarters in Brooklyn in 1924. At the time he granted me
this interview Mr. Sullivan had been serving for more than
a dozen years as a director of the Witnesses' principal corporation, the Watch Tower Bible & Tract Society.

Once outside his bustling department in the Society's publishing plant at 117 Adams Street, I noted, Mr. Sullivan's irrepressible spirits were apt to betray the Irish in him. I remember one morning, riding down the elevator from the Bethel apartments to the dining room. At that hour more than four hundred members of the Bethel family were making the elevators hum as they all converged toward breakfast. Our elevator had just filled up, with Mr. Sullivan one of the last to crowd aboard. Down at the next floor its automatic mechanism stopped the elevator, and the doors rolled back. A rush of faces in the corridor filled the elevator door, took one look, and hope faded. In the momentary silence Mr. Sullivan's wry "Too bad" set off a burst of chuckles that rippled over into the corridor as the elevator door closed out the stranded faces.

But when you ask him what it is that makes Jehovah's witnesses tick, Mr. Sullivan sheds his pungent wit.

"Their doctrines are what make Jehovah's witnesses the people they are," he told me immediately. "They are not the product of a commercial organization—the Society's publishing business, itself is not commercial, and our factories operate not on profits but on contributions.

"Neither," he continued, "are they the product of some political organization using religion as a blind. Jehovah's witnesses are the only truly international neutralists, with no designs to influence politics, overthrow governments, or set up a regime of their own. Their allegiance is to the heavenly Theocratic Kingdom ruled by Christ Jesus and which, Jesus said, is not political in any sense."

Lastly, Jehovah's witnesses "are not the product of some new religious sect or cult, because they have no organizational objective similar to any orthodox church. While their religion may seem new to the world, it is as old as the Bible, and that is what makes it seem strange and different."

Would the Superintendent of Evangelists explain, in terms of doctrines, what makes Jehovah's witnesses distinctively different?

"Well, the difference stems from a basic approach to the Bible," he suggested. By that he meant that when you read something, if your mind is already set to look for a particular thing, you are liable to note that one special thing and let most of the rest slip by. "What if you were already conditioned to think, for example, that the main theme of the Bible is soul salvation?" he demonstrated. "No matter how much you read and study the Bible, the things which strike you as pertaining to soul salvation will stand out. Someone comes along and suggests that the main theme of the Bible is something different, and points out texts supporting that view, and the texts will sound strange and new to you."

That is why Bible doctrines sound strange to the world, coming from Jehovah's witnesses. The world in general believes that soul salvation is the Bible's main theme. Jehovah's witnesses believe the main theme to be something else.

"What do they believe it is?"

"God's vindication. Human salvation is secondary to that."

Would my informant please explain?

"Suppose we put it this way," he illustrated. "Let's say that you and I read the Lord's prayer together. Jesus gave it to us to line our viewpoint up in the proper perspective. It starts out asking that our Father's name be sanctified, His Kingdom installed over the earth, His righteousness established. It ends up asking for our personal daily welfare and salvation.

"Now," he said, emphasizing the point with a lifted finger, "if, to you, the principal theme is soul salvation, only the latter part of the prayer will stand out. How much will the first part, the part of first importance, register with you?"

On the other hand, if to a man the main theme is the vindication of God's name and truth and purposes, then look what a different relationship of values he would derive from the same Lord's prayer!

To emphasize that people in general overlook God's vindication in their concern for personal salvation, the Superintendent noted that much is made of the Golden Rule, of doing to others as you would have them do unto you. "But are they not overlooking the fact that the Golden Rule is secondary to a first commandment?" He cited Matthew 22: 37-40: " 'You must love Jehovah your God with your whole heart and with your whole soul and with your whole mind.' This is the greatest and first commandment. The second, like it, is this: 'You must love your neighbor as yourself.' On these two commandments the whole Law hangs, and the Prophets." —*New World Translation of the Christian Greek Scriptures.*

This basic approach to understanding the Bible, then, is what distinguishes Jehovah's witnesses. Their insistence that God's vindication comes first, and all else after. Mr. Sullivan felt that one of the strongest proofs that this is the proper perspective was this: "It is impossible to see the Bible as a really and truly coherent whole unless you discern in the first place that its main theme is God's vindication by His chosen means."

I asked: "Just what, specifically, do Jehovah's witnesses mean by God's vindication?"

"When you study the Bible to find out what that means," he explained, "then you are able to grasp the Bible as a whole, as one Book, telling one coherent story. You see it as a drama, revealing a great work that God originally purposed to perform. You read of how that work was interrupted by a challenger. You find that God set to work a strategy by which to throw down the challenger and bring to fulfillment His original purpose in perfection. How God accomplishes this victory is what is meant by His vindication."

"Have you just now outlined to me the plot of the Bible's story?" I suggested.

"The Bible's central drama is as simple as that," he replied.

Here was something that did strike a new chord in Bible treatment. It reminded me of the time when I was in my twenties, working on a Southern newspaper. A couple of young writers used to come down from New York each summer and we three would hole up in a cabin on the river and try to fathom how dramatic writing is put together. Plotting stories was our daily occupation. Most story plots boiled down to a simple 1) THE SETTING—boy meets and falls for girl. 2) DRAMATIC SITUATION—obstacle stands in way of boy getting girl. 3) CONFLICT—boy's tussle to overcome obstacle. 4) CLIMAX—boy wins tussle, carries off girl and lives happily ever after. Disturbing the setting is the situation which creates conflict which generates drama which holds you to the climax. The fiercer the conflict the hotter the drama.

Now this overseer of peripatetic Jehovah's witnesses was about to plot the Bible for me like that—the setting, the dramatic situation, the conflict and the climax. It would show me the Bible in a new dimension, reveal a religion built around the concern to see God vindicated over His challenger, and explain what it is that motivates the most phenomenal group of people in modern Christendom.

Setting

Said Mr. Sullivan, the setting of the Bible drama, as told in the first two chapters of the Book, is Paradise. "There we find the creation of man. He is given a Paradise home. He is told to multiply and populate the earth. He is to wield dominion over all earthly life, subdue it, spread the boundaries of Paradise farther and farther, as his family grows. Eventually the whole habitable earth would become transformed like the garden of Eden. This was man's destiny. This was the Creator's purpose, to make His footstool, the earth, a glorious habitation for His visible creature, man, who imaged Him in His attributes of wisdom, power, justice and love."

Dramatic Situation

Why did not God's purpose advance? Why did not man in Paradise "multiply and transmit perfect life, through his God-given powers of procreation to his offspring"? Why was not Paradise extended over the globe? The reason must present the most dramatic situation that ever arose. Indeed it did. The reason was rebellion.

"The Bible tells us in Deuteronomy 32:4 and 5 that Jehovah's works are perfect and that any creatures that willfully fall from their perfection are disowned by Him. He had created Adam perfect. But He gave Adam a free will to exercise."

Free will was necessary if man was to demonstrate his Godly attributes of love and wisdom. However, free will, if wrongly employed, would certainly give rise to a dramatic situation!

"To test Adam's obedience," continued my informant, "that is, to test his exercise of love and wisdom toward his Creator, God had placed a restriction upon the eating of one fruit in the garden. Man was to let it alone."

But alas, the third chapter of the Bible rings down the curtain on Paradise. Man's life-right is lost. It is blotted out by a dramatic situation that has embroiled the universe in a conflict that has grown hotter ever since and is about to reach its frightful but glorious climax soon. "The man and his wife ate the forbidden fruit. They disobeyed. They did not show love and wisdom in dealing with their Creator. They turned their power to love inward upon themselves. They set their minds to devising rebellious works."

True, a challenger was behind it. "Selfish ambition had been stirred in their breasts by an intruder."

Mr. Sullivan described the intruder as a mighty spirit creature. Originally Jehovah had placed him as a "covering cherub" over man, to guide man in filling the earth with a paradise of everlasting life. "The twenty-eighth chapter of Ezekiel and the fourteenth chapter of Isaiah describe this mighty spirit creature as having been perfect until iniquity was found in him by virtue of conceiving a rebellion against Jehovah. He aspired to exalt himself above other creatures. He would challenge God's supremacy. He would match the Most High.

"The rebel opened his attack at the earth. He induced

the woman first to eat the forbidden fruit. He told her that
God had lied about it. Eating it would not bring death upon
her. In fact, she would herself become like gods."

So drama entered. Conflict shook the universe. The issue
was that of Universal Domination. Who is Supreme Sov-
ereign? No wonder then, that God's vindication is the main
thing.

Conflict

Drama flared, as the Bible outlines in its third chapter,
when Jehovah held a trial in Eden. God officially identified
the great "covering cherub" as having transformed himself
into a deceiving Serpent, a slandering Devil, the great ad-
versary Satan. He had made his challenge, now he must try to
answer it. The whole universe was invited to a ringside seat.
Satan would build up an organization to confront Jehovah's
organization of faithful creatures. Out from Jehovah's organization or "woman" in due time would proceed a cham-
pion or "seed" to crush the Devil's head. Jehovah's "seed"
the Bible proved to be Christ Jesus. The instrument he
would use to annihilate the Devil and his works would be
a new ruling Government set in power over heaven and
earth, a Government identified as the Kingdom of Heaven.

Climax

"The last book of the Bible," concluded the Society
director, "describes how the great heavenly King, Christ
Jesus, destroys Satan's works. How he restores righteous
Theocratic rule over the earth. How, during his thousand-
year Kingdom rule, he ushers in the global Paradise which
Jehovah originally purposed. Jehovah emerges from the
drama, His name and word of truth vindicated, His Sovereignty established, His righteousness prevailing forever-
more."

This greatest of all themes, he said, holds the Bible compactly together. All of its typical dramas foreshadow the great Drama of Ultimate Vindication. The typical theocracy of Israel, with its Divine constitution and particularly during its golden reign of Solomon, pictures the real Theocracy, Christ's Kingdom. This brings the Bible to life, a living breathing drama that involves every person from the Almighty God on down. It is not a story that happened only in the past. It reaches its most intense conflict, my informant declared, right here in our day. "Much of the Bible is prophecy," said he. "Jehovah, through His prophets, tells the end from the beginning of this mighty universal drama. The grand finale is described in such prophetic detail that students of His Word are enabled to discern the very generation of life on earth upon which that finale, 'Armageddon,' would fall."

Did Mr. Sullivan have some idea as to when that fateful generation would appear?

"It is this generation," he replied gravely. "Yours and mine."

The Leading Performer Named Jehovah

His announcement portended some awesome possibilities, but here I raised my hand. "Before we get into the action of the great climax," I suggested, "perhaps it would be better if you filled me in on some of the principal characters." I was checking my notes. "You have mentioned God. And Christ. There is Satan. There is the Kingdom. And man. The earth. And Armageddon."

If Jehovah's witnesses viewed the Bible as a whole in such a different light, it was reasonable to anticipate that their conception of its major characters offered fascinating prospects.

And I was not disappointed. Witness Sullivan thought that we ought to start with the Leading Character and Personality, the Most High God Himself. But here, right at the start, he warned, we were confronted with the most astounding circumstance. The Bible was the most widely distributed book in the world. Yet its readers could not agree as to the name of its own Author. "His name is in there, six thousand eight hundred and twenty-three times in the Hebrew Scriptures or Old Testament alone," he cited. "Some translators keep it in the text. Others throw it out and replace it with substitutes."

He was, of course, referring to God's Hebrew name, *YHWH*, or Jehovah.

I inquired: "Don't some authorities object to the name on the grounds that it is merely a name the Jews applied to God?"

"That is one argument," he agreed. "But a translator cannot throw God's name out of His own Book without changing the original inspired wording. Think how inconsistent that is."

"Inconsistent?"

"If they throw out the divine name *Jehovah* because of its Jewish background, why not throw out *Jesus* because of its Greek origin?"

Jesus, he pointed out, is the Greek for the shortened form of the Hebrew *Jehoshua*. It literally means "Jehovah is the Savior."

"Some people declare they hate Jehovah but they love Jesus. Yet every time they pronounce the name Jesus they are saying, in fact, 'Jehovah is the Savior.' Other people deny Jehovah while they shout halleluja to the Lamb, never realizing that the word halleluja means 'Praise Jah.' "

But why should Jehovah have a personal name? "There are gods many and lords many," quoted Witness Sullivan. The reason why God is entitled to His own identifying name is clearly shown by Psalm 83:18, which he cited: "That men may know that thou, whose name alone is JEHOVAH, art the most high over all the earth."

Strange, indeed, this controversy over God's own Name. "But it is the very essence of the issue raised in Eden," I was told. "The name Jehovah expresses God's personality as the Purposer of things. Well, who was the God of Purpose there in Eden? Whose designs for creation would prevail? That was the issue. Thirty-five centuries ago that was still the issue when Pharaoh demanded of Moses, 'Who is Jehovah, that I should harken unto his voice?' (Exodus 5:2, American Standard Version) Nineteen centuries ago Jesus was declaring, in John 17:6, 'I have made your name manifest to the men you gave me.' Jehovah's witnesses in modern times are turning out fifteen tons of literature a day to acquaint men with God's name. Pharaoh lost his world-ruling power and his life for scorning Jehovah. The ancient Israelites lost their position as God's name-people for denying Jehovah and killing His Son. This modern world is destined to lose its very existence at Armageddon for ignoring Jehovah and His Kingdom."

Jesus Christ, Champion of God's Vindication

We had come to the second greatest Character in the Drama of the Universe, Jesus Christ. Mr. Sullivan quoted Jesus's words in Revelation 3:14 where He refers to Himself as "the faithful and true witness." That made Jesus Jehovah's Chief Witness, my narrator reasoned.

Jehovah's witnesses, it developed, distinguish sharply between Jehovah and Jesus as individual personages.

"Psalm 90:2 states that God Almighty, the Father, Jehovah, is from everlasting to everlasting—without beginning. Jesus, in Revelation 3:14, identifies himself as the beginning of God's creative works." Hence Jesus could not be "co-eternal" with his own Father. "Men can understand how a human father can have a human son," he illustrated. "But they make all kinds of mystery out of the fact that the spirit Father has a spirit Son existing in spirit form like Himself."

"How does Jesus figure in the great Universal Conflict?" I prompted.

"Jesus came to earth to answer the Devil's challenge on at least three scores," he replied.

"What was the first?"

"To prove that God can put a perfect man on earth who will keep integrity under test."

"The second score?"

"To bear witness to the truth about the great Issue. He explained it in much more detail. His faithful disciples were able to record twenty-seven more books of the Divine Script."

"And the third?"

"To provide a ransom by which Adam's fallen children could be reinstated as children of God."

At this point it was proposed that we hold back from the chain of dramatic action touched off by Jesus in his three-fold role, until the stage was set with a fill-in on the Arch Villain and the Villain's pawn in the conflict, Man.

Man the Soul

"After thousands of years of creative work in preparing the earth for man's paradisaical habitation," began my narrator, "Jehovah God formed man of the dust of the ground, and breathed into his nostrils the breath of life; and man became a living soul." He quoted Genesis 2:7.

I was to note, please, that man did not become possessor of a soul. He *"became* a living soul." The point was, if you did not watch you might be taken by the Devil's original lie, that you do not really die but are like gods. "The point is, if you *have* a soul inside your body, as is generally taught, your body might die and your soul live on. But if you *are* a soul, as the Scripture says, when you die it is you, the soul, that perishes," he stressed. Adam sinned. His sentence was, "For dust thou art, and unto dust thou shalt return," Mr. Sullivan read from Genesis 3:19. He added that Jehovah's law on the matter is stated succinctly in Ezekiel 18:4, "The soul that sinneth, it shall die"; as well as in Romans 6:23: "The wages sin pays is death."

The point being stressed here was that Jehovah's witnesses do not go along with the "immortal soul doctrine" that the Devil insinuated back there at the rebellion. "The only Bible character who ever said that man does not really die, that he lives on like gods, was the serpent in Eden, deceiving Eve, as the record shows in Genesis 3: 4,5." The text there reads:

"And the serpent said unto the woman, Ye shall not surely die: For God doth know that in the day ye eat thereof, then your eyes shall be opened, and ye shall be as gods, knowing good and evil."

The sentence for wrongdoing is death, Mr. Sullivan summarized; the reward for rightdoing is life. Life and death were the two opposites that God set before His creatures. (Deuteronomy 30:19) Whether the prize were heavenly life or earthly life, the prize was still life. From Jesus' first coming until Armageddon, God selects a small number, limited by Revelation, chapters 7 and 14, to 144,000 "purchased from among mankind" to be with Christ in heavenly glory and share with him in the Kingdom, ruling with him as kings and priests for a thousand years over the earth. (Revelation 1:6; 5:10) I was to note, however, that man's natural destiny is earthly life, and this "little flock" of heavenly body members of Christ bend their kingly and priestly efforts during the Millennium to share with Christ in tending to his "other sheep," the earthly class, who were to be restored from Adam's curse to the standing of children of God and established in a global Paradise.

Mr. Sullivan returned to his original point: The "immortal soul" doctrine, with its subsequent "eternal torment" doctrine, was unscriptural. "If the Devil invented immortal souls, then he would have to invent a place somewhere outside of heaven or earth for such wicked immortal souls that could not die to go. What else could he do but fall on the explanation of a place of eternal conscious torment?"

These matters of the soul, and death, and hell, accentuated how far-reaching the mighty drama went in its consequences. The destiny of all living persons was swept up in

the Conflict. Life or death. No drama can play on farther
extremes than these. Paradise created. Paradise lost. Could it
be restored?

"Before Adam began to produce offspring he had lost his
right to perfect life, for himself and consequently for his offspring. He had lost his perfect home, his perfect start in life,"
it was explained. "If Satan could cause a perfect man to fall,
could he not by some means break the integrity of all men?
The first two chapters of Job indicate that it was Satan's boast
that Jehovah could not place a man on earth who would be
faithful under test. If true, then Jehovah's original purpose to
make the earth a paradise of life, inhabited by perfect creatures, stood forever thwarted."

How could the mighty struggle ever be settled in Jehovah's favor? How could Satan's rebellious works be undone?
How could the blemish of sin and the blight of death be
removed from fallen Adam's family?

"The question has never been more burning than now,"
he went on to say. "Today, in the closing hours of his reign,
Satan has succeeded in deceiving the whole world, says Revelation 12. To some, God's cause looks more lost than ever.
But Christians are wise to Satan's designs and can thereby
avoid being overreached by him, says II Corinthians 2:11."

The Arch Villain Satan

I asked: "Why did not Jehovah settle this issue with Satan
back there at Eden?"

"That would not have answered Satan's challenge."

"Why not?"

"Satan boasted that he could upset God's arrangements.
He could turn any of God's creatures away from Him. It
took time for that challenge to be answered."

Satan, I was told, must be permitted to devise every possible scheme to grasp universal sovereignty. He built up a
terrible system of world rule before the Flood, but he failed
to make all men break integrity. And 1,656 years after man's

creation Jehovah destroyed Satan's vicious system in the Flood, preserving faithful Noah and his family.

"Since then Satan has set up numerous world-ruling arrangements, from ancient Egypt down to his present world combine."

Again the Society director focused attention to the present. "The world has never been so completely under Satan's thrall as now. Yet there has never been a greater witness to Jehovah's name and supremacy than during this generation. This is an indication that the Climax of the Ages is upon us. Satan will not tolerate this witness to Jehovah's vindication to go on forever in his world. Jehovah dares Satan to touch the people who proclaim His name. When Satan in his rage strikes at Jehovah's people, Jehovah will strike him. That will mean Armageddon."

Paradise Restored

But even after Jehovah delivers His people from Satan's attack at Armageddon, I was reminded, there is still one problem. They are still Adam's offspring. They are still under bondage to death, just as much as Noah was after he stepped from the ark into a cleansed earth. In other words, a ransom was required.

"Do you realize what a privilege Adam forfeited?" suggested this reviewer of the Divine Drama.

Adam, he indicated, not only was given the right to perfect life for himself, but was granted the power to propagate life to his offspring, and become the princely father of the human race. "Jehovah does not create human souls in heaven and bring them down and plant them in earthly bodies. He does not put a soul into each baby at birth. What is born is the soul. If Adam had remained faithful his children and their children would have been born perfect and in Paradise."

Conversely, what had been born was a human race outside of God's favor, outside of Paradise, with no real right to life. What would it take to buy back Adam's heritage?

"The human race would have to be given a new father,"
I was informed. "Another perfect parent, with the power to
transmit the right to life to men, and the power to make the
earth once more yield its increase. He would have to adopt
the degenerate human race."

"Is that the role that Jesus played?"

That, I learned, was correct. "Jesus came to earth not
only to prove that a perfect man can withstand Satan's temp-
tations. And not only to state the great Universal Issue in
unmistakable terms. He came also to 'give his soul a ransom
in exchange for many.' " All this was explained, he said, in
Matthew 20:28; John 17:14 and 18:37.

"How would you describe Jesus in his earthly role?" I
inquired. "Was he a God-man?"

"He could not have been that, and served as a corresponding ransom."

"Why not?"

"Well," countered the Superintendent of Evangelists,
"what had been lost?"

The perfect human liferight, he reminded me, "God's
perfect law requires like for like. An eye for an eye. A life
for a life. If a God gave his life for a man, would that be a
corresponding ransom? Could a lion redeem a mouse?"

Jesus, he said, had to be one hundred per cent human.
But how could such a thing have been—this mighty spirit
creature becoming actually human?

"Men can change solids into gases. They unite a metal
and a gas and produce salt. Artificial insemination is used
today in cattle breeding, by unnaturally introducing sperm
cells from the male into the virgin womb of the female
bovine to produce high-bred calves. Could not an all-powerful God transfer the life force of His glorious spirit Son by
means of a sperm seed to fertilize a human egg and produce
a human embryo and let him be born from a virgin? 'The
Word became flesh.' "

That was how Jesus came to earth, in the role, as I Corinthians 15:45 described him, of "the second man Adam."

Now I asked the big question: "How could this 'second Adam' adopt the imperfect offspring of the 'first Adam'?"

"If the first Adam lost the liferight through disobedience, could not the second Adam earn that liferight through obedience?" he suggested.

Romans, chapter five, described the matter in that light, he said. But I countered: "Did not Jesus lose his life? Was he not killed?"

Mr. Sullivan responded: "Did Satan's murdering Jesus force his Father to withdraw the liferight from His Son?"

As Acts 2:24 declared, "It was not possible for the pangs of death to hold Jesus if Jehovah willed to resurrect him." That is what happened. And it was demonstrated that others could thereafter be resurrected if they had shown integrity while they lived.

I prompted the narrative by saying: "How does the resurrected Jesus redeem the human race?"

"He was restored to spirit life, I Peter 3:18, tells us. But he had not forfeited his right to perfect human life."

"So he returns again and takes up his humanity?"

This drew a negative shake of the head. "Hebrews, chapter seven, describes how the resurrected Jesus offers this liferight once and for all as a propitiatory sacrifice to his Father. If he never takes it up again for himself, then the right to it can be transferred to Adam's offspring who were born without the liferight."

That way, by adoption, all those of Adam's offspring exercising faith in Jesus' sacrifice can be restored to the right to life, whether in heaven with Jesus or in the new cleansed earth where Paradise will be restored, said my informant.

Meanwhile in his role of Jehovah's King, Christ Jesus climaxes the great Universal Struggle in battle against Satan and his hosts, his invisible demons and visible "earth." King Jesus vanquishes the enemy. He and his heavenly body members or true "Church" drawn from among men and transformed through a resurrection to spirit life, reign for a thousand years, says Revelation 20. And as Revelation 21 continues, Christ the King becomes the new overlord of earth. He takes up the assignment forfeited by the unfaithful covering cherub in Eden. He directs men, those passing alive through Armageddon and those resurrected from death, bringing the earth to the paradise state of life that Jehovah originally intended.

This meant that the greatest event in human history since Eden would be Jesus Christ's second presence, to inaugurate his Theocratic rule over the earth, have the Kingdom announced so that "sheep" like subjects might rally to his side, direct the fighting of Armageddon and clear the way for the Millennial age of peace, security and happiness.

Second Presence of Christ

Why, I asked Mr. Sullivan, had he threaded his whole narrative with burning intimations that we have reached the showdown in this great Conflict between Jehovah and Satan?

"Because the drama crashes to its Armageddon climax in this generation," he replied.

"You mean that sometime within this generation Christ will come again?"

"Christ Jesus was enthroned as King over the earth forty years ago, in the year 1914."

"Just a minute," I interrupted. "Does not Christ come back visibly?"

"And take back his humanity which he presented to God as a propitiatory ransom?" reminded Mr. Sullivan.

"But," I insisted, "doesn't the Bible say that every eye shall see him?"

"See him literally," he asked, "or symbolically?"

"Well, people in general are looking for him in a visible appearance, I always thought."

He dropped his tone. "Do you believe that the earth is round?"

"I rather think so. Yes."

"And still Christ returns from heaven visibly, on a cloud?"

The intimation was that if the earth is round and Christ comes on a cloud, how can everybody look up into the sky, all around the globe, and see Christ sitting on a cloud at one spot? After his chuckle Mr. Sullivan started off on a new tack.

"Did you know that the disciples did not expect Christ to return visibly?"

"How do you get that?"

"In Matthew 24:3, the disciples asked Jesus. 'What will be the *sign* of your presence and the consummation of the system of things?' "

Jehovah's witnesses, like the disciples, were looking for the *sign,* not any visible manifestation, of Christ's presence. "That is what Christians are told to look for," he emphasized. "The sign."

And what would the "sign" be? The balance of Matthew 24 detailed Jesus' description of what it would be. "The increase of total wars. Increase of food shortages, disease pestilences, earthquakes," recounted the minister. "The setting up of a disgusting substitute for Christ's Kingdom rule. They are all enumerated in Matthew 24."

It would be not just one thing (that is why people had been so wrong in the past when they thought the world's end was at hand—they had not witnessed the full composite picture of the sign). It would be a whole pattern of world events taking place together inside one generation (Matthew 24:34).

Jesus' enthronement meant the ousting of Satan from any longer intimidating the heavenly creatures and his being hurled to the earth's vicinity. (Revelation 12). Therefore Satan would vent his rage at the earth, stirring up unprecedented woes.

And the chiefest of all indications that Christ has started ruling as King would be the world-wide proclamation of the

Kingdom's establishment in fact. "This good news of the kingdom," Jesus declared in verse fourteen, "will be preached in all the inhabited earth for the purpose of a witness to all the nations, and then the accomplished end will come."

Verse nine forewarned that, as an attendant condition, the Kingdom proclaimers would be "hated by all nations on account of my name" as King ruling in their midst.

"Now let me see," I was reflecting. "You told me that Kingdom rule began in 1914?"

The Year 1914

"That is right," acknowledged the witness of Jehovah.

"Why 1914?"

"When," he prompted, "did total wars break out?"

In 1914, I acknowledged. Jesus had warned in verse six that mere wars and rumors of wars would not mark the signs —it would take total wars, nation against nation, kingdom against kingdom, verse seven specified.

Said Mr. Sullivan: "Try to imagine all the 901 major wars of the preceeding twenty-four centuries being rolled into one. Multiply all that by seven. Then you get some idea of the size of World War I."

A different kind of war indeed. And then within the same generation World War II. "It was nearly four times as great, in terms of costs, casualties, and countries involved, as World War I."

And now mankind faces the prospect of the nations preparing for more war that will make the previous conflagrations seem as tame as a firecracker celebration. Verse eight was hardly exaggerating when it stated that the outbreak of these woes was only "a beginning of pangs of distress" that would grow worse until the final holocaust when God puts a stop to it all at Armageddon.

Another feature of the Sign, quoted the Witness, citing verse seven, would be widespread famines. He had in mind, for instance, China following World War I. Each day fifteen thousand Chinese died. Thirty million were affected. India saw thirty-two million of her people clawed by starvation— "a situation which we were told was unparalleled elsewhere in the history of the world." By 1923 the Russian people were dying like flies, with thirty-five million hungry—ten years later six million Russians starved to death in eighteen months. One-fourth of the world was reported hungry in 1946. In 1954 we were told that upwards of two-thirds of the people of the world go to bed each night hungry and undernourished. "Since 1914," he concluded, "food shortages have affected more than twice as many people than were affected in the 900 years before."

There was also the matter of pestilences, mentioned in verse seven. "The 'Spanish influenza' following World War I took twenty million lives and put two hundred million people to bed in a few months. It was called one of the worst plagues of all times. Meanwhile, cancer, degenerative diseases of the heart, liver, kidneys and other organs go on increasing over the world. Mental and nervous disorders are reaching the proportions of a global calamity."

Earthquakes were also foretold in the same seventh verse, along with total wars, famines and pestilences. Mr. Sullivan said that from 1915 to 1949 mighty seismic disturbances took a toll of 848,450 lives, injured 577,876, made 14,639,169 people homeless, and destroyed billions of dollars' worth of property. The yearly toll in lives lost from earthquakes since 1914 has been ten times greater than before that year.

Anticipated 35 Years in Advance

Not only by foretelling these circumstantial evidences but also by chronologies the Bible marked 1914 as the time for the Kingdom's advent, I was told. "We knew thirty-five years in advance that 1914 would mark the year." He referred me to *The Watchtower* magazine which, as early as 1879, warned that 1914 would see Satan's rule interrupted by the Kingdom.

Kingdom Preaching vs. Kingdom Substitute

Announcing the good news of the Kingdom's arrival, as foretold in verse fourteen, constitutes the most outstanding part of the great Sign. This work by Jehovah's witnesses counteracted what Mr. Sullivan identified, from verse fifteen, as "a disgusting substitute that world leaders have foisted before the peoples to take the place of Jehovah's Kingdom by Christ."

"What substitute would the world have to offer?"

"A proposed world-dominating organization of political rule," he replied. "In 1919 the organized clergy of Christendom labeled it 'the political expression of God's Kingdom on earth.' "

"What was it?"

"The League of Nations."

"Why call it a disgusting substitute?"

Matthew 24:15 calls it the "abomination that maketh desolate" or "the disgusting thing that causes desolation." If the clergy point people away from the real Kingdom to a man-made political substitute, set up in the holy place of God's rightful rule, would not that desolate people's faith in the real Kingdom? "Would not that make it a disgusting thing in God's sight?"

Daniel 2:44 and John 18:36 clearly state that "God's kingdom has no earthly political form or expression," it was pointed out. When the Real Thing comes along it never, like the League of Nations, flickers out and has to be revived in a new United Nations form. No, the real Kingdom, a heavenly governmental power, "breaks and consumes all earthly kingdoms and stands forever in their stead." The real heavenly Kingdom government is Jehovah's chosen instrument under the indomitable leadership of Christ that vindicates God's name and power and winds up the age-long struggle over universal domination. By it Christ Jesus destroys Satan and his works. He restores the universe, heavenly and earthly, to Jehovah's rightful sovereignty. "The nations cannot repudiate these facts with impunity," warned Mr. Sullivan.

Kingdom Announced Worldwide

"How far along are Jehovah's witnesses in announcing the Kingdom's advent to all nations?" I inquired.

"As of 1954, we have established some 580,000 Kingdom publishers in 159 lands. Since 1914 we have published the good news in more than 100 languages. We have distributed more than 600 million bound books and booklets bearing this message. By 1955 we expect to be printing something like seven million magazines a month announcing Jehovah's established Kingdom."

Only Hope for Peace

Looking at things from this viewpoint, Jehovah's witnesses have made the Bible come alive with shocking impact for all of us. When you listen to them you catch something of the excitement, the awe, and the terrible prospect of being one among the generation overtaken. How will you play your little individual role across the stage as the Drama of the Ages crashes to its awful crescendo? If Jehovah's witnesses are right, the present world will never return to real stability, never know real peace, sense true security; for these are the last days. The only hope for peace, I was assured, is "inside Jehovah's New World Society," which alone will pass through and survive the world's terrible end, "just like the ark and its passengers came through the cataclysmic flood of ancient times."

Kingdom Fruits Now

As this interview drew to a close I was trying to round out some final assessment of Jehovah's witnesses. This conversation with the jovial man from County Kerry was winding up an investigation that stretched back over two years. Here was a religion which the world was waking up to find the most phenomenal and fastest-growing, proportionately, of any in Christendom. I had examined their recorded history covering some eighty years. I had seen them put across the most unacceptable religion, by all of them going out actively in preaching it, to gain a two thousand per cent increase during the most perilous of all generations—part of the time preaching underground in many nations.

I had followed their exploits as they—one of the smallest groups—staged the biggest dynamic Christian assemblies of this twentieth century. I saw them baptize more people at one time—4640, than were immersed at Pentecost. With my own eyes I watched them construct and settle tent-trailer cities up to 45,000 population and live together without a policeman, a jail, or a law court, in pure peace. Among their congregations, which I visited from New York to Minnesota to Tennessee, I had found a constant vigilance maintained to keep their inner ranks morally and socially clean. Swiftly, uncompromisingly they disfellowshipped any member high or low who tried to bring in immoral practices, drunkenness, lying, cheating, defrauding, extortion, and the like. I had learned why they do not entrust their children's spiritual welfare to Sunday-school teachers—because each parent shoulders the responsibility to carry out Ephesians 6:4 and Deuteronomy 6:6, 7, to bring up his own in the "discipline and authoritative advice of Jehovah."

This trait of guiding each living habit, each principle of social intercourse, by some specific, quotable and applicable Bible principle—whether in matters of rearing children, marriage, dealing with "Caesar" or whatever—this making the Bible their rule-of-thumb guidebook is what distinguished the Witnesses in my mind most of all.

They had pursued such a strenuous, never-ending course in Bible education among their congregations and among the public that they transformed their entire membership into a dynamic preaching body, that went out, each and every one, to make disciples for the Kingdom from among all nations.

What was I to conclude about Jehovah's witnesses? Or was my personal opinion important? I had tried to study them to the point where I could speak their language, think their thoughts, catch their vision. If I could translate that vision into language that you, the reader, can understand, would not this be enough on the part of a reporter?

Living under the Kingdom

Their vision?

Mr. Sullivan had led me to the essence of it now. A people impelled by the group of doctrines he had outlined, a people who can plot the Bible Drama on a dime, who see it as a mighty universal conflict between Jehovah God and Satan reaching its fearful crescendo here in our day, with a New World of righteousness certainly victorious—a people who believe implicitly that God's heavenly Kingdom started ruling in 1914, is drawing men of good will of all races together, like a magnet picking up iron filings out of the dust, and incorporating them into a New World Society—such a people naturally lead your mind to the Ultimate Question.

And now I asked it of Mr. Sullivan:

"What is it like to begin life under Jehovah's Kingdom?"

"Even during this pre-Millennial period, this period of world judgment, even here amid Satan's violently adverse old world," he responded, "Jehovah's witnesses have found ultimate peace of mind and realized their heart's desire. They have conquered fear. They are livened by unquenchable confidence in a glorious future. They are already a real New World Society."

Already they have learned, in a literal as well as spiritual way, to apply one of the foremost fruits of Kingdom living, as described in Micah 4:3, said my informant, quoting: "They shall beat their swords into plowshares, and their spears into pruning-hooks; nation shall not lift up sword against nation, neither shall they learn war any more." There are at least 159 countries today among whom resides a people joined together internationally in this unbreakable peace, he declared. No matter how these nations, as political or ideological entities, might quarrel, bicker and fight each other, the resident Witnesses within each would not be pro-jected by worldly frays into killing each other. "For they are through with 'swords and spears' and instead are devoting their wealth and equipment to the peaceful, constructive activities of the New World Society."

What if you honestly and truly expected to inherit, here in your present lifetime, the promise that "The meek shall inherit the earth; and shall delight themselves in the abun-dance of peace" because the time has come when "evil doers shall be cut off"?—Psalm 37:11,9.

Would that anticipation transform your viewpoint? Would it change your sense of values? Would your personali-ty be made over if you really, truly expected to exchange an uncertain future, sickness and old age for the rejuvenating work of building a paradise? If you could get on a boat and sail to a new, quiet, peaceful continent; or board a space ship for another planet forever out of the grasp of this system of things, would you go? Would you go if you had the iron-clad guarantee of becoming a charter member of a new society which "shall build houses, and inhabit them; they shall not plant and another eat: for as the days of a tree shall be the days of my people, and my chosen ones shall long en-joy the works of their hands. They shall not labor in vain, nor bring forth for calamity. . . ."? Jehovah's witnesses have no new continents or planets in mind. But for almost a generation they have nourished the confident hope of shar-ing in the fulfillment of these promises in Isaiah 65: 2-23, here on a cleansed earth, after a thorough and lasting rid-dance of its trouble-makers, within the next few years.

Total peace backed up by the Supreme God of the Uni-verse, I was assured, is the destiny of the New World Society. A peace reaching down even to the animal kingdom. "And the wolf shall dwell with the lamb, and the leopard shall lie down with the kid; and the calf and the young lion and the fatling together; and a little child shall lead them."—Isaiah 11:6.

When We Grow Young Again

What if you knew that soon you will feel the wrinkles of age fade from your face and from the faces of your loved ones—as you watched the gray hairs vanish and felt the surge of perfect health invigorating your flesh with supernal youth? Hundreds of thousands of people believe that this will literally happen to them in the coming years. Millions now living are contemplating the prospects of never dying. If you doubt this, get acquainted with these people. See if they do not give you the tangible impression, as this sixty-six-year-old witness for Jehovah was now giving me—the feeling that inwardly, spiritually, the Witnesses are already drinking from the fountain of youth. Mr. Sullivan was quoting Job 33:25: "His flesh shall become fresher than a child's; he returneth to the days of his youth."

The smashing of death-dealing forces of disease, calamity, wars and the like at Armageddon, will leave the "new earth" free for the physical rejuvenation to begin, he explained. "Man was naturally made to live forever." And so, with the causes that produce death gone, the life-producing, healing effects of the Millennium will reach the peak of perfection described in Revelation 21:1-5, until no pain, sorrow, sickness or even death will mar the joy and health and happiness of earth's inhabitants.

The thousand-year reign described in the Bible's closing book fulfills Jehovah's original purpose as outlined in the Bible's opening book. No scars of Satan's infliction, no imperfections from the first father Adam will sear its beauty any more. Jehovah makes a new world! That resolves the mightiest drama ever perpetrated or ever to be experienced again. It brings to a perfect conclusion the story told by the perfect Book.

This, Jehovah's witnesses believe. They are strong in this, a dynamic faith. Their vision ahead is paradisaic for beauty. Behind them are the sorrows and troubles of this "dying, desolate old world system." And because this is their conviction I know of no more apt words to describe them in than those of the prophet in Joel 2:3: "The land is as the garden of Eden before them, and behind them a desolate wilderness."

APPENDIX

CORPORATIONS OF JEHOVAH'S WITNESSES

Jehovah's witnesses world-wide make up a society of ministers.[1] There is no clergy class or laity class. They are dedicated to the work of "preaching the good news of God's Kingdom" in all the world as official notice to all nations that Jehovah's kingdom has begun under Christ as King; that with the completion of the preaching work the end will come for present world systems at the Bible Armageddon. Survivors of that "battle of the great day of God the Almighty" will start life anew under the thousand-year reign of Christ.

Watch Tower Bible and Tract Society

Jehovah's witnesses are adequately organized to carry out their mission. Throughout the earth they use many corporations. Their principal corporation is the Watch Tower Bible and Tract Society, of Pennsylvania, U.S.A. This corporation was set up in 1884 under the name of Zion's Watch Tower Tract Society. This was changed to its present name in 1896. The corporation maintains a registered head-

[1]The information in this section is taken from various *Yearbooks* of Jehovah's witnesses.

173

quarters at Pittsburgh, Pennsylvania, where its annual meetings are held. At the October 1, 1953 meeting, there were 393 members of the corporation, scattered over several continents.

In 1909, the staff of the corporation was transferred to Brooklyn, New York. There it functioned alongside a sister corporation at first known as the Peoples Pulpit Association.

Its Functions: It serves as the principal corporation. It supervises the Bible educational activities and ministerial work of Jehovah's witnesses in the United States. It sets up, wherever necessary, branch offices in foreign countries. It distributes the literature provided by the New York corporation. It sends missionaries all over the world. These include the graduates of the Watchtower Bible School of Gilead, an institution owned and operated by the New York corporation.

CORPORATIONS OF JEHOVAH'S WITNESSES
Chief Offices and Official Address of the following:
124 Columbia Heights, Brooklyn 1, New York, U.S.A.

NAME	FOUNDED	CHANGED TO	DATE
Zion's Watch Tower Tract Society of Pennsylvania, U.S.A.	1884	Watch Tower Bible & Tract Society Headquarters moved from Pittsburgh, Pa., to Brooklyn, N.Y., in 1909	1896
Peoples Pulpit Association of New York, U. S. A.	1909	Watchtower Bible & Tract Society, Inc.	1939
International Bible Students Association of Great Britain	1914		

People throughout the world contribute to the Pennsylvania corporation, direct or through its branches in about seventy countries. The money goes into a "Good Hopes" fund. Under direction of the corporation board, the fund is used to spread the work world-wide.

Watchtower Bible & Tract Society, Inc.

Organized in 1909 as the Peoples Pulpit Association of New York, this corporation owns the property used by the Pennsylvania corporation. It also serves as publisher. The following details are taken from the *1944 Yearbook of Jehovah's Witnesses.*

Its charter provides in part:

"The purposes for which it is to be formed are, the moral and mental improvement of men and women, the dissemination of Bible Truths in various languages by means of the publication of tracts, pamphlets, papers and other religious documents, and by the use of all other lawful means which its board of directors, duly constituted, shall deem expedient for the purposes stated, and for religious missionary work . . . 'its corporate purposes are, Charitable, benevolent, scientific, historical, literary, and Religious purposes, and for the purpose of maintaining and conducting classes for the gratuitous instruction of men and women, on the premises or by mail, in the Bible, Bible literature, and Bible history, and for the gratuitous teaching, training and preparing of men and women as teachers, and as lecturers on the Bible and preachers of the Gospel, and to provide and maintain a home, place, building, or buildings for the gratuitous housing, sheltering, and boarding of such students, lecturers, teachers, and ministers, and to gratuitously furnish to such students, lecturers, teachers, and ministers suitable meals and lodgings, and to prepare, support, maintain, and send out to the various parts of the world religious missionaries, teachers and instructors in the Bible and Bible literature, and for public religious worship, and for the purpose of the publication and distribution of Bibles and Bible and religious literature. . . . The operation of a radio broadcasting station . . . to carry out the present purposes and powers of the corporation.' "

The president's office and the office of the secretary-treasurer, and one of the Society's homes for "gratuitous teaching, training and preparing of men and women as teachers . . . on the Bible and . . . gratuitous housing, sheltering, and boarding of such students," are located at 124 Columbia Heights, Brooklyn 1, New York. The general offices of this corporation, and its printing plant, are located at 117 Adams Street. It is from there that all magazines, books, and tracts are shipped. Its Bible school, to "maintain and send out to various parts of the world . . . missionaries, teachers and instructors in the Bible and Bible literature," is located at South Lansing, New York. Its broadcasting station is located on Staten Island, New York City.

The New York corporation, known as the Watchtower Bible and Tract Society, Inc., is not the subsidiary of any legal corporation, but is an agent used by Jehovah's witnesses to carry on the work of preaching the gospel of the Kingdom, primarily in New York state, and generally throughout the United States.

For Jehovah's witnesses, the New York corporation prints Bibles, magazines, books, booklets, and tracts, and does generally all the work and business necessary as a corporation of Jehovah's witnesses. It purchases all materials for printing and publishing of literature. It makes shipments to all congregations, pioneers, and others desiring the Society's literature. It sends out circuit servants (these are traveling ordained ministers) throughout the country to aid in the organization of the congregations and to assist generally Jehovah's witnesses in advancing the preaching of God's Kingdom.

The contributions that Jehovah's witnesses receive in their house-to-house work distributing literature are sent to the New York corporation so that this corporation can print more such literature for other persons of good-will; but these contributions do not cover the entire cost of operating the Society. The difference is made up each year by donations to the Society by Jehovah's witnesses. The New York corporation is a nonprofit organization organized to carry on benevolent and charitable work, and all funds it receives are used to this end.

The corporation maintains a home at 124 Columbia Heights, Brooklyn 1, N. Y. This home houses all the workers who supervise the corporation's activities in the City of New York. The men and women living at 124 Columbia Heights, known as the Bethel Home, all being Jehovah's witnesses and ordained ministers, have volunteered their services freely to aid in the advancing of the Kingdom interests. All, including the officers and directors, receive the same allowance each month, namely, $14 for clothing and incidental expenses. All other things are provided for them, such as room and board. No officer or director receives any profit from the operation of the Society, and all services are voluntarily contributed to the cause of preaching the gospel. Some work at the Bethel Home; others in the printing plant, at 117 Adams Street, where books, booklets, and magazines are manufactured and shipped to all parts of the world. Many spend their time in the office, handling correspondence and doing other work necessary for the proper functioning of the organization and the activities of Jehovah's witnesses. The use of the properties owned by the Society is exclusively for chartered purposes and to carry on its philanthropic work.

The New York corporation also has property on Staten Island. There its radio transmitter is located. WBBR broadcasts no commercial announcements, and accepts no money for programs broadcast. Its sole purpose is the preaching of the gospel, and for announcements of interest, convenience, and necessity to the public.

There is also a truck garden on the Staten Island property. The food raised is used immediately on the table at the Bethel Home or is canned for use in the winter. No products of this farm are sold to anyone; all are used by the corporation exclusively for the family at Bethel. No one profits from the operation of the farm, but the food produced enables the Society to operate the Bethel Home at a much smaller cost than if all food had to be bought from outside producers or dealers. By this kind of economy more money is made available for preaching the gospel of God's kingdom among the poor and people of good will. All persons engaged in food production are members of the Bethel family and receive no money profit for their work. Each is a minister of the gospel and does ministerial work, as does every member of the family.

The charter of the New York corporation provides that schools for ministers, missionaries, traveling evangelists, and teachers may be established. To this end, the New York corporation has established the Watchtower Bible School of Gilead, at South Lansing, New York, where further training in Bible study is given to ordained ministers brought in from all parts of the United States. There, too, a farm is operated that provides food for the school and Bethel Home. Like the Staten Island farm, its workers receive no money in pay.

The corporation's work in connection with all its properties is wholly educational, benevolent, and nonprofit-making, and its activities are in the interests of all persons of good-will.

The New York corporation, being one of the legal agents used by Jehovah's witnesses, would naturally work in co-operation and full accord with other corporations established by Jehovah's witnesses, carrying out like purposes. To this end, the New York corporation co-operates fully with the Pennsylvania corporation and supplies it with all literature needed in further spreading the gospel of the kingdom.

The New York corporation has an account with the Pennsylvania corporation and prints all necessary publications that the Pennsylvania corporation uses in the foreign countries. The Pennsylvania corporation has no printing plant of its own in the United States. Therefore the New York corporation, as an agent of Jehovah's witnesses, prints such books, booklets, magazines, and so on, as the Pennsylvania corporation requires. Both corporations do much the same work, but in different areas.

When the Pennsylvania corporation was originally established, in 1884, printing was contracted for with commercial concerns. In 1909, it was found that the work in general could be carried on better from New York City. The main offices and operating headquarters were moved to Brooklyn, therefore, and the Peoples Pulpit Association, now the Watchtower Bible and Tract Society, Inc., was organized. Eventually the Watchtower Bible and Tract Society, Inc., established its own printing plant. Their purposes being parallel, both being agents of Jehovah's witnesses, the New York corporation began to print for the Pennsylvania corporation, all of which is done at no profit to either corporation. The Pennsylvania corporation still operates in Pennsylvania and has its home and registered office in Pittsburgh. Because the president of both corporations is the same individual, and for the convenience of officers and other reasons, the Pennsylvania corporation uses offices at 124 Columbia Heights, Brooklyn, to direct its corporate activities.

International Bible Students Association

The Pennsylvania corporation, operating in foreign lands, has in several instances set up its own printing plants in other countries. In some foreign branches it was found necessary to establish local corporations to manage the property and handle certain legal matters of local origin.

For this purpose the International Bible Students Association was organized in 1914, in London, England. This association owns several properties. It houses a branch office of the Watch Tower Bible & Tract Society. It operates a printing plant and shipping department. In other words, it serves the Pennsylvania corporation in Great Britain as the New York corporation serves it in the United States.

A corporation by the same name—International Bible Students Association, Ltd.—was also organized in Canada. And in several other nations similar legal instruments have been set up. All charters are modeled after that of the Pennsylvania corporation.

How the Corporations Co-ordinate

These legal agents—the Watch Tower Bible & Tract Society (Pennsylvania), the Watchtower Bible and Tract Society, Inc. (New York), the International Bible Students Association (United Kingdom), and any others—are all organized for the same purpose and do the same work. They are used by Jehovah's witnesses in whatever locality they are legally recognized to further the activities of preaching and teaching God's Word.

The principal officers of all three corporations are virtually the same men. The corporations are separate and distinct, however. Each corporation has its separate set of books and records. Each corporation also has its own board of directors. Sometimes there are joint meetings of the boards of directors, because the policies affecting one corporation often affect the others, since all are agents of Jehovah's witnesses.

Jehovah's witnesses themselves are not a corporate body. They cannot own or operate factories, homes, institutions or carry on any legal business under the name "Jehovah's witnesses." While the work of Jehovah's witnesses is a world-wide activity they must use agents or corporations so that, as far as the world is concerned, they have legal recognition in the preaching of the gospel of the Kingdom. They have full right to proclaim the message of the Kingdom throughout the world, because Jehovah God has given them that right. But they must conform to the laws of the various lands, and thus must have organized corporations for convenience and effective operation. No corporations are ever formed by Jehovah's witnesses in any state or country unless it is a necessary expedient, and then they are formed only with the consent of the president of the Pennsylvania and New York corporations.

THEIR DAY IN COURT

*Forty-six United States Supreme Court Cases
Involving Jehovah's Witnesses*

1. *Lovell* v. *Griffin,* 303 U. S. 444, (March 28, 1938). The Court held that an ordinance prohibiting distribution of literature without written permission from the City Manager of Griffin, Georgia, constituted prior censorship of the press in violation of the First Amendment to the Constitution.

2. *Schneider* v. *New Jersey,* 308 U. S. 147, (Nov. 22, 1939). An ordinance of the Town of Irvington, New Jersey, providing that solicitors and distributors provide certain information to the police and obtain a permit from the chief of police, was declared an abridgment of freedom of the press contrary to the First Amendment to the Constitution.

3. *Cantwell* v. *Connecticut,* 310 U. S. 296, (May 20, 1940). The Connecticut statute prohibiting solicitation for contributions to charities or a religious cause without approval thereof by the Connecticut secretary of public welfare was held to be a violation of the freedom of religion provision of the First Amendment. The common-law conviction for breach of the peace by playing of a phonograph record attacking the doctrines of the Catholic Church was held to abridge freedom of speech and freedom of worship guaranteed by the First Amendment to the Constitution.

4. *Minersville* v. *Gobitis,* 310 U. S. 586, (June 3, 1940). The compulsory flag-salute regulation of the Minersville, Pennsylvania, school district, which the Gobitis children refused to comply with because of their conscientious objections based on the Bible was held to be valid. Mr. Justice Stone alone dissented.

5. *Cox* v. *New Hampshire,* 312 U. S. 569, (March 31, 1941). The New Hampshire statute regulating parades, requiring an application for a permit and payment of a fee to pay part of the expense of policing the parade, was held to be a valid police regulation. The

conviction for not complying with the statute was held not to abridge the liberties of Jehovah's witnesses to march single file with placards down the streets of Manchester.

6. *Chaplinsky* v. *New Hampshire,* 315 U. S. 568 (March 9, 1942). The New Hampshire statute prohibiting offensive, derisive, and annoying words was held not to infract the liberties of the First Amendment when Chaplinsky, after a police officer refused to protect him from a mob on the streets of Rochester, New Hampshire, called him a "damned fascist" and added that all the officials of the town were fascists.

7. *Jones* v. *Opelika, Jobin* v. *Arizona, Bowden* v. *Arkansas,* 316 U. S. 584 (June 8, 1942). Ordinances of Opelika, Alabama; Casa Grande, Arizona; and Fort Smith, Arkansas, providing for the payment of license taxes for peddlers, solicitors, and agents on application for a license, were held to be valid when applied to the preaching activity of Jehovah's witnesses. The decision was 5 to 4. A petition for rehearing was granted. On a reargument the Court reversed itself and held the ordinances to be invalid as applied (319 U. S. 103). This decision was also 5 to 4 (May 3, 1943).

8. *Jamison* v. *Texas,* 318 U. S. 413 (March 8, 1943). In this case the Dallas ordinance prohibited the scattering of leaflets, the holding of advertisements, and the throwing of handbills upon the streets. Mere distribution of handbills by the appellant was held to be a violation. The Court held that the enforcement of the ordinance abridged appellant's liberty of press contrary to the First Amendment.

9. *Largent* v. *Texas,* 318 U. S. 418 (March 8, 1943). The Paris, Texas, ordinance provided that on application to the Mayor for a permit, after investigation and approval, he may issue the permit to sell or canvass in the residential area. The conviction under the ordinance was set aside because it provided for prior censorship of the press in violation of the First Amendment.

10. *Murdock* v. *Pennsylvania,* and seven others, 319 U. S. 105 (May 3, 1943). The Court held to be an abridgment of freedom of press and worship an ordinance of Jeannette, Pennsylvania, applied to the missionary work and distribution of literature by Jehovah's witnesses, which provided that solicitors and canvassers pay a license tax and obtain a license from the Burgess.

11. *Martin* v. *Struthers,* 319 U. S. 141 (May 3, 1943). An ordinance making unlawful the ringing of doorbells to aid the door-to-door distribution of handbills or other advertising matter was declared to be an abridgment of the freedom of the press. The Court set aside the conviction because the rights of appellant were violated.

12. *Douglas* v. *Jeannette,* 319 U. S. 157 (May 3, 1943). The Court held that Jehovah's witnesses did not have the right to enjoin by federal injunction the enforcement of the penal provisions of the Jeannette, Pennsylvania, license-tax law involved in the Murdock

case, but that the remedy of defense to the criminal charge in the state courts was sufficient.

13. *Taylor* v. *Mississippi,* and two others, 319 U. S. 583 (June 14, 1943). The Court held unconstitutional the enforcement of the anti-sabotage and sedition statute of Mississippi in convicting Jehovah's witnesses for distributing literature explaining their reasons for not saluting the flag or bearing arms. The Court concluded that the conviction deprived appellants of their rights to freedom of speech and press guaranteed by the First Amendment.

14. *Busey* v. *District of Columbia,* 319 U. S. 579 (June 14, 1943). The Court vacated the decision of the Court of Appeals for the District of Columbia, 129 F 2d 24, so that it could reconsider the case in the light of *Murdock* v. *Pennsylvania,* 319 U. S. 105. On remand the Court of Appeals reversed a conviction and dismissed the prosecution (138 F 2d 592).

15. *West Virginia State Board of Education* v. *Barnette,* 319 U. S. 624 (June 14, 1943). The Court affirmed the judgment of the district court in refusing to follow its decision in *Minersville* v. *Gobitis,* 310 U. S. 586. Here the Court held the compulsory flag-salute regulation unconstitutional because it abridged freedom of speech contrary to the First Amendment. Thereby the Court reversed its *Gobitis* decision.

16. *Mathews* v. *Hamilton,* 320 U. S. 707 (October 18, 1943). Here the Court vacated a judgment enjoining the distribution of literature explaining why Jehovah's witnesses do not salute the flag and bear arms. The state court later dismissed the case.

17. *Falbo* v. *United States,* 320 U. S. 549 (January 3, 1944). This case involved prosecution for failure to report for induction by one of Jehovah's witnesses. The Court held that Falbo failed to exhaust his administrative remedies. The conviction was affirmed.

18. *Prince* v. *Massachusetts,* 321 U. S. 158 (January 31, 1944). The Court held to be valid a conviction of a foster parent of a child who was allowed to accompany the parent on the streets and distribute literature under the child-labor law of Massachusetts. The Court held that the conviction did not violate the rights of the parent under the First Amendment.

19. *Follett* v. *McCormick,* 321 U. S. 573 (March 27, 1944). The Court here held that the Constitution protected an itinerant minister as much as it did a local minister in door-to-door preaching and distribution of literature, and added that earning a livelihood from the ministry did not justify the imposition of the license-tax law. The Court reaffirmed its position in the Jones and Murdock decisions.

20. *Marsh* v. *Alabama,* 326 U. S. 501 (January 7, 1946). The Court set aside a trespass conviction on the grounds that it violated the rights guaranteed to the appellant by the First Amendment. Appellant was ordered to discontinue distribution of religious magazines on the streets of a private town near Mobile. The town was company-

owned by a shipbuilding concern. The Court held that the Constitution shielded the appellant.

21. *Tucker* v. *Texas,* 326 U. S. 517 (January 7, 1946). A similar trespass conviction was set aside for the same reason in this case. Here the preaching and distribution took place from door to door in Hondo, Texas, Navigation Village, a wholly owned Government defense housing project. The distribution was over the protest of the manager who commanded Jehovah's witnesses to cease going from door to door.

22. *Estep* v. *United States* and *Smith* v. *United States,* 327 U. S. 114 (February 4, 1946). The decision here reversed all the lower federal courts in the country in that no challenge to a draft-board classification was permitted in defense to an indictment charging a refusal to submit to induction. The Court held that invalidity of draft-board orders could be shown where the registrant had exhausted his administrative remedy.

23. *Dodez* v. *United States* and *Gibson* v. *United States,* 329 U. S. 338 (December 23, 1946). The Court here extended the doctrine of the Estep decision to permit defenses by persons charged by indictment with failing to report to or remain at conscientious-objector camps.

24. *Alexander* v. *Kulick* and *Sunal* v. *Large,* 332 U. S. 174 (June 23, 1947). The Court held that failure to permit a challenge against the validity of a draft-board order in a prosecution charging refusal to submit to induction, while erroneous, was not sufficient to warrant release from prison by writ of habeas corpus. The Court held the only remedy was by appeal, which was not exhausted in these cases.

25. *Cox* v. *United States, Thompson* v. *United States,* and *Roisum* v. *United States,* 332 U. S. 442 (November 24, 1947). The Court decided it could not hold there was no basis in fact for the denial of the ministerial exemption under the draft law to the petitioners who carried on their ministry part time and devoted a major or substantial portion of their time to secular vocations.

26. *Saia* v. *New York,* 334 U. S. 558 (June 7, 1948). Here the Court held invalid an ordinance of Lockport, New York, that required a permit before a sound device could be used in the city. The Court held that the right of freedom of speech and assembly had been violated.

27. *Niemotko* v. *Maryland* and *Kelley* v. *Maryland,* 340 U. S. 268 (January 15, 1951). This case held unconstitutional a policy of Havre de Grace that required a permit from the city council before a meeting of Jehovah's witnesses could be held or speech be given in the local city park.

28. *Fowler* v. *Rhode Island,* 345 U. S. 67 (March 9, 1953). Pawtucket prohibited religious and political meetings in its park. This was

unconstitutional. The Court found discrimination in favor of popular religions and against Jehovah's witnesses in the use of the park.

29. *Poulos* v. *New Hampshire,* 345 U. S. 395 (April 27, 1953). This case held valid the requirement that Jehovah's witnesses sue the City of Portsmouth for a permit to use the park. The Court said that Poulos was properly convicted for using the park without a permit. The Court sustained the holding of the state courts in denying Poulos his defense that the illegal refusal of his application for permit by the city council violated the Constitution.

30. *Dickinson* v. *United States,* 348 U. S. 389 (November 30, 1953.) Prosecution for refusal to be inducted into the armed forces. Dickinson claimed exemption as a minister. The Court held that it was illegally denied him because it was shown by the undisputed evidence that he worked in the ministry as a vocation, being called a pioneer. It was held that the exemption was denied without basis in fact and that the final classification was arbitrary and capricious.

31. *Gonzales* v. *United States,* 75 S. Ct. 409, March 14, 1955, No. 69, October Term, 1954.—The procedure of the Department of Justice is to make a recommendation to the appeal board, either in favor of or against the conscientious objector claim of the registrant. No copy of the advice is sent to the registrant, thus denying a chance to answer the recommendation. The Court held that due process of law demanded a chance to answer the recommendation before the appeal board acted. The Court said the procedure followed denied that right and violated the rights of Gonzales so as to call for an acquittal. The judgment was reversed.

32. *Witmer* v. *United States,* 75 St. Ct. 392, March 14, 1955, No. 164, October Term, 1954.—The registrant in quick succession made two groundless claims for exemption, known to be baseless. Shortly before making the ministry claim he informed the board that it did not apply. In making an agricultural claim he told the board he was willing to contribute to the war effort; yet at his conscientious objector hearing he said he would not indirectly participate as a conscientious objector. The local board made a memorandum of certain inconsistencies. The Court held the conscientious objector claim was subjective and that these circumstances could be considered as sufficient basis in fact for the denial of the conscientious objector status. The judgment of conviction was therefore affirmed.

33. *Sicurella* v. *United States,* 75 S. Ct. 403, March 14, 1955, No. 250, October Term, 1954.—The Department of Justice recommended to the appeal board that it deny the conscientious objector claim because Sicurella believed in theocratic warfare mentioned in the Bible and in defense of himself and his brothers. The Court held that the recommendation was illegal. It said that the classification and

order based thereon were invalid so as to require an acquittal. The judgment was reversed.

34. *Simmons* v. *United States,* 75 S. Ct. 397, March 14, 1955, No. 251, October Term, 1954.—The hearing officer and the Department of Justice had in their possession evidence that was unfavorable to the conscientious objector claim of Simmons. At his hearing in the Department of Justice on his claim the unfavorable evidence was not called to his attention. The Court held that this failure was a denial of due process of law. The judgment of conviction was reversed.

35. *Bates* v. *United States,*—S. Ct.—, March 28, 1955. No. 450, October Term, 1954.—The local board and the appeal board for the district gave Bates a conscientious objector classification. The state Director appealed the case to the President. The National Selective Service Appeal Board, without referring the case to the Department of Justice for a recommendation, changed the I-O Classification to I-A, making him liable for unlimited military service. The Court held that the failure to refer the case to the Department of Justice for a recommendation on the conscientious objector claim was a denial of due process of law. The case was reversed and an acquittal ordered by the Supreme Court.

36. *Simon* v. *United States,*—S. Ct.—, March 28, 1955, No. 526, October Term, 1954.—Reversed and acquittal directed for the reasons stated in *Simmons* v. *United States,* 75 S. Ct. 397, March 14, 1955, No. 251, October Term, 1954.

37. *Bradley* v. *United States,*—S. Ct.—, March 28, 1955, No. 565, October Term, 1954.—Reversed and acquittal directed for the reasons stated in *Gonzales* v. *United States,* 75 S. Ct. 409, March 14, 1955, No. 69, October Term, 1954.

38. *DeMoss* v. *United States,*—S. Ct.—, April   , 1955, No. 595, October Term, 1954.—Reversed and acquittal directed for the reasons stated in *Bates* v. *United States,*—S. Ct.—, March 28, 1955, No. 450, October Term, 1954.

THE CANADIAN DOCKET

From 1946 to 1953, Jehovah's witnesses were involved in 1,665 prosecutions in Quebec. Of these, 780 cases were decided in favor of the Witnesses. Meanwhile 864 prosecutions and eleven civil actions had been pending since December, 1952, awaiting the decision of the Supreme Court of Canada on the test case, *Saumur* v. *Quebec.*

FLAG SALUTE: In 1945, the Ontario Court of Appeals adopted the reasoning of the United States Supreme Court and unanimously held that the compulsory flag salute was an unlawful infringement on religious liberty of those who object to it. The case was *Donald* v. *Board of Education,* Ontario Reports 518.

SEDITION: In 1951, in *Boucher* v. *The King* (Supreme Court Reports 265), a landmark decision in Canadian legal history disposed of more than one hundred sedition and defamatory libel charges laid by the Attorney General of Quebec. It culminated a fight against sedition charges dating back to 1933. The Witnesses had won, on a point of procedure, a previous case in 1936, when the Supreme Court (Reports 188) ruled in favor of the Witnesses in *Brodie* v. *The King*. In the Boucher case, the Supreme Court ordered it back for a new trial. But a rehearing was granted and held before nine justices. A majority of five held that the Witnesses' denunciation of Quebec law enforcement was not seditious but was a justifiable complaint against mistreatment of them.

CHILD CUSTODY: *In re Bennett Infants* (Ontario Weekly Notes 621) the High Court of the Province of Ontario ruled, in 1952, that "it is not for the Court to decide as between the two religions," in refusing to deny custody of her child to a mother who happened to be a Witness of Jehovah.

KIDNAPING: A 1935 Quebec case, *Parsons and Lundell* v. *Masse et al.*, No. 9522, District of Joliette, involved two young women missionaries who had been kidnaped by Roman Catholic mobsters, transported to Montreal, warned under threat not to return to their homes in Joliette, and abandoned. The Attorney General of the Province refused to prosecute the kidnapers under the criminal law. Damage actions were instituted. Roman Catholic Justice André Demers denounced the kidnapers and assessed damages of six hundred dollars.

CENSORSHIP: In *Saumur* v. *City and Province of Quebec*, the Supreme Court of Canada, on October 6, 1953, ruled that the following censorship by-law of Quebec City could not be applied to the preaching activities of Jehovah's Witnesses: "It is forbidden to distribute in the streets of Quebec any book, pamphlet, booklet, circular, tract whatsoever without having previously obtained for so doing the written permission of the Chief of Police."

BILL OF RIGHTS PETITION: No guarantees of civil liberty are set forth in the Canadian Constitution. Jehovah's Witnesses, feeling that such a guarantee "would help put a stop to the scandalous persecutions" they suffered, particularly in the Province of Quebec, circulated a petition that gathered 500,967 names and presented it to Parliament on June 9, 1947. This was twice as big as any other petition ever submitted.

A second petition on the same subject was presented on the request of Jehovah's Witnesses in February, 1949, which contained 625,510 signatures.

IN THE COMMUNIST "PARADISE"

Czechoslovakia

November, 1948: The Society's office staff of thirteen and five others arrested in Prague and consigned to protective custody.

July, 1949: All eighteen released for lack of evidence and turned over to a Communist labor commission of nine members. The commission sentenced them to two years in labor camps. In December, 1949, and January, 1950, they were released.

A letter dated November 20, 1950, said that "about sixty were tried for conscientious objection and sentenced each to two years in prison." A later communication (1951) spoke of about three hundred being tried and sentenced by military courts.

The next big action against Jehovah's witnesses by the Czech authorities was carried out on the night of February 3, 1952, when arrests were made throughout the country. "The actual number of arrests is estimated to have been between 500 and 600." (Letter dated September 22, 1952.)

"At present (September, 1952) only about one hundred men and five women are in prison," the others having been released sometime after the arrests in February.

One Witness, Franz Kapinus, died in prison, on July 4, 1952.

March 27 and 28, 1953: The Prague District Court sentenced eight of Jehovah's witnesses: two to eighteen years each; three to fifteen years each; the other three respectively to twelve, eight, and five years. Total 106 years.

To the 106 years, add three hundred sentenced by military courts to two years each. Grand total: 706 years.

This is only a cross-section report. For instance, it does not account for the one hundred men and five women reported in prison in September, 1952.

Hungary

November 14, 1950: The presiding minister for Hungary and two other men of the Budapest office of the Society imprisoned. No trial had taken place as late as July, 1953.

August, 1951: At this time, two hundred younger Witnesses were serving prison terms from ten months to four years. "The number increases from day to day; here and there one or the other is dismissed under threat." (Letter of August, 1951).

August, 1952: "At present there are 500 of Jehovah's witnesses (men and women) in confinement with sentences ranging from three to ten years. They are held in three working camps." Taking the average to be six and a half years, the total sentence would be 3,250 years.

Poland

June, 1950: Approximately six thousand Jehovah's witnesses were arrested. About half this number were released after thorough questioning. By the end of 1950, all were released except 282. The total of their sentences was 838 years.

At the end of September, 1952, 171 (out of the 282) were still in prison. Since June, 1950, thirteen had died in the hands of the police and judicial authorities.

July 1952: 259 more imprisoned for conscientious objection.

October 16, 1952: "Today the number would be considerably higher, and that for every category."

November 15, 1952: "During the past two months about 130 workers were arrested, among them eleven circuit ministers."

February, 1953: Additional arrests, including the four most responsible representatives of the group.

This incomplete report totals 564 arrests since November, 1952.

Rumania

August, 1949: Branch office in Bucharest raided by police.

January, 1950: Presiding minister for Rumania and other co-workers, men and women, were arrested.

July, 1950: A Bucharest court sentenced the three principal Witnesses to ten years each, at forced labor; three others to five years each; two women to two years each. Total: 64 years.

January, 1951: M. Magyarosi, one of the three, national presiding minister, died in prison.

The Rumania report is very incomplete.

Russia

In 1947 and 1948, several delegations of Jehovah's witnesses tried to get to Moscow to submit a petition to the government setting out the purposes of Jehovah's winesses. They were arrested before they reached the city.

In the spring of 1946, four hundred of two thousand of Jehovah's witnesses then in Bessarabia were deported to the Urals and Siberia.

Last news showed that there were at least ten thousand Jehovah's witnesses in the USSR. Many of these were held in Siberia.

Yugoslavia

From 1948 till June, 1953: Seventeen men and four women, members of Jehovah's witnesses, were sentenced from six months to fifteen years. Of these, two women died, one in Reichenburg and the other in Lubljana. Cause of deaths unknown. One man, a prisoner, died accidentally while employed constructing an electric power plant. Sentences total 76 years 5 months.

East Germany

1. Total number of persons arrested during the time of persecution (Since end of August, 1950): to August, 1953:
   1,316 men
     742 women
   ‾‾‾‾‾‾
   2,058 Total

2. Released:
   515 men
   411 women
   ‾‾‾‾‾‾
   926 Total

3. Still being held to date:
   794 men
   324 women
   ‾‾‾‾‾‾
   1,118 Total

4. Total numbers of persons sentenced till now:
   738 men
   292 women
   ‾‾‾‾‾‾
   1,030 Total

5. Minors:
   A number of minors were given sentences, but no figure can be reported yet, since the ages of the ones arrested have not been registered.

6. Killed during imprisonment or died because of bad treatment:
   7 men
   7 women
   ‾‾‾‾
   14 Total

7. Given penitentiary sentences for "life":
   14 men
    0 women
   ‾‾‾‾
   14 Total

8. Finally, 1016 men and women were sentenced to a total of 6,865 years and five months in prison or penitentiary, which gives an average of 6 3/4 years in prison or penitentiary for each.

Bulgaria

Much persecution, but no statistics available.

WHAT DID THE PRESIDENT'S PARENTS BELIEVE?

MANY words have been spoken and printed about the religion of the parents of Dwight D. Eisenhower, President of the United States. But well-meaning though his biographers may have been, the story has been presented poorly.

What actually was the faith to which his parents began exposing Dwight D. Eisenhower when he was a lad of five summers? From that time, what was the religious atmosphere in which he and his four living brothers were reared?

In "The President's Religious Faith," as described in *Life* for March 22, 1954, Paul Hutchinson tried to clear away some of the haze surrounding the President's mother at least, saying, "The evidence is to be seen in her withdrawal from the River Brethren to become a Jehovah's witness."

And after that, on July 7, 1954, the President himself, with a critical word for some of his biographers, declared, according to *The New York Times,* that his parents were deeply religious people and that his mother ultimately became a member of an organization identified as Jehovah's witnesses.

But what of the President's father? The answer to that the *Life* article left in the fog. "Whether the President's father ever joined the Witnesses is disputed," it said. "River Brethren—the President's bishop cousin among them—say that he did."

The President's brother, Edgar Newton Eisenhower, Tacoma attorney, cut through the fog on that point. "My father," *Woman's Home Companion* (August, 1954) quoted Edgar as saying, "broke away from the River Brethren Church and joined what was then referred to as 'Bible Students.' "

Anyone with even the scantiest knowledge of the background of Jehovah's witnesses recognizes "Bible Students" as the name used by them for decades up to 1931.

What are the facts about President Eisenhower's parents? Had they been Catholics, Presbyterians, or Jews, or even Mennonites, do you agree that the logical place to go for the answer is their church, their associates in the faith, and to their own statements?

As to David Jacob Eisenhower and his wife, Ida, parents of the President, the natural and reasonable place to find substantial evidence is in the archives of Jehovah's witnesses, for that is what those parents were.

Here is a glimpse at some of that evidence:

It begins at Abilene, Kansas, early in the year 1895. A young mother was grieving over the death of her infant son—the mother's name, Ida Eisenhower. Paul, her fifth son, born May 12, 1894, had just succumbed to scarlet fever. Three of her neighbors, Mrs. Clara Witt, Mrs. Emma Holland, and Mrs. Mary Thayer, were trying to console her.

Those women were ardent students of the *Millennial Dawn* Bible helps written by Charles Taze Russell and published by the Watch Tower Society. Indeed those three women were "skilled students and talkers of Bible truths." What they had to say led both Ida Eisenhower and her husband to look more deeply into the Bible with help of those Watch Tower books. Both grieving parents were "strongly attracted to those books" with their "comforting and sound Scriptural explanations of Almighty God's declared purposes."

Ida Eisenhower then was thirty-three. One year later, 1896, when their third-born son David Dwight (now Dwight David) was approaching his sixth birthday, the Eisenhowers opened their home for a neighborhood Bible class, using the Watch Tower study books and the *Watch Tower* magazine.

For the next twenty years the Eisenhower home served as the public meeting place for the nucleus of the Abilene congregation of Bible Students, known today (and since 1931) as Jehovah's witnesses.

Meeting in the Eisenhower home until 1915, that Abilene group of Bible Students was one of hundreds of growing congregations that met regularly each week, in their respective localities, throughout most of the United States and in several foreign countries. As class textbooks, all of these congregations used the Watch Tower Bible-study aids. Charles Taze Russell, who in those days edited their official magazine, *The Watch Tower,* was then known around the globe as Pastor Russell. In 1884 he had incorporated the Watch Tower Bible and Tract Society at Allegheny (now Pittsburgh), Pennsylvania. In those days, too, folks in Abilene, when speaking of the group that regularly met in the Eisenhower home, sometimes called them "Russellites," a name then elsewhere also tacked onto the Bible Students, just as in the 16th century "Lutheran" was tacked onto former Roman Catholics.

During most of the twenty years while the Bible Students of Abilene held Sunday meetings in the Eisenhower home, David Jacob Eisenhower served that class as its chosen "elder" or Bible-study conductor. There the father of the future American President sometimes alternated in conducting the Bible class with L. D. Toliver, another regular attender.

Recalling these home religious services, R. G. Tonkin, "Dwight Eisenhower's first intimate friend," reflected: "Whatever the re-

To substantiate this factual narrative, four never-before published letters are reproduced in facsimile in the following pages.

The Abilene (Kansas) *Daily Reflector-Chronicle,* having shared in misleading biographers and others by sending out erroneous information on the religion of Ida Elizabeth Stover Eisenhower, was duly visited. Mrs. Lotta Thayer, an almost lifelong close friend of David and Ida Eisenhower, accompanied by Naomi Engle, spoke to the newspaper's editor, Charles Moreau Harger, deceased, age 92, April 3, 1955, and its business manager, Henry B. Jameson, about the inaccurate reports then being given out. She promptly received a written apology. In fairness to all, Mrs. Thayer has granted permission for reproduction of this letter.

ABILENE DAILY REFLECTOR-CHRONICLE
ASSOCIATED PRESS

C. M. HARGER, Editor
H. B. JAMESON, Business Manager

Abilene, Kansas

May 25, 1953

Mrs. Lotta Thayer
510 N. Cedar
Abilene, Kans.

Dear Mrs. Thayer:

Pursuant to our conversation Saturday afternoon, may I once again thank you for calling to my attention the error about the religious affiliation of the late Mrs. Eisenhower.

As I explained to you, soon after writing the letter in question--based on erroneous information given to me at the time--I discovered the error, but too late to rectify it as I did not keep a carbon copy and did not have the address.

I am more than happy to acknowledge the error, since it was by no means intentional but left me in a bad position because of incorrect information given to me. And I would appreciate it very much if you would please be so kind as to pass this information on to the proper persons who questioned you about it.

During the period of the last campaign we received scores of inquiries about President Eisenhower's religious beliefs and affiliations. The subject of Mrs. Eisenhower's religious affiliations never was an "issue" so far as any of us were concerned. As you know, I was gone from Abilene for a number of years and returned just a matter of weeks before her death. Therefore, I personally knew little or nothing about her personal life.

When this particular inquiry was received I made a check with a source whom I considered reliable. Although I was led astray I do not believe this was intentional either--I think it was a case of complete misunderstanding on the part of my source, too. That would account for the discrepancy in names which I explained to you. I later learned that there was no question about Mrs. Eisenhower's affiliation with your group, and that she had been for many years. However, I think the fact that it was previously known here by one or two other names accounted for the belief of some that she only on late years became a member of Jehovas Witness.

Please accept my apologies and again may I ask that you pass them along to the right people--for there was indeed no intent on my part to mislead or misinform anyone.

Sincerely yours,

Henry B. Jameson

With her own hand Ida E. Eisenhower, at 81, wrote on June 4, 1943, to Mrs. B. I. Lawson, one of Jehovah's witnesses, stating that she had been "in the truth" as a Witness of Jehovah since 1896. Her handwritten letter, reproduced in facsimile, reads:

Mrs. Lawson,

Your letter reached me and I can give you the facts. I have been in the truth since ninety-six, am still in, and glad that I found the truth. It has been a comfort to me. I am now alone since my husband has pass away. My sons are scattered from East to West. I am still living in my own home. Naomi Engle stay with me and she is a witness too, so my hope are still good. The Lord knows what is best for us; so I put my trust in the Lord.

Ida E. Eisenhower

Mrs Lawson
        Your letter reached me
and I can ~~cannot~~ give you the
the facts I have been in the
truth since ninty six
an still in & glad that I
found the truth it hes been
acomfort - to me - I am now
alone since my husband
has pass away my sons are
scatered from east to west
I am still living in my
own home Mamna Engle
stay with me and she is
a wittness too so my hoope
are still good the Lord -
knows what is best for us
so I put my trust in the
Lord Ida E Eisenhower

Abilene,Kansas.
August-20-'44.

Mr.Richard Boeckel,
35 Garland Drive
Eggertsville.21,New York.

Dear Sir:-

A friend returning from the United Announcers Convention of
Jehovah's witnesses,informs me of meeting you there. I rejoice
with you in your privilege of attending such convention.

It has been my good fortune many times in the years gone by
to attend these meetings of those faithfully proclaiming the
name of Jehovah and and his glorious Kingdom which shortly now
will pour out its rich blessings over all the earth.

My friend informs me of your desire to have a word from
General Eisenhower's mother whom you have been told is one
of the witnesses of Jehovah. I am indeed such and what a
glourious privilege it has been in association with those of
the present time and with those on back through the annals
of Biblical history even to Abel.

Generally I have refused such requests because of my desire
to avoid all publicity. However,because you are a person of
good will towards Jehovah God and his glorious Theocracy I am
very happy to write you.

I have been blessed with seven sons of which five are living,
all being very good to their mother and I am constrained to
believe are very fine in the eyes of those who have learned to
know them.

It was always my desire and my effort to raise my boys in the
knowledge of and to reverence their Creator. My prayer is that
they all may anchor their hope in the New World,the central
feature of which is the Kingdom for which all good people have
been praying the past two thousand years.

I feel that Dwight my third son will always strive to do his duty
with integrety as he sees such duty. I mention him in particular
because of your expressed interest in him.

And so as the mother of General Eisenhower and as a witness of
and for the Great Jehovah of Hosts (I have been such the past
49 years) I am pleased to write you and to urge you to faithfulness
as a companion of and servant with those who "keep the commandments
of God and have the testimony of Jesus".

There can be no doubt that what is now called the post-war period
is the "one hour"mentioned at Revelations chapters 17 and 18.
Ten here being a symbol not of just ten nations but rather of the
whole number or all of the nations,then if we have a real League of
Nations acting efficiently as a super guide to the nations of earth
at the close of this war,should be ample proof.

Mr. Richard Boeckel. #2.

Surely this portends that very soon the glorious Theocracy, the long promised Kingdom of Jehovah the Great God and of his Son the everlasting King will rule the entire earth and pour out manifold blessings upon all peoples who are of good will towards Him. All others will be removed.

Again may I urge your ever faithfulness to these the "Higher Powers" and to the New World now so very near.

Respectfully yours in hope of and as a
fighter for the New World,

Ida E. Eisenhower

At 82, Ida E. Eisenhower wrote on August 20, 1944, to Richard Boeckel, then a member of the United States Army. While in the Army, Boeckel had become one of Jehovah's witnesses. This letter, coming to him in a time of trouble, from the mother of General Eisenhower, telling how she had been one of Jehovah's witnesses for 49 years, gave Boeckel great encouragement. He has given permission for this letter's reproduction.

WAR DEPARTMENT
THE CHIEF OF STAFF
WASHINGTON

1 February 1946

Dear Mr. Southworth:

Thank you very much for your letter giving
me news of my mother's health. It is indeed
comforting to know that she is happy and in
good spirits.

Again my thanks,

Sincerely,

Dwight D. Eisenhower

Mr. Fred K. Southworth
319 E. 5th Street
Hutchinson, Kansas.

A letter of Dwight D. Eisenhower, dated 1 February, 1946,
to his parents' long-time friend and fellow Witness of Jehovah,
Fred K. Southworth.

HOW A NEW MINISTER IS MADE

The-House-to-House Ministry. When the knock came on Tott Wilson's door that afternoon, the farthest thing from the young chemical worker's mind was to become a minister. A church member, maybe; but he, actually a preacher and a teacher of what he was going to learn about the Bible?

"My name is Martin," said Tott's caller. "And this is my son, Teddy. Teddy wants to give you an invitation to a free Bible talk to be given Sunday."

"The Conquering Power of Faith," read Teddy's invitation.

"This lecture is sponsored by the Watchtower Bible & Tract Society," Mr. Martin was saying. Then he asked: "Have you ever read *The Watchtower* magazine?"

It all started as simply as that, one casual morning in 1953. The call took only five minutes out of the 72,344,728 hours spent by Jehovah's witnesses world-wide in the public ministry, that year.

Does such a method of preaching sound unorthodox to you? Jehovah's witnesses say you do not need a special building in which to worship God, for He "does not dwell in houses made with hands." The house-to-house method follows the Bible example, they point out. It goes right to the people, just as did the apostles and disciples of Jesus, who preached "every day in the temple and from house to house." They taught "publicly and from house to house."—Acts 5:42; 7:48; 20:20, *New World Translation of the Christian Greek Scriptures.*

HOME BIBLE STUDIES

Cliff Martin and his eight-year-old son Teddy called back on Tott Wilson every week or so for a couple of months. They brought him new invitations to the Bible talks, new magazines, and other literature. Each time they called Cliff had a new Bible theme to talk about.

"What is this about the new earth?" Tott asked one day.

"Suppose we come over next week, about this same time, and really go into that subject from the Bible?" Cliff suggested.

That was how the two families—Cliff and his wife Doris, and Tott and his wife Sue—got acquainted. The Martins held a home Bible study with the Wilsons, free of charge, one night a week. Sometimes they gathered in the Wilson home. Sometimes they gathered in the Martin home. But the study went on week after week, for six months.

Sue and Tott liked what they learned. One night their attention was alerted by Cliff's remark that "Home Bible studies like these lay the groundwork for a thousand new ministers to enter the field every week."

They were taught that this method of home study was not only practical but Scriptural; that "where two or three meet together in my name, there I am in their midst."—Matthew 18:20, *New World Translation of the Christian Greek Scriptures.*

THEIR BIBLE HELP

Let God Be True was the name of the Bible help they used. Its circulation of more than twelve million copies in thirty-one languages makes it the most popular publication ever produced by Jehovah's witnesses.

"This book is not to take the place of the Bible," Cliff explained. "But it contains twenty-six major Bible doctrines. In each chapter the Scriptures are gathered from the whole Bible explaining the doctrine involved. When we go through a chapter we are going through the Bible in a topical manner."

THE KINGDOM HALL

But not all Christian instruction is in the home. One Sunday the Wilsons went with the Martins to the Kingdom Hall, not far from their home. There they met "all the brothers" including the theocratic ministry school instructor, Brother Humphries.

The Wilsons' little girl, Jan, was just as curious as Tott and Sue.

For one thing, they learned that Jehovah's witnesses, in 1953, maintained more than 14,000 of these educational centers throughout the world, for free Bible instruction and public worship. All are called Kingdom Halls.

A course of study that never ends, and from which nobody ever graduates, is provided in these halls by the Watch Tower Bible & Tract Society. A minimum of four one-hour classes are held every week—two topical Bible studies, a public-speaking course, a service meeting in which every one trains in all features of the ministry. One of the Bible studies is the weekly Watchtower lesson. *The Watchtower,* official publication of the New World Society, is used as the textbook for presenting Biblical facts and practical information for daily Christian living.

In addition to the four weekly classes, a public lecture is given in most Kingdom Halls every Sunday, the year around.

Impressed by these meetings, the Wilsons commenced to attend Kingdom Hall regularly. Soon they no longer just sat and listened. They participated in the questions and answers.

They learned that the Bible instructs Christians to meet congregationally, "not forsaking the gathering of ourselves together." (Hebrews 10:25, *New World Translation*) They began to catch "the joy of Christian fellowship," and to appreciate that "such meetings are interesting, informative and worthwhile."

"Jehovah's witnesses are dedicated to reaching every living soul with the good news that the Kingdom is here," Doris remarked to Sue one day. "Even if it takes standing on the streets to catch people we don't find at home."

It was a simple, if courageous, way to start becoming a "publisher," Sue observed.

She went along with Doris for an hour. Doris (on the left in the preceding picture) explained that she would face the traffic coming one way, and Sue could face it coming the other. At first, Sue showed herself the novice by looking Doris's way and letting her own traffic walk by without seeing her.

She noticed that Doris made no effort to attract attention, except to smile and ask the passers-by if they would like the latest copy. Also, Doris found a station against a blank wall. "We do not stand in front of display windows and spoil the merchants' advertising displays," Doris cautioned.

Sue was astonished to discover that *Awake!* magazine, of which 1,300,000 copies are published every two weeks (1954), enjoyed a bigger circulation than any other religious journal except *The Watchtower,* of which 1,950,000 copies are circulated twice a month, in 40 languages.

Sue also learned the role of women Witnesses. They do not dictate organizational policy, preside over men, or deliver public addresses. But they do share in congregational commenting and training, and they take part in the ministry, house to house, on the streets, and in private studies.

Street witnessing is also in harmony with Bible principles, Doris assured her. "Wisdom cries aloud in the streets, she lifts up her voice in the squares; at the head of noisy thoroughfares she calls, at the openings of the city gates she utters her words." (Proverbs 1:20,21, *American Translation*) This and other Scriptures, Doris said, proves that public streets from time immemorial have been used as a vital spot for the dissemination of information. "Christ and the apostles made use of them, and so do Jehovah's witnesses today."

THEOCRATIC TRAINING IN THE PUBLIC MINISTRY

The theocratic ministry school trains males of all ages in public speaking, while the entire congregation participates in class coverage of grammar, diction, and composition, as well as doctrines, history, geography, comparative religions, characters, and chapter-by-chapter coverage of the Bible.

Tott and Sue Wilson, having studied for a year with Jehovah's witnesses, symbolized their life-dedication to the public ministry by water immersion. Thereupon Tott became eligible for enrollment in the weekly theocratic ministry school.

Came the night for Tott to give his first ministry talk at the Kingdom Hall. The instructor followed his student presentation with three minutes of counsel on his delivery, articulation, facial and body expressions, poise, modulation, and other points involved in making a mature and polished speaker. The entire congregation learned something not only from Tott's eight-minute discourse, but also from the counsel he received.

Again, he learned, that the Scriptural example is followed. Christ's original followers themselves learned to be teachers, to teach wherever they had the opportunity, "whether to a small group in a private home or to a large throng." Tott Wilson and the others enrolled in the ministry school were training to be efficient ministers. A year from the date of his immersion, Tott qualified to give his first public discourse, like the one little Teddy Martin invited him to attend that afternoon two years before.

"BRINGING IN THE SHEEP"

Soon after his dedication, Tott took out his own house-to-house territory. Before long he found his own "good-will person," just as the Martins had found him, in his own home.

The day arrived when he brought this interested person, A. H. Lowery, to the Kingdom Hall. Tott showed him the theocratic library, then the congregation-service chart.

"Here at Kingdom Hall of Jehovah's witnesses," Tott told Lowery, "you see no donations chart, no membership-drive chart. All you see is the public-ministry chart."

The chart tells the story, Tott explained. "There are no clergy and laity distinctions among Jehovah's witnesses, because each dedicated Witness is a minister."

Lowery was impressed. He followed Tott's finger as it pointed out the 40-per-cent increase in publishers from 1953 to 1954.

"You notice in May," Tott indicated, "there were thirty-eight publishers in this congregation." They put in 385 hours of field ministry, he told Lowery, an average of 10.1 hours.

"We made ninety-five back-calls on interested persons like yourself. We conducted twenty different Bible studies in homes, like the one I started with you a few weeks ago."

So the cycle that commenced with the first home call on Tott Wilson had now moved on to A. H. Lowery. If he should maintain interest, it will not be long until he is bringing *his* "good will" into the New World Society.

Multiply by more than a thousand times a week what happened to Tott Wilson and his wife Sue and you have a small picture of the activities of Jehovah's witnesses. The principle of "each one a minister" is producing for this group the fastest growing religion in the world.

"REMEMBER ALSO THY CREATOR IN THE DAYS OF THY YOUTH." (Ecclesiastes 12:1, *American Standard Version*) Young Witnesses enjoy an active part in the ministry, including inviting the public to hear Bible lectures. The youth are taught early in life to worship Jehovah God. Parents know they must "train up a child in the way he should go, and even when he is old he will not depart from it." (Proverbs 22:6, *American Standard Version*) The children find in Jesus, Samuel, Jeremiah, and Timothy examples of faithful men who served God in their youth.

ligious convictions of the boys may have been, they did not talk about them. I never knew any of the family to attend the River Brethren church; they seemed to have organized a schismatic branch of their own. Every Sunday afternoon about fifteen people would gather at the Eisenhower house. There was a small organ and the group would sing and pray for hours—at least it seemed that long to me." ("I Grew Up with Eisenhower," *The Saturday Evening Post,* May 3, 1952.)

Each spring, from 1896 to 1915, members of that Eisenhower home-Bible class, like the hundreds of other associated classes of Bible Students, met on a selected date, according to their understanding of the Biblical rule, to celebrate the Lord's supper or annual Memorial of Christ's death. For example, as part of its official report, the *Watch Tower* magazine of April, 1899, published the fact that at Abilene, on March 26, ten persons shared in that year's Memorial observance.

During those two decades up to 1915 the *Watch Tower* magazine also published the itinerary of the Watch Tower Society's traveling ordained ministers. These official records show that the Abilene group made an annual request, like the Bible Students' classes in other places, to be served twice a year or more often by such traveling speakers. Sent out from the Bible Students' national headquarters, those traveling or "pilgrim" speakers visited Abilene on two-day assignments. Their coming was widely advertised in advance by the Eisenhowers and their fellow Bible Students. Those speakers' talks were delivered in the Eisenhower house. Often the visiting speaker was entertained at the Eisenhower home during his entire stay in Abilene.

The advance notices of many of such special speakers' visits to Abilene, the speakers' names, dates of their visits, are part of the published record still accessible to anyone who desires to see the bound volumes of the *Watch Tower* magazine for those years (1896-1915) in the New York Public Library or other public and private libraries. There still survive some of the traveling ministers themselves who, in those days, visited Abilene; and even now they are active as witnesses of Jehovah in California, New York, and elsewhere.

By 1915 the Bible Students' class in Abilene had outgrown the capacity of the Eisenhower home. From then on a hired local hall has served as the group's regular meeting place.

With friends from Abilene and vicinity both David and Ida Eisenhower repeatedly traveled near and far to attend district and national Bible Students' conventions. For instance, in 1912 they were delegates to an eight-day national convention that ended Sunday, July 14, at Washington, D. C. Before returning home the Eisenhowers and another Abilene couple, James L. Thayer (dental-surgeon son of Mary Thayer) and his wife, Lotta Jessop Thayer, traveled on together by train to New York and then by Hudson River steamer to West Point. There, at the United States Military Academy, they visited Cadet Dwight D. Eisenhower. The young West Pointer "graciously showed them around the grounds."

In March, 1942, David Jacob Eisenhower died. He had requested that his funeral service be conducted by James L. Thayer. For more than twenty-five years Dr. Thayer had been serving as appointed leader of the Abilene Bible class. Assisting at the funeral was Fred K. Southworth, another long-time ordained minister of that Bible Students' group at Abilene. Today he resides at Hutchinson, Kansas. For more than forty years Fred Southworth had been an intimate friend of both David and Ida Eisenhower.

After the death of her husband, Ida Eisenhower continued to attend the conventions of Jehovah's witnesses. In 1943 one of such conventions was held in Wichita, Kansas, and her presence there was publicized, with a front-page picture of her, in the April 19 issue of the Wichita *Beacon*. She had become known among Jehovah's witnesses in other countries as well as in the United States as "one who faithfully and regularly, in wartime and in peacetime, engaged in the work of announcing Jehovah's kingdom," from house to house and on the streets, like any other dedicated witness of Jehovah. Such dedication she had publicly confessed in 1897 at her baptism.

In September, 1946, shortly after her death, Ida Eisenhower's youngest son, Milton Stover Eisenhower, presented a gift to his mother's friend, Mrs. James L. Thayer. It was the year-by-year collection of his parents' subscription copies of the *Watch Tower* magazine. During the entire half century from 1896, mail deliveries at the Abilene Eisenhower home had included the semimonthly issues of the *Watch Tower*, sent there by the publisher on regular subscription. To Mrs. Thayer (the former Lotta Jessop) that gift was a "grief-burdened but generous gesture," a kind of climax to an unbroken friendship with David and Ida Eisenhower that had begun at Hope, Kansas, several years before the birth of their third son David Dwight (now Dwight David—born at Denison, Texas, October 14, 1890). At Hope, in the 1880's the newlywedded Eisenhowers, David and Ida, carried on their first joint business venture, a grocery store. One of their regular customers was a schoolgirl, Lotta Jessop, who loved to spend time with those "two humble, earnest Kansans" whenever her mother sent her to that store for the family food. In 1895, Lotta, upon her mother's death, removed from Hope to Abilene, becoming in 1903 Mrs. James L. Thayer; and since her husband's death in 1951 she continues, to this writing, to reside in Abilene, Kansas.

CHARITABLE WORKS OF JEHOVAH'S WITNESSES

"GIFTS of mercy, or help and assistance for the welfare of others toward Jehovah God, publicly or privately, either individually or in an organized way, will gain God's favor."

Thus do Jehovah's witnesses define charitable works.

They do not tithe. They have no laity class to do the tithing. All together are in the ministerial class. They feel that "Christian" means being a minister of the Word. "The Bible tells us to follow in Christ's footsteps. Where do they lead? To the public ministry."

Tithing, they feel, went out with the Jewish law and Levite priesthood. In *The Watchtower,* Dec. 1, 1953, it is put this way:

"Is not tithing approved by the Bible? Under the law of Moses, yes! But we do not find Jesus recommending tithing to his followers. His disciples were sent out to preach the gospel free, not to demand tithes. (Matthew 10:8, 9) True, Christ upheld tithing while the Jewish law was in effect, but tithing came to an end when the law was abolished by God through Christ Jesus. (Ephesians 2:15; Colossians 2:13, 14) The Bible is definitely clear that the early Christians had no system of tithing; all giving was on a voluntary basis. (I Corinthians 16:1, 2; II Corinthians 9:1-5) Hence, insistence on tithing, a practice no longer Scripturally required, is peddling the Word of God and making dishonest gain by means of it."

Spiritual Gifts More Important

The Witnesses feel that giving spiritual things is more important than giving material gifts. (Luke 10:38-42; John 6:26,27; Amos 8:11; Acts 3:2-8; Matthew 5:3,6) The bulk of their giving is to support their local Kingdom Halls as continual public educational and religious centers; and to contribute to the publishing and missionary work of their central Society.

"The Watch Tower Bible and Tract Society is a nonprofit organization, and what monies it receives it uses for the spreading of the gospel unto the ends of the earth," states the 1949 *Yearbook of Jehovah's Witnesses.* And as a typical example it describes for the work of foreign missionaries, as follows:

"During the 1948 service year the Brooklyn office sent money and literature to its Branch offices valued at $488,821.22. In addition to that, for foreign service or expansion work in various countries where Branches are not established, assistance was required to the amount of $110,851.11. Literature and supplies were sent to some countries as gifts, and this amounted to $118,608.04. This meant a total outlay of $718,280.37 to assist the preaching of the gospel outside the United States. A few of the large Branches were able to

remit to the Brooklyn office to cover the cost of some of the shipments made, and these remittances amounted to $296,119.58. That
left a balance of $422,170.79 that the Watch Tower Bible and Tract
Society paid out during 1948 for the expansion work in territories
outside the United States of America."

The work was carried on in 96 lands in 1948. Seven of these
were opened up that year.

Material Assistance

In regard to material assistance, Jehovah's witnesses feel that the
Christian's special responsibility is to his family and his brothers in
the faith. (I Timothy 5:8; Acts 2:44,45; Matthew 25:34-40; James
2:15; II Corinthians 8:1-15) If some individual or family within a
congregation is in need, the congregation takes measures to provide
modest assistance. Dependence upon congregational handouts is definitely not encouraged. Even full-time missionaries, "pioneers," must
not expect the congregation to perpetually feed, clothe, and support
them.

Sometimes Jehovah's witnesses help each other on a national or
international scale. A relief drive may be announced by the Society.
The charity is organized and carried out in the manner of Paul, who
collected some free-will offerings from the congregations in Rome,
Corinth, and elsewhere to distribute among "the poor of the holy
ones in Jerusalem." The contributions were for the brothers, not for
promiscuous charity.

By financing their own Kingdom Halls, their cases of need within their own congregations, their Society operations, and sometimes
their brothers in need in foreign territories, Jehovah's witnesses do
an extensive work of material giving. Their charitable work is carried
out through their own organization, whether on a local or an international scale.

Giving to community charities outside their organization is a personal and individual matter among the Witnesses. The usual answer
to such a request is: "I have already given all I can afford through
our society." Then the Witness makes as much of the opportunity as he can to describe to the solicitor of outside charity the
nature of the work of the New World Society.

IMPORTANT COURT BRIEFS

Witnesses not Seditious

The courts have held that preaching by Jehovah's witnesses and
the distribution of the literature, as well as the contents thereof, do

not violate the laws of the various nations forbidding sedition and subversive activity.

The Supreme Court of the United States, in *Taylor* v. *Mississippi,* 319 U. S. 583, 589-590, 63 S. Ct. 1200, 1203-1204, 87 L. Ed. 1600 (1943), held that the distribution of literature and the speaking of words that explain the reason why Jehovah's witnesses do not participate in worldly controversy and wars between nations, and why they cannot salute the flag of the United States, cannot be made the basis of a conviction under a sedition statute which prohibits the distribution of literature which tends to create disloyalty and causes an attitude of stubborn refusal to salute the flag. In that case the Supreme Court said:

"If the state cannot constrain one to violate his conscientious religious conviction by saluting the national emblem [*West Virginia State Board of Education* v. *Barnette,* 319 U. S. 624, 63 S. Ct. 1178, 87 L. Ed. 1628], then certainly it cannot punish him for imparting his views on the subject to his fellows and exhorting them to accept those views.

"Inasmuch as Betty Benoit was charged only with disseminating literature reasonably tending to create an attitude of stubborn refusal to salute, honor, or respect the national and state flag and government, her conviction denies her the liberty guaranteed by the Fourteenth Amendment. Her conviction and the convictions of Taylor and Cummings, for advocating and teaching refusal to salute the flag, cannot be sustained.

"The last mentioned appellants were also charged with oral teachings and the dissemination of literature calculated to encourage disloyalty to the state and national governments. Their convictions on this charge must also be set aside.

"The statute as construed in these cases makes it a criminal offense to communicate to others views and opinions respecting governmental policies, and prophecies concerning the future of our own and other nations. As applied to the appellants it punishes them although what they communicated is not claimed or shown to have been done with an evil or sinister purpose, to have advocated or incited subversive action against the nation or state, or to have threatened any clear and present danger to our institutions or our government. What these appellants communicated were their beliefs and opinions concerning domestic measures and trends in national and world affairs.

"Under our decisions criminal sanctions cannot be imposed for such communication."

In *McKee* v. *Indiana,* 219 Ind. 247, 37 N. E. 2d 940 (1941), the Indiana Supreme Court held that the distribution of literature by Jehovah's witnesses did not violate a sedition statute designated as the Riotous Conspiracy Statute and "Criminal Syndicalism" Act. It held that the distribution did not advocate or incite the overthrow of the government by force and violence.

In *Beeler* v. *Smith,* 40 F. Supp. 139 (1941), the United States District Court for the Eastern District of Kentucky held that the activity and literature distributed by Jehovah's witnesses were not in violation of the Kentucky sedition statute.

More recently the Supreme Court of Canada, in *Boucher* v. *The King,* (1950) 96 Can. Cr. Cases 48, ruled in favor of Jehovah's witnesses in a case involving a prosecution in the Province of Quebec, Canada, under the charge of sedition. Mr. Justice Rand, in his judgment filed in the Supreme Court of Canada, among other things, said, p. 73:

"The incidents as described, are of peaceable Canadians who seem not to be lacking in meekness, but who, for distributing, apparently without permits, Bibles and tracts on Christian doctrines; for conducting religious services in private homes or on private lands in Christian fellowship; for holding public lecture meetings to teach religious truth as they believe it of the Christian religion; who, for this exercise of what has been taken for granted to be the unchallengeable rights of Canadians, have been assaulted and beaten and their Bibles and publications torn up and destroyed, by individuals and by mobs. . .

"The conduct of the accused appears to have been unexceptionable; so far as disclosed, he is an exemplary citizen who is at least sympathetic to doctrines of the Christian religion which are, evidently, different from either the Protestant or the Roman Catholic versions: but the foundation in all is the same, Christ and his relation to God and humanity. . . .

". . . but it is not challenged that, as they allege, whatever they did was done peaceably, and, as they saw it, in the way of bringing the light and peace of the Christian religion to the souls of men and women. To say that is to say that their acts were lawful."

The Supreme Court of South Africa, in *The Magistrate, Bulawayo* v. *Kabungo,* 1938 S. A. Law Reports 304-316, held that the literature of Jehovah's witnesses did not violate the Sedition Act of Southern Rhodesia. The court ordered all of the literature belonging to Jehovah's witnesses and that had been seized and detained by the magistrate returned because it was proper for distribution and did not violate the sedition laws.

The High Court of Australia, in *Adelaide Company of Jehovah's Witnesses, Inc.,* v. *The Commonwealth,* (1943) 67 C. L. R. 116, 124, ruled in favor of Jehovah's witnesses and against The Commonwealth. The court held that The Commonwealth had unlawfully declared the Adelaide Company of Jehovah's Witnesses, Inc., and the unincorporated association of persons known as Jehovah's witnesses a subversive organization and prejudicial to the official prosecution of the war. The court held that Jehovah's witnesses were not engaged

in any seditious enterprise or engaged in publishing or printing literature which was seditious within the meaning of the criminal law of
Australia. The court held that the Order-in-Council, banning Jehovah's
witnesses in Australia, was illegal and *ultra vires*. In discussing the
guarantee of freedom of worship in the Australian Constitution, Chief
Justice Latham, speaking for the court, said, in part:

"... it should not be forgotten that such a provision as s. 116 [free
exercise of religion] is not required for the protection of the religion
of a majority. The religion of the majority of the people can look
after itself. Section 116 is required to protect the religion (or absence
of religion) of minorities, and, in particular, of unpopular minorities.

"It is sometimes suggested in discussions on the subject of freedom
of religion that, though the civil government should not interfere
with religious *opinions*, it nevertheless may deal as it pleases with
any *acts* which are done in pursuance of religious belief without in-
fringing the principle of freedom of religion. It appears to me to be
difficult to maintain this distinction as relevant to the interpretation
of s. 116. The section refers in express terms to the *exercise* of religion,
and therefore it is intended to protect from the operation of any
Commonwealth laws acts which are done in the exercise of religion.
Thus the section goes far beyond protecting liberty of opinion. It pro-
tects also acts done in pursuance of religious belief as part of religion."

It is submitted that neither Jehovah's witnesses, nor literature
published and distributed by them, nor their preaching activity violates
the sedition laws of the nations. They are definitely not subversive,
being engaged in preaching the gospel of God's kingdom in the same
manner as did Jesus and his apostles.

Flag Salute

The courts have held that Jehovah's witnesses have the right to
refuse to salute the flag and to explain orally or distribute literature
giving reasons why they do not salute and they may not be denied
their legal rights because of such refusal to salute.

Jehovah's witnesses respect the flag of every nation where they
reside. They refuse to salute it because to do so requires them to
violate their covenant obligation with Jehovah God. In Exodus 20:3-5,
Almighty God forbids his people to ascribe salvation to any other
god, or to an image or likeness. To salute the flag of any nation is
to do an act of obeisance to the flag which attributes to it salvation in
violation of such Scriptural command.

Jehovah's witnesses do not teach others not to salute the flag.
They do not encourage others not to salute it. If others choose to
salute, that is their affair. Jehovah's witnesses believe it would be
wrong to prevent others from saluting. They merely claim for themselves the right to refuse to salute the flag of any nation.

Jehovah's witnesses respect the flag and the things for which it stands. They have valiantly fought on the "home front" in many lands for liberty for which the flag stands, namely, freedom of speech, press, conscience and worship of Almighty God, and they push these fights through the courts so as to maintain these liberties for all.

On June 14, 1943, the Supreme Court of the United States reversed its adverse decision of June 3, 1940, in *Minersville* v. *Gobitis,* 310 U. S. 586, 60 S. Ct. 1010, 87 L. Ed. 1375, when it rendered its decision in *West Virginia State Board of Education* v. *Barnette,* 319 U. S. 624, 63 S. Ct. 1178, 87 L. Ed. 1628 (1943), and held that the school board did not have the right to expel from school and deny education to children of Jehovah's witnesses who refuse to salute the flag. In that case the court said:

"To sustain the compulsory flag salute we are required to say that a Bill of Rights which guards the individual's right to speak his own mind, left it open to public authorities to compel him to utter what is not in his mind. . . .

"The very purpose of a Bill of Rights was to withdraw certain subjects from the vicissitudes of political controversy, to place them beyond the reach of majorities and officials and to establish them as legal principles to be applied by the courts. One's right to life, liberty, and property, to free speech, a free press, freedom of worship and assembly, and other fundamental rights may not be submitted to vote; they depend on the outcome of no elections. . . .

"The case is made difficult not because the principles of its decision are obscure but because the flag involved is our own. Nevertheless, we apply the limitations of the Constitution with no fear that freedom to be intelligently and spiritually diverse or even contrary will disintegrate the social organization. . . . When they are so harmless to others or to the State as those we deal with here, the price is not too great. But freedom to differ is not limited to things that do not matter much. That would be a mere shadow of freedom. The test of its substance is the right to differ as to things that touch the heart of the existing order.

"If there is any fixed star in our constitutional constellation, it is that no official, high or petty, can prescribe what shall be orthodox in politics, nationalism, religion, or other matters of opinion or force citizens to confess by word or act their faith therein. . . .

"We think the action of the local authorities in compelling the flag salute and pledge transcends constitutional limitations on their power and invades the sphere of intellect and spirit which it is the purpose of the First Amendment to our Constitution to reserve from all official control.

"The decision of this Court in *Minersville School District* v. *Gobitis,* and the holdings of those few *per curiam* decisions which preceded and foreshadowed it are overruled, and the judgment enjoining en-

forcement of the West Virginia Regulation is affirmed. 319 U. S. at
pp. 634, 638, 641-642, 63 S. Ct. at pp. 1183, 1185, 1186, 1187."

Based on the decision of the Supreme Court of the United
States in the *Barnette* case, the Supreme Court of Colorado, in
Zavilla v. *Masse,* 112 Colo. 183, 147 P. 2d 823 (1944), held that a
school board's rule requiring that school children must pledge allegiance to the flag of the United States, or suffer expulsion, was inappli-
cable to children of Jehovah's witnesses. The court said, among other
things:

"Unauthorized explusion from school under our laws, constitution
and decisions, deprives them of a civil right. In the instant case
plaintiffs were denied the civil right to attend the public schools because of their opinion that it is a violation of one of God's commandments to salute the flag, and their consequent refusal to do so. They
contend that their opinion concerning this matter is, in the constitutional sense, a religious opinion, and we think their contention is
supported by our Constitution and laws. . . .

". . . As a matter of elementary psychology, it is apparent that
compelling the expression of a sentiment not felt or the doing of an
act that it is feared will subject the actor to punishment hereafter, will
not only fail to create and foster respect for the compelling authority,
but will engender a sentiment of rebellion against it. It is not, as we
believe, a trespass on the legislative function that enacts or authorizes
the promulgation of a rule having such an effect, admittedly establishing a method or means only by obtaining an objective that can and
has been otherwise attained, to declare that such rule is an unwarranted
invasion of the constitutional guarantee of liberty and a guarantee
against the deprivation of civil rights and privileges by reason of
one's opinions concerning religion, and to hold that as to these plaintiffs the rule is not enforceable."

The Court of Appeals of Ontario, Canada, followed the decision
of the Supreme Court of the United States in the celebrated *Barnette*
case, in *Donald* v. *Board of Education* (1945) Ontario Reports 518.
There the court protected the right of Jehovah's witnesses to refuse
to salute the flag. Mr. Justice Gillanders, speaking for the court, said:

"Perhaps those who framed the regulations so providing never
considered that any well-disposed person would object to its inclusion
in their programme on religious grounds. There is no doubt that the
teachers and the school board, in the case now being considered, in
good faith prescribed the ceremony of the flag salute only with the
thought of inculcating respect for the flag and the Empire or Commonwealth of Nations which events of recent years have given more
abundant reason than ever before to love and respect. If I were permitted to be guided by my personal views, I would find it difficult
to understand how any well-disposed person could offer objection to
joining in such a salute on religious or other grounds. To me, a com-

mand to join in the flag salute or the singing of the national anthem
would be a command not to join in any enforced religious exercise,
but, viewed in proper perspective, to join in an act of respect for a
contrary principle, that is, to pay respect to a nation and country
which stands for religious freedom, and the principle that people may
worship as they please, or not at all.

"But in considering whether or not such exercises may or should,
in this case, be considered as having devotional or religious significance, it would be misleading to proceed on any personal views on
what such exercises might include or exclude. Although various cases
in the United States dealing with questions arising out of the flag
salute are not binding here, and are not concerned with the legislation
here being considered, I desire respectfully to adopt a portion of what
was said by Mr. Justice Jackson in his interesting opinion in the
case of *West Virginia State Board of Education et al.* (1943), 319
U. S. 624, at 632: . . .

"That certain acts, exercises and symbols at certain times, or to
certain people, connote a significance or meaning which, at other times
or to other people, is completely absent, is a fact so obvious from
history, and from observation, that it needs no elaboration.

"The fact that the appellants conscientiously believe the views which
they assert is not here in question. A considerable number of cases
in other jurisdictions, in which a similar attitude to the flag salute
has been taken, indicates that at least the same view has been conscientiously held by others. The statute, while it absolves pupils
from joining in exercises of devotion or religion to which they, or
their parents, object, does not further define or specifiy what such
exercises are or include or exclude. Had it done so, other considera-
tions would apply. For the Court to take to itself the right to say that
the exercises here in question had no religious or devotional significance might well be for the Court to deny that very religious freedom which the statute is intended to provide."

It is submitted that Jehovah's witnesses have the legal right to
refuse to salute the flag of any nation, and to explain to others the
reason why they refuse to salute the flag. They also have the right to
print literature explaining why they do not salute the flag. They may
not be prosecuted or penalized for refusal to salute the flag, for teaching their children that it is improper to salute or for explaining to
others why they and their children do not salute the flag.

MILITARY

Jehovah's witnesses are recognized as ministers constituting a legal
religious organization; and the Watch Tower Society, because of its

religious status, has been found by the state and federal governments of the United States to be exempt from the payment of taxes.

General Lewis B. Hershey, director of Selective Service, United States of America, had for determination the ministerial status of Jehovah's witnesses in 1942. After considering all the facts, he found that Jehovah's witnesses and the Watchtower Bible and Tract Society are recognized as a religious organization. He said, among other things:

"FACTS: Jehovah's Witnesses claim exemption from training and service and classification in Class IV-D as duly ordained ministers of religion under Section 5 (d), Selective Training and Service Act of 1940 . . .

"Section 5 (d): " 'Regular or duly ordained ministers of religion . . . shall be exempt from training and service (but not from registration) under this Act.'. . .

"*Question.*—May Jehovah's Witnesses be placed in Class IV-D as regular or duly ordained ministers of religion exempt from training and service?

"*Answer*: 1. The Watchtower Bible and Tract Society, Inc., is incorporated under the laws of the State of New York for charitable, religious, and scientific purposes. The unincorporated body of persons known as Jehovah's Witnesses hold in common certain religious tenets and beliefs and recognize as their terrestrial governing organization the Watchtower Bible and Tract Society, Inc. By their adherence to the organization of this religious corporation, the unincorporated body of Jehovah's Witnesses are considered to constitute a recognized religious sect.—Vol. III Opinion No. 14, National Headquarters, Selective Service System, November 2, 1942."

On April 3, 1943, General Hershey made his Second Report of the Director of Selective Service to the president, which was published in a book entitled *Selective Service in Wartime* (Government Printing Office, Washington, 1943). In that report to President Roosevelt, he said, in part, with respect to the definition given by National Headquarters to the vocation of ministers of religion:

"The principle was extended to persons who were not, in any strict sense, ministers or priests in any sacerdotal sense. It included Christian Brothers, who are religious, who live in communities apart from the world and devote themselves exclusively to religious teaching; Lutheran lay teachers, who also dedicate themselves to teaching, including religion; to the Jehovah's Witnesses, who sell their religious books, and thus extend the Word. It includes lay brothers in Catholic religious orders, and many other groups who dedicate their lives to the spread of their religion." (page 241)

In discharging one of Jehovah's witnesses from the custody of the Selective Service System, the United States Court of Appeals for the

Seventh Circuit, in *Hull* v. *Stalter,* 151 F. 2d 633 (1945), said:

"Relator alleged that at the time of his registration and at the time of his final classification, the proof submitted by him to the Selective Service System showed that he was exempt as a minister of religion under § 5 (d) of the Selective Training and Service Act of 1940, as amended, in that he was a duly ordained minister of Jehovah's Witnesses and the Watchtower Bible and Tract Society, constituting a recognized religious organization under the Act. . . .

"Much is said in the briefs both complimentary and derogatory to Jehovah's Witnesses. With this argument we are not concerned. Whatever a draft board or a court, or anybody else for that matter, may think of them is of little consequence. The fact is, they have been recognized by the Selective Service System as a religious organization and are entitled to the same treatment as the members of any other religious organization. . . .

". . . The Selective Service System has even more broadly defined the term 'regular minister of religion.' Under the heading, 'Special Problems of Classification' (*Selective Service in Wartime,* Second Report of the Director of Selective Service, 1941-42, pages 239-241), it is stated:

" 'The ordinary concept of "preaching and teaching" is that it must be oral and from the pulpit or platform. Such is not the test. Preaching and teaching have neither locational nor vocal limitations. The method of transmission of knowledge does not determine its value or effect its purpose or goal. One may preach or teach from the pulpit, from the curbstone, in the fields, or at the residential fronts. He may shout his message "from housetops" or write it "upon tablets of stone." He may give his "sermon on the mount," heal the eyes of the blind, write upon the sands while a Magdalene kneels, wash disciples' feet or die upon the cross . . . He may walk the streets in daily converse with those about him telling them of those ideals that are the foundation of his religious conviction, or he may transmit his message on the written or printed page, but he is none the less the minister of religion if such method has been adopted by him as the effective means of inculcating in the minds and hearts of men the principles of religion. . . . To be a "regular minister" of religion the translation of religious principles into the lives of his fellows must be the dominating factor in his own life, and must have that continuity of purpose and action that renders other purposes and actions relatively unimportant.' . . .

" . . . We have serious doubt that there was any justification for the Board's refusal originally to classify relator in 4-D. Whatever be thought, however, of the Board's original action in this respect, there can be no question but that subsequent proof conclusively demonstrated that he was entitled to such classification.

"Such being the situation, the Board abused its discretion in its refusal to so classify him. Its action was arbitrary and unauthorized. The order discharging relator is AFFIRMED."

The Supreme Court of the United States, in *Dickinson* v. *United States,* 346 U. S. 389, declared that Jehovah's witnesses who follow the ministry as their vocation, and give evidence of this by devoting the bulk of their time to preaching, are exempt under the terms of the Universal Military Training and Service Act. In that case the Supreme Court said:

"We think Dickinson made out a case which meets the statutory criteria. He was ordained in accordance with the ritual of his sect and, according to the evidence here, he meets the vital test of regularly, as a vocation, teaching and preaching the principles of his sect and conducting public worship in the tradition of his religion. That the ordination, doctrines, or manner of preaching that his sect employs diverge from the orthodox and traditional is no concern of ours; of course the statute does not purport to impose a test of orthodoxy.

"Why, then, was Dickinson denied IV-D? It may be argued that his five hours a week as a radio repairman supplied a factual basis for the denial. We think not. The statutory definition of a 'regular or duly ordained minister' does not preclude all secular employment. Many preachers, including those in the more traditional and orthodox sects, may not be blessed with congregations or parishes capable of paying them a living wage. A statutory ban on all secular work would mete out draft exemptions with an uneven hand, to the detriment of those who minister to the poor and thus need some secular work in order to survive. To hold that one who supports himself by five hours of secular work each week may thereby lose an exemption to which he is otherwise entitled, would be to achieve a result that Congress so wisely avoided. . . .

". . . when the uncontroverted evidence supporting a registrant's claim places him prima facie within the statutory exemption, dismissal of the claim solely on the basis of suspicion and speculation is both contrary to the spirit of the Act and foreign to our concepts of justice. *Reversed.*"

In 1941 the United States District Court for the Northern District of Texas, in *Borchert* v. *Ranger,* 42 F. Supp. 577, in enjoining local officials from interference with the door-to-door and street preaching of Jehovah's witnesses in four Texas towns said that Jehovah's witnesses constituted a recognized religion under the United States Constitution. In part the court said:

"In the disposition of this case I must look to the facts alleged and established, not to mere opinions of the pleader. Though it is not binding upon the mentality of these plaintiffs, I hold their faith constitutes a religion under our Constitution and under all definitions found in dictionaries and in the decisions of the courts of this country; also that preaching such religion, orally, by phonographs, the distribution of pamphlets, or printed sermons, carrying information or opinions about it to others, is a legitimate exercise of such religion . . ."

By orders of the commissioner of Internal Revenue, United States Treasury Department, under dates of November 9, 1934, March 22, 1935, April 24, 1935, April 23, 1938, September 1, 1942, and June 17, 1946, Watchtower Bible and Tract Society, Inc. (a New York corporation) and Watch Tower Bible and Tract Society (a Pennsylvania corporation), were held to be entitled to exemption from the making of income tax returns under the Federal Internal Revenue Act because such societies were charitable corporations engaged in religious activity. A similar ruling has been made in favor of the Society by the British government in England and in Canada. Copies of these orders are available in letter form to anyone who has reason for obtaining them upon request in writing addressed to the Society (legal office) at 124 Columbia Heights, Brooklyn 1, New York.

Watch Tower Bible and Tract Society and Watchtower Bible and Tract Society, Inc., have been declared exempt also from the payment of taxes on real estate owned and used by them for carrying out the chartered purposes of the societies because such societies are benevolent and engaged in religious activity. *Watch Tower Bible & Tract Society* v. *Allegheny City, Pa.,* 14 Dist. 695 (1905); *Peoples Pulpit Association* (name changed by law to Watchtower Bible and Tract Society, Inc.) v. *Purdy,* New York Supreme Court, Kings County, May 1, 1915, affirmed (New York Supreme Court, Appellate Division, Second Department) 170 App. Div. 950 (1915).

Real estate owned and used by congregations of Jehovah's witnesses as places of assembly, called "Kingdom Halls," have been declared entitled to the benefit of church exemptions from the payment of real estate taxes. *Syracuse Center of Jehovah's witnesses, Inc.,* v. *City of Syracuse,* 163 Misc. 535, 297 N.Y.S. 587 (New York Supreme Court, Onondaga County, July 7, 1937).

It is submitted that the Watch Tower Society and Jehovah's witnesses are a legal religious organization and that their representatives engaged in preaching the gospel are legally recognized as ministers of religion, which entitles them to all privileges accorded to all religious organizations and ministers.

Witnesses May Do Secular Work

The courts have held that the performance of secular work by Jehovah's witnesses does not deny them the right to their status as ministers of religion.

The earliest ministers of Christianity performed secular work to maintain themselves in their ministry. It is quite common in many parts of the earth today to find ministers of religion who regularly and customarily preach on their Sabbath day while doing secular work during the week. All that is required, to claim that one is a minister of religion, is that he teach and preach *regularly and customarily*. Jehovah's witnesses do just that.

Some of Jehovah's witnesses are full-time ministers. Others are part-time ministers who preach and teach on week-ends, week-days and at nighttime. The sum total of their preaching and teaching usually equals and often exceeds the actual time devoted to the ministry by the orthodox clergy, many of whom preach only on their Sabbath day.

The apostle Paul regularly performed secular work during his ministry, although his primary occupation was preaching "publicly, and from house to house." (Acts 20:20) He spent much time in tent-making, so as to earn money and thus avoid being a charge upon those to whom he preached. (I Thess. 4:10-12; II Thess. 3:7-12) Peter and other apostles were fishermen, while regularly and customarily performing their duties as apostles. (Matt. 4:18-21; Mark 1:16, 19; John 21:2, 3) Luke was a physician. (Col. 4:14) Jesus had been a carpenter. (Mark 6:3) He and his apostles were called "unlearned and ignorant" by the orthodox clergy who did not work.—Acts 4:13; John 7:15.

The only way the preaching job could be successfully done in the early days of the settlement of the United States was said to be "by the preaching and teaching, under Episcopal direction, by laymen deriving their support from their own secular labors." *The Missouri Valley and Lay Preaching,* Wharton, 1859, New York, p. 18.

"The church has always been more successful in winning kingdoms for her Christ, when she has adopted just this lay preaching method. . . . The whole church a royal priesthood, and so the whole church a preaching church, that is the New Testament ideal." *Lay Preaching* (Secretary's Annual Report), Hoyt, American Baptist Publication Society, 1869, New York, p. 21.

The English Court of Appeals held that the conscription law of that country, passed during World War I, should be given an interpretation so as to include a part-time minister of unorthodox Strict Baptist Church. (*Offord* v. *Hiscock,* 86 L.J.K.B. 941) In that case the person held to be a minister was a lawyer's secretary (known as a solicitor's clerk) during six days of the week. He was invited to preach on one occasion and it appeared that he was satisfactory, so he was engaged as the minister. In that case Viscount Reading said: "I have come to the conclusion that there is an absence of any evidence from which the Justices could draw the conclusion that he had not brought himself within the exception to the statute enforcing military service.

In my view it is clear that he had determined to devote himself to the ministry."

Under the Canadian National Selective Service Mobilization Regulations the Supreme Court of Saskatchewan held that a registrant was entitled to exemption from all training and service as a minister of religion. (*Bien* v. *Cooke,* (1944) 1 W.W.R. 237) There the minister spent six days a week farming. No special educational requirements were necessary. All that was required was that he satisfy the general secretary, who was a railroad engineer, that he believed the New Testament, and that he met the necessary moral requirements.

The United States Court of Appeals for the Second Circuit, in *Trainin* v. *Cain,* 144 F. 2d 944 (1944), held that the regular performance of secular employment was not incompatible with the claim for exemption as a regular minister of religion: "While the two positions are not mutually exclusive, and a validly draft-exempt minister of religion could still maintain a legal practice on the side, the existence of the latter can be taken into consideration in determining whether registrant is in fact a regularly practicing minister."

The Supreme Court of Alabama, during the Civil War, said in respect to this matter that a minister of religion includes a minister belonging to a sect of religionists who perform ministerial labor gratuitously and rely on secular employment as a means of subsistence. Ex parte *Cain,* 39 Ala. 440, 441.

Thousands of urban ministers in the United States and other countries enjoy large incomes from their ministry. Many more thousands of rural ministers of the orthodox religions are forced to engage in farming and other occupations during the week so as to preach in the pulpit on their Sabbath day. Likewise the performance of secular work by Jehovah's witnesses does not negative their fitness to preach the gospel of God's kingdom.

It is submitted that performance of secular work by Jehovah's witnesses does not prevent their claiming all the benefits that the clergy who perform no secular work claim under the law.

PUBLICATIONS

With the nineteenth century came the Bible societies: in Great Britain (1804), Germany (1806), United States (1808), Switzerland (1812), Finland (1812), Russia (1813), Holland (1813), Sweden (1814), Denmark (1814), Norway (1815), France (1818). Such societies reached a climax in 1884 with the Watch Tower Bible and Tract Society.

The Society has quoted more than seventy Bible translations in its literature. It distributes versions of all faiths. Bibles published on the Society's own presses are described below.

Bibles Published by Watch Tower Bible & Tract Society

BIBLES	ACQUIRED	COMMENTS
The New Testament by J. B. Rotherham. He was not associated with the Watch Tower Society.	1896 Twelfth Edition, Revised	Printed for the Watch Tower Bible and Tract Society, Allegheny, Pa., U.S.A. by Samuel Bagster and Sons, Limited, London, England
Emphatic Diaglott by B. Wilson. He was not associated with the Watch Tower Society	1902 First printed on Society presses, 1926	Three versions in one: (1) Greek text with readings from Vatican MS. 1209. (2) Interlineary literal word-for-word English. (3) New version with signs of emphasis. Copious references and footnotes. Comprehensive Introduction. Alphabetical Appendix.
Authorized or King James Version	1907	Printed for the Watch Tower Bible and Tract Society, Allegheny, Pa., U.S.A., by Samuel Bagster and Sons, Limited, London, England and James Pott & Co., New York. Popularly called "Bible Students Edition" containing in the Appendix the "Berean Bible Teachers' Manual" of 555 pages as compiled by the Watch Tower Society.
Authorized or King James Version	1942	First complete Bible printed on Society's presses. Marginal cross references. Maps. New World Concordance. Appendix helps.

American Standard Version	1944 Purchased right to plates only	Renders God's name "Jehovah" 6,823 times in Hebrew Scriptures. Cross References. Footnotes. New World Concordance. Maps.
New World Translation of Christian Greek Scriptures (New Testament)	1950	New translation by New World Bible Translation Committee of Jehovah's Witnesses. In modern English idiom. Illustrated Foreword. Extensive Appendix. Alphabetical Chain References. Footnotes. Maps. Illustrations. Uses name "Jehovah" 237 times in text, 72 times in margin.
New World Translation of Hebrew Scriptures (Old Testament) Vol. 1 Genesis—Ruth inclusive	1953	First part of Hebrew Scriptures translated by New World Bible Translation Committee. Foreword. Appendix. Chain and Cross References. Footnotes. Maps. Illustrations.

Magazines

Nsanja ya Olonda, Ang Bantayan, Nqabayokulinda: these odd names are translations into Cinyanja, Tagalog, and Zulu of a familiar name, *The Watchtower.*

Its 1955 circulation soaring to approximately two million (average yearly increase 600,000), *The Watchtower* is published in 40 languages.

Its companion magazine, *Awake!* was printing 1,300,000 copies in 13 languages in 1955. A one-month campaign in 1953 netted 161,800 new subscriptions.

Both magazines contain 32 pages of solid matter, no advertising, They are published semi-monthly. American subscriptions, $1.00 a year each.

Books

By 1954, the Bible study book, *Let God Be True* was being published in 31 languages. It had then been seven years in print, and a total of 12,006,774 copies had been distributed.

Jehovah's witnesses publish first printings of books like *Let God Be True* in editions of one and two million. Their world-wide, house-to-house missionary work, featuring the distribution of the literature, assures global circulations at astronomical figures.

Let God Be True contains 320 pages. It is cloth bound and gold stamped. The paragraphs are numbered with accompanying questions for class study. Indexed by subjects and by Scriptures cited. American Witnesses ask a public contribution for this book and its companions of fifty cents a copy.

CHARLES TAZE RUSSELL

Charles Taze Russell, known the world over as Pastor Russell, author, lecturer, and minister of the Gospel, was born in Pittsburgh, Pennsylvania, February 16, 1852. He died October 31, 1916. He was the son of Joseph L. and Eliza Birney Russell, both of Scottish-Irish ancestry.

He was educated in public schools and by private tutors.

In 1879, he was married to Maria Frances Ackley. Seventeen years later they disagreed about the management of his journal; a separation followed. The couple had no children.

Reared under the influence of Presbyterian parents, at an early age he became interested in theology. He joined the Congregational Church and the Y.M.C.A. and became active in local mission work.

The doctrine of eternal torment for all mankind except the few elect became so abhorrent to him that about the age of fifteen he became a skeptic. He turned his attention to the investigation of heathen religions. He found all of them unsatisfactory.

But naturally of a reverential mind, and desiring to worship and serve the true God, he reasoned: "All the creeds of Christendom claim to be founded on the Bible, and these are conflicting. Is it possible that the Bible has been misrepresented? It may not teach the terrible doctrine of eternal torment."

He turned again to the Bible. He determined to make a careful, systematic study of it without reference to creeds of men. The remainder of his life was wholly devoted to teaching the Bible, writing and publishing religious books and papers, lecturing, and proclaiming the message of Messiah's kingdom.

He was not the founder of a new religion. He never made such a claim. He "revived the great truths taught by Jesus and the apostles," and turned the light of the twentieth century upon them.

He made no claim of a special revelation from God. He held that it was God's due time for the Bible to be understood; and that he, being fully dedicated to the Lord and to his service, was permitted to understand it.

He was editor of *The Watch Tower* from 1879 until his death in 1916. He stressed in its first issue and throughout his tenure as editor the doctrine that "the merit toward God lies not in these moral virtues, but in Christ's perfect sacrifice."

He was president of the Watch Tower Bible and Tract Society from its organization, in 1884, until his death. He was also president of the Peoples Pulpit Association incorporated in New York in 1909, and of the International Bible Students Association incorporated in London in 1914. Through these religious corporations, as well as by word of mouth, he promulgated the Gospel of Messiah's kingdom.

In 1874, he wrote and published the booklet *Object and Manner of Our Lord's Return*. This, his initial literary venture, was widely circulated for several years. The aggregate circulation of his books and booklets alone is upward of sixteen million copies, in thirty-five languages.

He was the author of numerous books and booklet publications, issued at intervals between the years 1874 and 1914. Most notable among them is his six-volume series of *Studies in the Scriptures*. Originally these were designated *Millennial Dawn*.

He organized and conducted a lecture bureau that constantly employed seventy Bible lecturers who traveled and delivered lectures on the Scriptures. Every year he wrote practically all the copy for the *Bible Students Monthly*, the annual distribution of which was approximately fifty million copies.

His weekly sermons were handled by a newspaper syndicate. More than two thousand newspapers, with a combined circulation of fifteen million readers, at one time published his discourses. All told, more than four thousand newspapers published these sermons.

NATHAN HOMER KNORR

THE man who became the third president of the Watch Tower Society and its affiliate corporations, succeeding J. F. Rutherford, is Nathan Homer Knorr.

Mr. Knorr was born April 23, 1905, in Bethlehem, Pennsylvania. He graduated from Allentown, Pennsylvania, high school, in 1923. He first came in contact with Jehovah's witnesses while he was in high school, at the age of sixteen. Some members of his family had received Watchtower literature from some of the Witnesses. The Knorr family studied the publications. Before long, the youthful Nathan was associating with Jehovah's witnesses, in Allentown, in their regular Bible studies. He withdrew from the Reformed Church. The year he graduated from high school, he entered the ministry of Jehovah's witnesses on a full-time basis.

That same year young Knorr was invited to become a member of the working family at Bethel, in Brooklyn, New York. This is the world headquarters and chief printing plant of Jehovah's witnesses. The first assignment Knorr received was in the shipping department. Next, he was appointed to co-ordinate all the printing activities in the Society's plant. He showed a flair for organization and for getting things functioning. Nine years after coming to Bethel, Nathan Knorr, at the age of twenty-seven, became general manager of the publishing office and plant. That was in 1932.

Two years later he was elected a director of the Peoples Pulpit Association (now Watchtower Bible and Tract Society, Inc., of New York). A year later he became vice-president.

In 1940, he became a director and vice-president of the Pennsylvania corporation, The Watch Tower Bible & Tract Society.

After Judge Rutherford died, the boards of directors unanimously elected Mr. Knorr president of both American corporations and the International Bible Students Association of England. These are lifetime offices.

Mr. Knorr grew up in the business end of the organization; but there is nothing commercial about any of the nonprofit charitable corporations he supervises. They are instruments used by Jehovah's witnesses to preach their message of Christ's Kingdom as having arrived, and every muscle and sinew of the Theocratic systems of things must function to the nth degree of effectiveness. Doing everything decently, orderly, and without loitering are Mr. Knorr's traits. His co-workers speak of him not as a driver type but as one who appreciates effectiveness.

It would be hard to set forth all his duties. He directs policy. He supervises the enormous amount of editorial work. He directs the Watch Tower Society's seventy-five missionary branches. He is president of the Watchtower Bible School of Gilead. He supervises such Society properties as the food farms that feed the headquarters workers. Radio station WBBR in Staten Island, New York, is also under his care.

Mr. Knorr's chief preoccupation, however, is with the world missionary work. It was during his day that the famous portable phonograph vanished as equipment of Jehovah's witnesses, in making their house-to-house calls. The Theocratic ministry school, inaugurated in every congregation during the early 1940's, produced preachers capable of doing their own talking. The Gilead School began in 1943 to send forth specially trained missionaries to go out to all the countries in the world that were open to them. Emphasis on the plain, common-sense, practical need for every Christian minister to be trained, skilled, mature in "giving every man a reason for the hope that is within you," has grown stronger under his supervision. These are the characteristics that seem to shape Mr. Knorr's attitude toward his mission of helping all his fellow witnesses of Jehovah to "mature in the ministry."

It was a concept shared wholeheartedly by Judge Rutherford. But while a shift of attention from the individual to the organization was the Judge's aim, attention was still centered around the Judge as the main voice, the key speaker, the one whose words came to life at the door from the phonograph record, and not the voice of the Witness holding the phonograph. The Judge's use of world-wide radio facilities and recorded sermons was replaced early in Knorr's career, and Jehovah's witnesses took up the message individually.

Every year President Knorr makes a service tour to some part of the globe, visiting the branches, opening new branches, paving the way for further expansion among nations. One time he completely circled the globe on such a tour. An average trip takes him almost half way around the planet. He estimates that he travels 50,000 miles a year. He has visited over 85 countries.

Like the two previous presidents, Pastor Russell and Judge Rutherford, Mr. Knorr is a public speaker of world reputation. At some of the places he speaks, in Africa, for instance, he requires one or more interpreters at a time. On some tours, peoples of a dozen tongues hear his talks translated into their own language or dialects. The largest single live audience Mr. Knorr ever addressed was the 1953 world convention of 165,829 people at Yankee Stadium, New York.

During the eleven years of Mr. Knorr's presidential career, the following world expansion of Jehovah's witnesses took place:

Year	No. Lands	Witnesses	Preaching Hours	Gilead Missionaries
1942	54	115,240	28,464,352	None
1947	86	207,552	43,842,305	486
1952	127	456,265	68,703,699	1,421
1953	143	519,982	72,344,728	1,626

Growing at the rate of 400 per cent a decade is no proof of personal prowess, Mr. Knorr says. "It is proof that Jehovah's spirit is at work, gathering in the New World Society." Rather than the effort of any individual, high or low, he declares (this is practically a slogan of his): "What counts is the individual ministry of each and every one."

HAYDEN COOPER COVINGTON

ATTORNEY COVINGTON succeeded Judge Rutherford as legal counsel for Jehovah's witnesses in 1942. He came to the world headquarters of the organization to work full time in 1939.

Covington was born, in 1911, in Hopkins County, Texas. He attended San Antonio Bar Association School of Law (now St. Mary's University School of Law). He became a preaching Witness of Jehovah in 1934.

He was admitted to the bar in Texas, in 1933; to ten U. S. Courts of Appeals and ten U. S. District Courts from 1933 to 1937; and to the New York bar in 1940.

He is a member of the Texas State Bar, New York County Lawyers Association, New York State Bar Association, American Bar Association.

Annually, Covington handles an average of fifty major cases for Jehovah's witnesses. He has personally argued forty-one major cases before the U. S. Supreme Court, involving Bill of Rights freedoms. Twice he persuaded the nation's highest tribunal to reverse its own decisions.

The United States decisions, hailed by the American Civil Liberties Union as having bolstered American freedoms more than anything since the adoption of the Bill of Rights, have been reviewed by law courts throughout the British Commonwealth of Nations, in Scandinavian countries, and elsewhere, in reaching decisions in similar cases. In this way the legal contributions of Jehovah's witnesses, under Covington's direction, have been acknowledged as benefiting people in many countries.

JOSEPH FRANKLIN RUTHERFORD

THE man who was to become known all over the world as Judge Rutherford was born in Morgan County, Missouri, November 8, 1869. He spent his boyhood on a farm. If he had fulfilled his father's wish he would have stayed there, taking care of the livestock.

But young Joseph had other plans. After he finished public school and the local academies, he wanted to go to college. His father consented, upon two impossible conditions: first, Joseph would have to hire a man to take his place on the farm; second, he would have to pay his own way through college.

Young Rutherford resolved both obstacles by giving a friend his own personal, unsecured note for enough money to see him through. That put him, at sixteen, on his own. He not only took the regular college course but studied shorthand and law at the same time.

While continuing his law studies, he spent two years under the tutelage of Judge E. L. Edwards, a noted Missouri jurist. At twenty, Joseph became official reporter of the Courts of the Fourteenth Judicial Circuit of Missouri. At twenty-two, he was admitted to the bar. He began his law practice in Boonville, Missouri. Advancement came early. He was taken into the firm of Draffen & Wright and made a trial lawyer.

From Boonville, he went on to practice law in all the courts in

Missouri, for about fifteen years thereafter. He appeared as counsel in the Federal Circuit Courts. In the same role, he appeared before the Supreme Court of the United States. In 1909, he became a member of the New York State Bar, and practiced in New York till his death.

Long before coming to New York, however, he had become known as "Judge Rutherford." The origin of that title goes back to his early Missouri law career. He had served at times as Special Judge in the Eighth Judicial Circuit Court.

Vouching for Mr. Rutherford's right to the title, his successor as counsel for Jehovah's witnesses, Attorney Hayden C. Covington, said this: "From records available to me I have proof of what Judge Rutherford told me during his lifetime. It is that he was elected on several occasions by the lawyers of the Eighth Judicial Circuit Court of Boonville, Missouri, to be judge of that court. He acted as special judge in the absence of the regular judge. This was before he came to New York, in 1909."

A Lawyer's View of God

About the beginning of the twentieth century, Judge Rutherford met Pastor Russell. He admired the Pastor's teachings. One day he was entertaining the Pastor in the Midland Hotel at Kansas City, Missouri. The Pastor was impressed by the Judge. "Why," suggested the Pastor, "don't you write something on the Divine Plan from a lawyer's viewpoint?"

Mr. Rutherford, at that point, did not even understand what it meant to be a dedicated Christian. But he liked what Pastor Russell preached. He liked what he was being taught from the Bible. And later on he turned out, at the Pastor's urging, a book entitled *Man's Salvation from a Lawyer's Viewpoint*.

The writing of that book led the Judge into a deep, searching study that changed the course of his life. "This Bible teaching must be true, and being true it is the panacea for all human ills," he concluded. "Henceforth I will give my life to this work."

The following year, 1907, Pastor Russell invited him to share the public platform. By mid-year he was sent on a lecture tour on his own, covering the Middle West. About the only time his law career got attention after that was when he took an occasional case for a friend or went to the defense of Pastor Russell and the Watch Tower Society.

That same year, 1907, Judge Rutherford defended several cases involving the Pastor and the Society, and in the Pastor's absence (Russell was in England) he wound up the whole litigation so successfully that thereafter all legal matters, whether personal or a Society matter, were turned over to him by the Pastor.

The Pastor's Successor

"Probably no man in the world was closer to Pastor Russell than Mr. Rutherford," said *The Watchtower* for December 1, 1916. How early the Pastor saw his likely successor in the Judge nobody knows, but the training as a Bible authority and lecturer Mr. Rutherford received from the start was all good grooming. By 1910 he was traveling far, seeing Egypt and Palestine, and lecturing in Germany, Finland, Denmark, Norway, Sweden, and Great Britain.

Commenting on his tour that year, the Leicester *Daily Post,* of England, said: "The De Montfort Hall was crowded last evening, when the Hon. J. F. Rutherford, of the United States, delivered his lecture on 'Where Are the Dead?' 5,000 persons were present. Judge Rutherford speaks clearly and fluently, and cites liberally from the Bible."

"Mr. Rutherford's speech is brief and distinctive and of an irreproachable logic," the Stockholm, Sweden, *Dagnes Nyheter* editorialized.

He spoke twice in one day at the University of Oregon. When the officers of the United States Naval Academy invited him to speak there, the Annapolis, Maryland, *Evening Capitol* reported that "the lecture was well received, the entire audience applauding the speaker vigorously." United States Senator George L. Wellington introduced the Judge on one occasion, and of his address the Cumberland, Maryland, *Evening Times* reported: "Mr. Rutherford fully maintained his reputation as an orator and Bible scholar, his points being made with telling force."

The Wheeling *Register,* of West Virginia, after announcing his introduction by Congressman B. B. Dovener, described the Judge on that occasion so as to make him live for the reader. "Standing over six feet tall, with a heavy voice and deliberate manner, his every utterance bearing intense earnestness, the speaker commanded marked attention. The theater was completely filled and many turned away."

Thus Mr. Rutherford traveled widely and was received with interest and enthusiasm until the persecution of the group, in 1918. After nine years on the lecture platform, *The Watchtower* said of him at the close of 1916:

"He has lectured in practically every city of any consequence in the United States and Canada. He has spoken in many of the colleges and universities by special request . . . He has never accepted a dollar from anyone for these lectures, deeming it a great privilege to tell the people the Glad Tidings concerning Messiah's Kingdom [heralded as taking power in 1914] and the blessings coming to mankind."

The Second Watch Tower President

Pittsburgh, Pennsylvania, news stories on January 6, 1917, announced: "Hon. Joseph F. Rutherford, of New York, was today unanimously chosen here to succeed the late Pastor Russell as President of the Watch Tower Bible and Tract Society."

He held this post until his death, January 8, 1942, just two days more than twenty-five years from the date of his election to the presidency of the Society.

Judge Rutherford died working, and his last act was to conclude the *1942 Yearbook of Jehovah's Witnesses.* He was producing an average of one book a year. During his last service year, 36,030,595 books and booklets were distributed. His radio broadcasts went out over the biggest networks ever used. He had carried on a work of "advertising the Kingdom" that compared well with that of his predecessor, Pastor Russell.

JEHOVAH'S WITNESSES' GIFTS FOR RELIEF
January, 1946, to August, 1948

	Pounds of Clothing	Value	Pounds of Food	Cost	Total Value
United States	919,302	$898,481.16	537,995	$208,416.76	$1,106,897.92
Misc.					6,709.46
Canada	72,807	80,699.88	87,913	36,084.90	116,784.78
Denmark			2,949	1,407.14	1,407.14
Norway			24,000	12,000.00	12,000.00
Switzerland	57,584	42,400.00	40,682	13,754.00	56,154.00
Misc.					3,851.00
Sweden	6,554	9,776.10	25,334	8,702.50	18,478.60
Misc.					124.00
TOTALS	1,056,247	$1,031,357.14	718,873	$280,365.30	$1,322,406.90

WHERE JEHOVAH'S WITNESSES SENT RELIEF GIFTS

	Pounds of Clothing	Pairs of Shoes	Pounds of Food	Pounds of Misc. Supplies
Austria	39,304	4,118	43,675	
Belgium	28,113	2,576	1,397	
Bulgaria			387	
China	553	43		
Czechoslovakia	33,458	2,435	6,450	
Denmark	35,219	3,832		
England	21,160	1,786	31,970	
Finland	23,973	1,944	6,450	
France	39,545	3,948	6,450	
Germany	544,749	72,804	564,025	80,459
Greece	17,888	2,813	2,150	
Hungary	32,054	3,349	21,500	251
Italy	9,266	597	4,300	
Netherlands	122,533	11,494	7,958	
Norway	20,514	2,244		
Philippine Republic	10,594	2,239		
Poland	77,324	7,888	11,411	
Rumania			10,750	
TOTALS	1,056,247	124,110	718,873	80,710

DATE	PLACE	No. PRESENT	BAPTIZED	REMARKS
1893(8/20-24)	Chicago, Ill.	360	20	
1904 (10/1-3)	St. Louis, Mo.	2,000 (peak)		
1908(8/29-9/7)	Put-in-Bay, O.	3,500	363	
1911(9/1-11)	Mountain Lake Park, Md.	5,000		
1919(9/1-8)	Cedar Pt. Ohio	8,000		
1922(9/3-10)	Cedar Pt. Ohio	20,000		
1926(5/25-31)	London, Eng.	7,000		
1927(7/18-26)	Toronto, Can.	15,000		53 radio stations carried feature lecture. Largest network carrying a single broadcast to that time.
1928 (7/30-8/6)	Detroit, Mich.	12,000		106 radio stations; new world record for single broadcast network.
1931(7/24-30)	Col'bus, Ohio	15,000		465 radio stations.
1935(5/30-6/2)	Wash., D.C.	20,000		
1938(9/10,11)	London, Eng.	150,000		London as key city for 50-city convention connected by wire.
1939(6/23-25)	N.Y., N.Y.	67,726		Main talks carried simultaneously to England, Switzerland, South Africa, Hawaii, Norway, Singapore, Sweden, Trinidad, Guatemala, Canada, and other lands, including U.S. cities from Chicago to Houston to Los Angeles.
1940(7/24-28)	Detroit, Mich.	79,335		Detroit as key city with 17 other U.S. cities tied in by wire.
1942(9/18-20)	C'land, Ohio	129,000		Cleveland as key city with 52 other cities tied in by wire.
1944(8/9-13)	Buffalo, N.Y.	140,612	3503	66 convention cities tied in.
1946(8/4-11)	C'land, Ohio	80,000	2602	First world convention at one city. 302 from 32 countries. Talks in 20 languages.
1950(7/30-8/6)	N.Y., N.Y.	123,707	3381	Second world convention at one city.
1953(7/19-26)	N.Y., N.Y.	165,829	4640	Third world assembly. More than 21,000 from 95 countries outside U.S.A.

GROWTH OF JEHOVAH'S WITNESSES

Country (Branches in capitals)	Average No. of Ministers Over 35-Year Period					Activities During 1953		
	1918	1928	1938	1948	1953	Congregations	Hours in Ministry	Home Studies (M'thly)
U.S. OF AMERICA	743	6,040	25,596	72,945	139,966	3,195	21,978,943	87,858
Alaska	—	—	5	30	101	5	16,890	69
Bermuda	—	—	—	6	17	1	3,243	42
French Equ. Africa	—	—	—	2	235	5	32,285	94
Guadeloupe	—	—	—	28	86	4	13,473	59
Guam	—	—	—	—	23	1	3,047	4
Iceland	—	—	—	3	7	1	7,345	18
Islands (served by missionary boat *Sibia*)	—	—	—	—	4	—	4,646	24
Israel	—	—	—	(b)	21	2	9,630	30
Korea	—	—	—	—	312	7	62,878	209
Lebanon-Syria	—	—	51	109	(a)	—	—	—
Morocco	—	—	—	—	1	—	25	—
Palestine	—	—	—	22	(b)	—	—	—
St. Martin, F.W.I.	—	—	—	—	4	1	1,671	5
ARGENTINA	—	34	128	927	2,579	85	411,879	2,057
AUSTRALIA	130	305	1,720	3,503	6,302	290	1,010,396	3,784
American Samoa	—	—	—	—	1	—	70	2
Fiji	—	—	—	10	36	1	8,349	40
Indonesia	—	—	21	9	(c)	—	—	—
Papua	—	—	—	—	5	1	1,359	9
Western Samoa	—	—	—	—	16	1	3,873	26

GROWTH OF JEHOVAH'S WITNESSES (*Continued*)

Country (Branches in capitals)	Average No. of Ministers			Over 35-Year Period		Activities During 1953		
	1918	1928	1938	1948	1953	Congregations	Hours in Ministry	Home Studies (M'thly)
AUSTRIA	—	261	471	1,286	3,101	162	453,565	1,632
BAHAMAS	—	7	10	33	92	2	16,950	135
BELGIUM	—	—	117	1,177	3,406	83	453,778	1,683
Luxembourg	—	—	22	47	109	4	17,856	67
BOLIVIA	—	—	—	36	95	4	43,078	228
BRAZIL	—	18	103	1,077	5,774	148	828,999	3,272
BRITISH GUIANA	—	15	30	174	325	15	82,033	408
BRITISH HONDURAS	—	—	—	38	76	3	21,211	134
BRITISH ISLES	2,784	3,066	4,959	14,676	26,104	729	3,582,887	12,509
Eire	—	—	—	52	143	4	68,503	159
Malta	—	—	—	3	2	—	33	4
BRITISH W. INDIES (TRINIDAD)	—	189	—	980	1,163	38	214,345	1,225
Anguilla	—	—	—	—	2	—	3	—
Antigua	—	—	—	—	37	1	8,018	42
Barbados	—	—	—	—	480	18	83,397	478
Carriacou	—	—	—	—	8	1	930	10
Dominica	—	—	—	—	53	2	6,303	45
Grenada	—	—	—	—	85	3	14,460	119
Montserrat	—	—	—	—	5	1	543	3

GROWTH OF JEHOVAH'S WITNESSES (*Continued*)

Country (Branches in capitals)	Average No. of Ministers Over 35-Year Period						Activities During 1953		
	1918	1928	1938	1948	1953	Congregations	Hours in Ministry	Home Studies (M'thly)
BRITISH W.I. (*continued*)								
Nevis	—	—	—	—	20	2	4,686	31
St. Kitts	—	—	—	—	43	1	8,645	41
St. Lucia	—	—	—	—	28	2	7,987	64
St. Vincent	—	—	—	—	40	5	11,054	81
Tobago	—	—	—	—	29	2	5,679	33
BURMA	—	—	28	36	108	2	24,343	110
CANADA	—	998	3,113	12,603	22,350	672	2,915,915	8,995
CHILE	—	—	26	191	824	15	163,942	1,096
CHINA	—	—	10	25	20	1	3,740	57
COLOMBIA	—	—	—	28	368	11	95,233	496
COSTA RICA	73	—	—	637	1,551	40	173,709	1,055
CUBA	—	—	—	4,352	9,085	252	1,117,748	5,474
CYPRUS	—	4	11	59	328	9	46,875	243
CZECHOSLOVAKIA	—	106	903	1,581	(d)	—	—	—
DENMARK	26	324	889	3,260	6,765	180	732,386	2,511
DOMINICAN REPUBLIC	—	—	—	128	273	7	29,437	213

GROWTH OF JEHOVAH'S WITNESSES (*Continued*)

Country (Branches in capitals)	Average No. of Ministers Over 35-Year Period					Congregations	Activities During 1953	
	1918	1928	1938	1948	1953		Hours in Ministry	Home Studies (M'thly)
ECUADOR	—	—	—	29	203	5	66,430	329
EGYPT	—	—	14	96	243	9	56,552	214
Anglo-Egyptian Sudan	—	—	—	—	17	1	2,479	5
EL SALVADOR	—	—	—	151	251	10	58,210	296
ETHIOPIA	—	—	—	—	40	4	19,220	107
FINLAND	—	305	429	2,610	5,029	393	718,392	2,379
FRANCE	—	447	845	2,627	7,371	169	763,287	2,873
Algeria	—	—	—	—	24	1	12,418	76
Indo-China	—	—	—	—	1	—	36	—
Saar	—	60	—	252	592	15	73,946	275
Senegal	—	—	—	—	2	—	430	4
Tunisia	—	—	—	—	4	—	1,180	6
GERMANY, WEST	—	9,755	—	29,172	40,158	899	5,999,597	19,781
GOLD COAST	—	—	30	735	4,728	91	1,095,044	3,004
Gambia	—	—	—	—	1	—	404	2
Ivory Coast	—	—	—	—	13	—	6,027	30
GREECE	12	77	189	2,338	3,784	240	288,767	1,114
Turkey	—	—	—	12	56	2	13,805	95
GUATEMALA	—	—	—	121	308	11	63,901	422

GROWTH OF JEHOVAH'S WITNESSES (*Continued*)

Country (Branches in capitals)	Average No. of Ministers Over 35-Year Period					Congre-gations	Activities During 1953	
	1918	1928	1938	1948	1953		Ministry Hours in	Home Studies (M'thly)
HAITI	—	—	—	36	201	8	49,943	294
HAWAII	—	—	13	156	661	12	134,358	962
HONDURAS	—	—	—	119	340	15	79,805	487
HONG KONG	—	—	—	—	58	1	15,424	158
HUNGARY	—	—	—	1,346	(e)	—	—	—
INDIA	2	69	291	267	562	36	139,644	558
Ceylon	—	—	—	25	42	1	21,047	75
Iran	—	—	—	2	(f)	—	—	—
INDONESIA	—	—	—	(c)	132	4	35,861	297
ITALY	—	—	—	329	2,170	96	317,710	1,330
Libya	—	—	—	—	22	1	3,405	16
JAMAICA	50	84	390	1,465	2,759	143	398,252	2,394
JAPAN	—	75	110	—	287	13	115,235	851
Okinawa	—	—	—	—	10	1	2,025	6
Taiwan	—	—	—	(a)	934	12	176,926	492
LEBANON	—	—	—	—	375	10	68,355	186
Aden	—	—	—	—	1	—	49	1
Iraq	—	—	—	—	2	—	759	1

GROWTH OF JEHOVAH'S WITNESSES (*Continued*)

Country (Branches in capitals)	Average No. of Ministers Over 35-Year Period					Congregations	Activities During 1953	
	1918	1928	1938	1948	1953		Hours in Ministry	Home Studies (M'thly)
LEBANON (*continued*)								
Jordan	—	—	—	(b)	79	3	19,567	50
Saudi Arabia	—	—	—	—	2	—	74	—
Syria	—	—	—	—	67	4	10,780	34
LIBERIA	—	—	—	9	70	2	24,930	131
MEXICO	—	—	309	4,711	9,759	380	1,194,818	5,051
NETHERLANDS	—	57	234	4,190	7,649	143	914,958	2,540
NETHERLANDS ANTILLES								
Aruba	—	—	—	—	108	2	18,650	101
Bonaire	—	—	—	—	4	1	2,139	7
Curaçao	—	—	—	36	95	1	16,337	91
NEWFOUNDLAND	5	—	13	85	224	24	47,612	147
NEW ZEALAND	—	73	—	790	1,643	68	223,486	973
NICARAGUA	—	—	—	72	123	8	46,759	270
NIGERIA	—	7	427	5,511	13,056	442	3,042,666	7,605
Cameroon	—	—	4	60	649	23	150,434	319
Dahomey	—	—	12	140	349	16	103,339	330
French Togoland	—	—	—	—	87	3	46,935	204
NORTHERN RHODESIA	—	—	939	9,873	20,373	324	3,668,906	11,236

GROWTH OF JEHOVAH'S WITNESSES (*Continued*)

Country (Branches in capitals)	Average No. of Ministers Over 35-Year Period					Activities During 1953		
	1918	1928	1938	1948	1953	Congregations	Hours in Ministry	Home Studies (M'thly)
NORTHERN RHODESIA (*continued*)								
Belgian Congo	—	—	—	14	16	2	3,113	9
Kenya	—	—	—	—	4	1	371	1
Tanganyika	—	—	—	136	194	13	50,277	174
Uganda	—	—	—	—	4	1	324	2
NORWAY	15	85	328	992	2,164	120	256,996	700
NYASALAND	—	—	1,065	4,918	11,296	624	2,611,154	9,863
Portuguese E. Africa	—	—	14	398	252	19	14,561	162
PAKISTAN	—	—	—	23	51	1	22,377	103
PANAMA	—	—	—	224	602	25	131,686	909
PARAGUAY	—	—	—	47	155	14	26,191	100
PERU	—	—	—	40	283	8	90,745	628
PHILIPPINES	—	—	—	3,589	18,053	487	2,614,496	9,585
PORTUGAL	—	—	2	10	77	2	17,046	53
Azores	—	—	—	—	28	1	1,647	17
POLAND	20	430	669	9,048	(g)			
PUERTO RICO	—	—	1	160	637	20	144,533	893
Virgin Islands	—	—	—	32	89	3	14,648	103

GROWTH OF JEHOVAH'S WITNESSES (*Continued*)

Country (Branches in capitals)	Average No. of Ministers Over 35-Year Period					Activities During 1953		
	1918	1928	1938	1948	1953	Congregations	Hours in Ministry	Home Studies (M'thly)
RUMANIA	—	—	—	1,992	(h)			
RUSSIA	—	16	—	8,000	(i)			
SIERRA LEONE	—	—	13	24	114	3	28,772	158
SINGAPORE	—	—	—	10	84	2	20,656	154
North Borneo	—	—	—	—	3	1	251	4
SOUTH AFRICA	—	58	378	4,440	10,492	496	2,854,446	7,992
Angola	—	—	—	—	23	1	5,804	34
Basutoland	—	—	—	—	67	8	26,223	77
Bechuanaland	—	—	—	—	100	7	29,808	67
Mauritius	—	—	—	—	14	2	4,269	38
St. Helena	—	—	—	10	40	2	5,113	23
South-West Africa	—	—	3	—	11	3	4,951	26
Swaziland	—	—	—	—	126	8	30,733	130
SOUTHERN RHODESIA	—	—	323	3,599	9,699	236	3,015,429	11,906
SPAIN	—	—	—	34	177	8	30,288	161
SURINAM	8	7	6	78	90	2	23,637	147
French Guiana	—	—	—	2	—	—	—	—
SWEDEN	—	253	982	3,231	5,435	333	754,213	2,332
SWITZERLAND	—	763	813	1,660	3,074	104	357,307	1,806

GROWTH OF JEHOVAH'S WITNESSES (*Concluded*)

Country (Branches in capitals)	Average No. of Ministers Over 35-Year Period					Activities During 1953		
	1918	1928	1938	1948	1953	Congregations	Hours in Ministry	Home Studies (M'thly)
THAILAND	—	—	1	48	150	10	48,651	221
URUGUAY	—	—	4	249	553	16	140,034	838
VENEZUELA	—	—	—	51	689	13	165,340	776
YUGOSLAVIA	—	—	79	—	807	—	32,649	312
4 OTHER COUNTRIES (j)	—	—	—	—	44,127	1,902	3,599,403	25,529
GRAND TOTAL	3,868	23,988	47,143	230,532	468,106	14,163	72,344,728	281,219

This table shows only the monthly averages, not the yearly peaks. As of 1953, there were 72 branches in 143 lands.

(a) Branch office opened at Beirut January 1, 1950.

(b) Witnesses in Palestine divided between Israel and Jordan.

(c) Branch office opened September, 1951.

(d) Communist rulers closed office November, 1948; work continues underground.

(e) Communists closed office November, 1950; preaching proceeds amid persecution.

(f) No reports; activity resumed 1954.

(g) Communists closed office June, 1950; underground ministry carried on.

(h) Communist police closed office January, 1950; preaching continues in secret.

(i) No reports received; worship underground.

(j) Reports from countries behind "iron curtain."

WATCHTOWER BROOKLYN FACTORY REPORT

	1950	1951	1952
Books and Bibles	3,742,420	4,731,329	5,281,878
Booklets	6,806,775	11,666,279	7,376,041
The Watchtower	18,038,800	21,737,200	26,135,600
Awake	16,493,600	18,037,900	19,999,824
Convention Reports			
(96 pages)		243,927	
(32 pages)	130,000		
(16 pages)	500,000		
Total	45,711,595	56,416,635	58,793,343

MISCELLANEOUS

	1950	1951	1952
Advertising Leaflets ..	95,061,000	111,855,000	103,163,000
Calendars	132,361	144,329	138,585
Miscellaneous Printing	26,061,440	35,622,496	30,746,921
Magazine Bags	26,322	21,439	30,543
Tracts			19,016,000
Total	121,281,123	147,643,264	153,095,039

PERIODICALS OF JEHOVAH'S WITNESSES

NAME	YEAR OF ORIGIN	TITLE CHANGES	CURRENT CIRCULATION
Zion's Watch Tower & Herald of Christ's Presence	1879	*The Watchtower* Announcing Jehovah's Kingdom	1,825,000 in 40 languages. (Circulation increasing one-quarter million yearly since 1949)
The Golden Age (Total circulation of 47,000,000 copies in 18-year period)	1919	*Consolation* (1937) (Total circulation of 57,500,000 copies in 9-year period) *Awake!* (1946)	1,250,000 in 13 languages (1954)